William Wills

An Essay on the Principles of Circumstantial Evidence

William Wills

An Essay on the Principles of Circumstantial Evidence

ISBN/EAN: 9783337313364

Printed in Europe, USA, Canada, Australia, Japan

Cover: Foto ©Andreas Hilbeck / pixelio.de

More available books at **www.hansebooks.com**

AN ESSAY

ON

THE PRINCIPLES OF

CIRCUMSTANTIAL EVIDENCE.

Illustrated by Numerous Cases.

BY THE LATE

WILLIAM WILLS, Esq.

EDITED BY HIS SON,

ALFRED WILLS, Esq.,

BARRISTER-AT-LAW.

Nulla denique est causa, in qua id, quod in judicium venit, ex reorum personis, non generum ipsorum universa disputatione quaeratur.—Cic. De Oratore.

FOURTH EDITION.

LONDON:

BUTTERWORTHS, 7, FLEET STREET,

Law Publishers to the Queen's Most Excellent Majesty.

HODGES, SMITH, AND CO., GRAFTON STREET, DUBLIN.

1862.

PRINTED BY
JOHN EDWARD TAYLOR, LITTLE QUEEN STREET,
LINCOLN'S INN FIELDS.

PREFACE

TO THE FOURTH EDITION.

BY THE EDITOR.

--◆

THE earlier sheets of this volume were in the press more than two years ago, and the remainder was very nearly ready for publication when the Author was seized with an illness, which proved speedily fatal. The subsequent delay has arisen from unavoidable circumstances, with which it is unnecessary to trouble the reader. The work, however, was so far advanced, that I have had little to do beyond correcting the press and occasionally verifying a quotation or a reference; and I append my name, only because I think my father would have wished that some one should appear to be responsible for even these mechanical operations.

I had intended to add to the " Illustrations of the force of circumstantial evidence " an instance of conflict between direct and circumstantial evidence more remarkable than any of those cited in this volume, presented by a case of disputed codicils to a will, twice tried at Derby; but as I have lately learned that it is not finally disposed of, I must leave it to be noticed hereafter, should a further edition be called for.

During the ten years which had elapsed between the publication of the last edition and the death of the author, he had been constantly on the watch for cases illustrative of the subject of this Essay, and this edition will be found rich in such additional materials. The section of Chapter III., on Scientific Testimony, is new ; many parts of the book have been rewritten, and it will be found, I trust and believe, not less worthy than before of the high reputation it has gained as the offspring of an accurate, clear, and philosophical mind.

A. W.

Inner Temple. November, 1862.

PREFACE

TO THE THIRD EDITION.

----&----

THE favourable reception which this Essay has met with has induced me again to commit it to the press.

I have incorporated with the text of the present edition the more recent cases of circumstantial evidence, in some of which the leading doctrines applicable to that department of moral and legal science have been declared with a clearness, precision, and completeness which are not to be found in connection with the earlier cases. Those parts of the Work which relate to the subject of presumptions have been considerably enlarged, and other portions of it have been wholly re-written.

I avail myself of this opportunity of recording my obligations to that profound jurist and upright magistrate, the late Chancellor Kent, to whose estimate of this Essay I have been indebted for its republication in the United States of America.

Nor can I quit my subject without expressing my admiration of the simplicity and harmony of our English system and rules of evidence, and of their incomparable superiority to those of all other nations which have adopted or modified the doctrines and practice of the Civil Law, so unworthy of the general excellence of that imperishable monument of human wisdom; a superiority for which we are mainly indebted to the uncompromising resistance made by our forefathers to every attempt to substitute the intangible subtleties and impracticable formulæ of the Roman jurisprudence for the plain and intelligible principles of our own Common Law.

W. W.

Edgbaston, February, 1850.

PREFACE

TO THE FIRST EDITION.

THE most important doctrines of Circumstantial Evidence have been so ably treated in the learned works of Mr. Bentham and Mr. Starkie, that an apology may be thought necessary for this publication. It will however be perceived, that the design of the following Essay is different in some important particulars from that of either of the above-mentioned authors; and that an attempt has been made to illustrate the subject by the application of many instructive cases, some of which have been compiled from original documents, and others from publications not easily accessible.

It has not always been practicable to support the statement of cases by reference to books of recognised authority, or of an equal degree of credit; but discrimination has uniformly been exercised in the adoption of such statements: and they have generally been verified by comparison with contemporaneous and independent accounts. A like discretion has been exercised in the rejection of some generally received cases of circumstantial evidence, the authenticity of which does not appear to be sufficiently established.

It is to be regretted that, with the exception of the State Trials, there is no authoritative collection of English cases of controverted fact, for which nevertheless there are extant abundant materials. Isolated and anomalous as such cases may appear to be, they, like every other part of the great system of jurisprudence, are reducible to consistent and immutable principles of reason and natural justice. There has existed hitherto little inducement to any such compilation, since (however pertinent and instructive such cases might be), by an unreasonable rule of legal procedure they were shut out from practical application. It is probable that, as the consequence of recent legislative changes, cases of circumstantial evidence will hereafter be treated with an amplitude of argument and illustration, both as to fact and principle, which will give them an increased value, and offer inducements to the satisfactory record of such cases for the purposes both of practical use and liberal curiosity.

In the course of my experience and reading, my attention has frequently been drawn to the consideration of the leading principles of circumstantial evidence. The matter which presented itself upon this favourite subject of study, and the thoughts which it suggested, it was my practice to preserve; and thus, without any view to publication, materials gradually and insensibly accumulated, which at length I have endeavoured to methodize and arrange in the present volume. Notwithstanding the originality of some of those materials, and the novelty of their arrangement and combination, it is probable that few of the generalizations and reflections advanced in this Essay can be considered as strictly original. The labour of composing these pages has nevertheless been an agreeable and useful employment, in the brief intervals of leisure from other pursuits; and though I am not insensible to their deficiencies, I am also not without the hope that they may be in some degree serviceable to others. At any rate, this Essay will be considerately received by those who rightly estimate the importance of the subject, and the difficulties of such an attempt.

W. W.

Edgbaston, near Birmingham,
    February, 1838.

TABLE OF CONTENTS.

CHAPTER I.

EVIDENCE IN GENERAL.

CHAPTER II.

CIRCUMSTANTIAL EVIDENCE.

CHAPTER III.

INCULPATORY MORAL INDICATIONS.

CHAPTER IV.

EXTRINSIC AND MECHANICAL INCULPATORY INDICATIONS.

CHAPTER V.

EXCULPATORY PRESUMPTIONS AND CIRCUMSTANTIAL EVIDENCE

CHAPTER VI.

RULES OF INDUCTION SPECIALLY APPLICABLE TO CIRCUMSTANTIAL EVIDENCE

CHAPTER VII.

PROOF OF THE CORPUS DELICTI.

CHAPTER VIII.

OF THE FORCE AND EFFECT OF CIRCUMSTANTIAL EVIDENCE.
CONCLUSION.

TABLE OF CASES AND STATUTES.

CIVIL CASES.

CRIMINAL CASES.

STATUTES.

THE PRINCIPLES

OF

CIRCUMSTANTIAL EVIDENCE.

CHAPTER I.

EVIDENCE IN GENERAL.

SECTION 1.

THE NATURE OF EVIDENCE.

IT will greatly conduce to the formation of clear and correct notions on the subject of Circumstantial Evidence, to take a brief introductory view of the nature of evidence in general, of some of its various kinds, and of the nature of the assurance which each of them is calculated to produce.

The great object of all intellectual research is the discovery of TRUTH, which is either OBJECTIVE AND ABSOLUTE, in which sense it is synonymous with being or existence, or SUBJECTIVE AND RELATIVE, in which acceptation it expresses the conformity of our ideas and mental convictions with the nature and reality of events and things.

The JUDGMENT is that faculty of the mind which is principally concerned in the investigation and acquisition of truth; and its exercise is the intellectual act by which

B

one thing is perceived and affirmed of another, or the reverse.

Every conclusion of the judgment, whatever may be its subject, is the result of EVIDENCE,—a word which (derived from words in the dead languages signifying to see, to know), by a natural transition is applied to denote the *means* by which any alleged matter of fact, the truth of which is submitted to investigation, is established or disproved.

The term PROOF is often confounded with that of evidence, and applied to denote the *medium* of proof, whereas in strictness it marks merely the *effect* of evidence. When the result of evidence is undoubting assent to the certainty of the event or proposition which is the subject-matter of inquiry, such event or proposition is said to be *proved;* and, according to the nature of the evidence on which such conclusion is grounded, it is either *known* or *believed* to be true. Our judgments, then, are the consequence of proof; and proof is that quantity of appropriate evidence which produces assurance and certainty; evidence therefore differs from proof, as cause from effect.

It is unnecessary, in relation to the subject of this section, to mention the inferior degrees of assurance, which will be more appropriately noticed in another place.

SECTION 2.

THE VARIOUS KINDS OF EVIDENCE.

TRUTH is either abstract and necessary, or probable and contingent; and each of these kinds of truth is discoverable by appropriate, but necessarily different kinds of evidence. This classification, however, is not founded in any essential difference in the nature of truths themselves, and has reference merely to our imperfect capacity and ability of perceiving them; since to an Infinite Intelligence nothing which is the object of knowledge can be probable, and everything must be perceived absolutely and really as it is.*

In many instances the correspondence of our ideas with realities is perceived instantaneously, and without any conscious intermediate process of reasoning, in which cases the judgment is said to be INTUITIVE, from a word signifying to look at; and the evidence on which it is founded is also denominated intuitive; though it would perhaps be more correct to use that word as descriptive of the nature of the mental operation, rather than of the kind of evidence on which it rests.

INTUITION is the foundation of DEMONSTRATION, which consists of a series of steps severally resolvable into some intuitive truth. Demonstration concerns only necessary and immutable truth; and its first principles are definitions, which exclude all ambiguities of language, and lead to infallibly certain conclusions.†

But the subjects which admit of the certainty of intuition and demonstration are comparatively few. Innumerable truths, the knowledge of which is indispensable to happiness, if not to existence, depend upon evidence of a totally different kind, and admit of no other guide than our own observation and experience, or the testimony of our fellow-men. Such truths involve questions of fact or of actual existence, which, as they are not of a necessary nature, may or may not have existed, without involving any contradiction, and as to which our reasonings and

* Butler's Analogy, Introduction.

† 2 Stewart's Elements of the Philosophy of the Human Mind, ch. ii. s. 3.

deductions may be erroneous.   Such evidence is called
MORAL EVIDENCE; probably because its principal application is to subjects directly or remotely connected with
moral conduct and relations.

Of the various kinds of moral evidence, that of TESTI-
MONY is the most comprehensive and important in its relation to human concerns; so extensive is its application,
that to enter on the subject of testimony at large, would
be to treat of the conduct of the understanding in relation to the greater portion of human affairs.   The design
of this essay is limited to the consideration of some of
the principal rules and doctrines peculiar to circumstantial
evidence as applicable to criminal jurisprudence,—one of
the leading heads under which philosophical and juridical
writers consider the subject of testimonial evidence. Nor
is it proposed to treat, except cursorily and incidentally,
of *documentary* circumstantial evidence; a subject which,
however interesting in itself, is applicable principally to
discussions upon the genuineness of historical and other
writings; and such cases of this description as occasionally happen in the concerns of common life, are referable
to general principles, which equally apply to circumstantial evidence of every kind.

Considering how many of our most momentous determinations are grounded upon circumstantial evidence, and
how important it is that they should be correctly formed,
the subject is one of deep interest and moment.   It
would be most erroneous to conclude that, because it is
illustrated principally by forensic occurrences, it especially
concerns the business or the members of a particular profession.   Such *events* are amongst the most interesting
occurrences of social life; the *subject* relates to an intellectual process, called into exercise in almost every branch
of human speculation and research.

SECTION 3.

NATURE OF THE ASSURANCE PRODUCED BY DIFFERENT KINDS OF EVIDENCE.

IN investigations of every kind it is essential that a correct estimate be made, of the kind and degree of assurance of which the subject admits.

Since the evidence of DEMONSTRATION relates to necessary truths (as to which the supposition of the contrary involves not merely what is not and cannot be true, but what is also absurd), and since MORAL EVIDENCE is the basis of contingent or probable truth merely, it follows that the convictions which these various kinds of evidence are calculated to produce must be of very different natures. In the former case ABSOLUTE CERTITUDE is the result; to which MORAL CERTAINTY, the highest degree of assurance of which truths of the latter class admit, is necessarily inferior.

Unlike the assent, which is the inevitable result of mathematical reasoning, BELIEF in the truth of events may be of various degrees, from moral certainty, the highest, to that of mere probability, the lowest; between which extremes there are innumerable degrees and shades of conviction, which the latency of mental operations and the unavoidable imperfections of language render it impossible to define or express. In subjects of moral science, the want of appropriate words, and the occasional application of the same word to denote different things, have given occasion to much obscurity and confusion both of idea and expression; of which a remarkable exemplification is presented in the words probability and certainty.

The general meaning of the word PROBABILITY is likeness or similarity to some other truth, event, or thing.* Sometimes the word probability is used to express the preponderance of the evidence or arguments, in favour of the existence of a particular event or proposition, or adverse to it; and sometimes as assertive of the abstract and intrinsic credibility of a fact or event.

In its former sense the word probability is applied as well to certain mathematical subjects, as to questions dependent upon moral evidence, and expresses the ratio of the favourable cases to all the possible cases by which an event may happen or fail; and it is represented by a fraction, the numerator of which is the sum of the favourable cases, and the denominator the whole number of possible cases, certainty being represented by unity. If the number of chances for the happening of the event be $=0$, and the event be consequently impossible, the expression for that chance will be $=0$; and so, if the number of chances of the failure of the event be $=0$, and the event be therefore certain, the expression for the chance of failure will also be $=0$. If $m+n$ be the whole number of cases, m the favourable and n the unfavourable ones, the probability of the event is $m : m+n$. It follows, that if there be an equality of chances for the happening or the failing of an event, the fraction expressive of the probability is $=\frac{1}{2}$, the mean between certainty and impossibility;† and probability therefore includes the whole range between those extremes.

The terms CERTAINTY and PROBABILITY are however essentially different in meaning as applied to moral evidence, from what they import in a mathematical sense;

* Butler's Analogy, *ut supra;* Locke's Essay concerning Human Understanding, b. iv. ch. xv.; Cic. De Inventione, c. 47.

† Kirwan's Logic, part iii. ch. vii. s. 1.

inasmuch as the elements of moral certainty and moral probability, notwithstanding the ingenious arguments which have been urged to the contrary, appear to be incapable of numerical expression, and because it is not possible to assign all the chances for or against the occurrence of any particular event.

The expression MORAL PROBABILITY, though liable to objection on account of its deficiency in precision, is for want of one more definite and appropriate, of frequent and necessary use; nor will its application lead to mistake, if it be remembered, that it denotes only the preponderance of probability, resulting from the comparison and estimate of *moral* evidence, and that if this were capable of being expressed with exactness, it would lose its essential characteristic and possess the certainty of demonstration.

The preceding strictures equally apply to the term MORAL CERTAINTY, or its equivalent MORAL CONVICTION, which must be understood, not as importing deficiency in the proof, but only as descriptive of the kind of certainty which is attainable by means of moral evidence; and it is that full and complete assurance which admits of no degrees and induces a sound mind to act without doubt upon the conclusions to which it naturally and reasonably leads.[*]

It has been justly and powerfully remarked by a noble and learned writer, that " the degree of excellence and of strength to which testimony may rise seems almost indefinite. There is hardly any cogency which it is not capable by possible supposition of attaining. The endless multiplication of witnesses—the unbounded variety

* 2 Stewart's Elements, ch. ii. s. 4; Encyclopædia Brit., art. *Metaphysics*, part i.

of their habits of thinking, their prejudices, their interests —afford the means of conceiving the force of their testimony augmented *ad infinitum*, because these circumstances afford the means of diminishing indefinitely the chances of their being all mistaken, all misled, or all combining to deceive us."*   But if evidence leave reasonable ground for doubt, the conclusion cannot be morally certain, however great may be the preponderance of probability in its favour.

Some mathematical writers have propounded numerical fractions for expressing moral certainty; which, as might have been expected, have been of very different values. But the nature of the subject precludes the possibility of reducing to the form of arithmetical notation the subtle, shifting, and evanescent elements of moral assurance, or of bringing to quantitive comparison, things so inherently different as certainty and probability.

Other writers have given, in a more general manner, mathematical form to moral reasonings and judgments; but it is questionable if they have done so with any useful result, however they may have shown their own ingenuity.†   Though it is true that some very important deductions from the doctrine of chances are applicable to events dependent upon the duration of human life, such as the expectation and the decrement of life, the law of mortality, the value of annuities and other contingencies, and also to reasoning in the abstract upon particular cases of testimonial evidence, yet it is obvious, that all such conclusions depend upon circumstances, which, notwithstanding that to the unreflecting

* Lord Brougham's Discourse on Natural Theology, 251.
† See Kirwan's Logic, part iii. ch. vii. s. 21 ; Whately's Logic, b. iv. ch. ii. s. 1.

observer they appear casual, uncertain, and irreducible to principle, unlike moral facts and reasonings in general, are really based upon and deducible from numerical elements.

A learned writer, whose writings, in despite of his eccentricities of matter and of style, have exercised great influence in awakening the spirit of judicial reformation, asks,* "Does justice require less precision than chemistry?" The truth is, that the precision attainable in the one case is of a nature of which the other does not admit. It would be absurd to require the proof of an historic event, by the same kind of evidence and reasoning as that which establishes the equality of triangles upon equal bases and between the same parallels, or that the *latus rectum* in an ellipse is a third proportional to the major and minor axes.

This conscript father of legal reforms† has himself supplied a memorable illustration of the futility of his own inquiry. He has proposed a scale for measuring the degrees of belief, with a positive and a negative side, each divided into ten degrees, respectively affirming and denying the same fact, zero denoting the absence of belief; and the witness is to be asked what degree expresses his belief most correctly. With characteristic ardour, the venerable author gravely argues that this instrument could be employed without confusion, difficulty, or inconvenience.‡ But MAN must become wiser and better before the mass of his species can be entrusted with the use

* Bentham's Traité des Preuves Judiciaires, b. i. ch. xvii.; Mackintosh's Discourse on the Progress of Ethical Philosophy, 290.

† 1 Hoffman's Course of Legal Study, 364.

‡ Bentham's Rationale of Judicial Ev., b. i. ch. vi. s. 1, and see in Kirwan's Logic, part iii. ch. vii. s. 21, a proposed scale of testimonial probability.

of such a moral gauge, from which the unassuming and the wise would shrink, while it would be eagerly grasped by the conceited, the interested, and the bold.

But though a process strictly mathematical cannot be applied to estimate the effect of moral evidence, a proceeding somewhat analogous is observed in the examination of a group of facts adduced as grounds for inferring the existence of some other fact. Although an *exact* value cannot be assigned to the testimonial evidence for or against a matter of disputed fact, the separate testimony of each of the witnesses has nevertheless a determinate *relative* value, depending upon considerations which it would be foreign to the present subject to enumerate. On one side of the equation are mentally collected all the facts and circumstances which have an affirmative value; and on the other, all those which either lead to an opposite inference, or tend to diminish the weight, or to show the non-relevancy, of all or any of the circumstances which have been put into the opposite scale. The value of each separate portion of the evidence is separately estimated, and, as in algebraic addition, the opposite quantities, positive and negative, are united, and the *balance* of probabilities is what remains as the ground of human belief and judgment.*

But, as has been already intimated, there is another sense in which the word probability is often used, and in which it denotes CREDIBILITY or INTERNAL PROBABILITY, and expresses our judgment of the accordance or similarity of events with which we become acquainted,

* See some remarks on this passage in a learned paper " On the Measure of the Force of Testimony in Cases of Legal Evidence," by John Tozer, Esq., M.A., 8 Camb. Phil. Trans., and 36 Phil. Mag., 3rd ser. 78.

through the medium of testimony, with facts previously known by experience.*

The results of EXPERIENCE are, expressly or impliedly, assumed as the standard of credibility in all questions dependent upon moral evidence. By means of the senses and of our own consciousness we become acquainted with external nature, and with the characteristics and properties of physical things and moral beings, which are then made the subjects of memory, reflection, and other intellectual operations; and thus ultimately the mind is led to the recognition of the principle of causality and other necessary truths, which become the basis and standard of comparison in similar and analogous circumstances. The groundwork of our reasoning is an instinctive and inevitable belief in the truthfulness and legitimacy of our own faculties and in the permanence of the order of external nature, as also in the existence of moral causes, which operate with an unvarying uniformity, not inferior to, and perhaps surpassing even, the stability of physical laws; though, relatively to our feeble and limited powers of observation and comprehension, and on account of the latency, subtlety, and fugitiveness of mental operations, and of the infinite diversities of individual men, there is apparently more of uncertainty and confusion in moral than in material phenomena.†

Experience comprehends not merely the facts and deductions of personal observation, but the observations of mankind at large of every age and country. It would be absurd to disbelieve and reject as incredible the relations of events, because such events have not occurred within

---

* Abercrombie on the Intellectual Powers, part ii. s. 3.

† Hampden's Lectures on Moral Philosophy. 150; Abercrombie's Philosophy of the Moral Feelings, Prelim. Obs. s. ii.

the range of individual experience. We may remember the unreasonable incredulity of the King of Siam, who when the Dutch ambassador told him that in his country the water in cold weather became so hard that men walked upon it, and that it would even bear an elephant, replied, " Hitherto I have believed the strange things you have told me, because I look upon you as a sober, fair man, but now I am sure you lie."*

By experience facts or events of the same character are referred to causes of the same kind; by ANALOGY facts and events similar in some, but not in all of their particulars to other facts and occurrences, are concluded to have been produced by a similar cause: so that analogy vastly exceeds in its range the limits of experience in its widest latitude, though their boundaries may sometimes be coincident and sometimes undistinguishable. It has been profoundly remarked that " in whatever manner the province of experience, strictly so called, comes to be thus enlarged, it is perfectly manifest that, without some such provision for this purpose, the principles of our constitution would not have been duly adjusted to the scene in which we have to act. Were we not so formed as eagerly to seize the resembling features of different things and different events, and to extend our conclusions from the individual to the species, life would elapse before we had acquired the first rudiments of that knowledge which is essential to our animal existence."† Every branch of knowledge presents instructive examples of the extent to which this mode of reasoning may be securely carried. Newton, from having observed that the refractive forces of different bodies follow the ratio of their densities, was

* Locke on the Human Understanding, b. iv. ch. xv. s. 5.
† 2 Stewart's Elements, *ut supra*, ch. ii. s. iv.

led to predict the combustibility of the diamond ages before the mechanical aids of science were capable of verifying his prediction ; nor is the sagacity of the conjecture the less striking, because this correspondence has been discovered not to be without exception. The scientific observer, from the inspection of shapeless fragments, which have mouldered under the suns and storms of ages, constructs a model of the original in its primitive magnificence and symmetry. A profound knowledge of comparative anatomy enabled the immortal Cuvier, from a single fossil bone, to describe the structure and habits of many of the extinct animals of the antediluvian world. In like manner an enlightened knowledge of human nature often enables us, on the foundation of apparently slight circumstances, to follow the tortuous windings of crime, and ultimately to discover its guilty author, as infallibly as the hunter is conducted by the track to his game.

The following pertinent and instructive observations may advantageously close this part of our subject, comprehending, as they do, everything which can be usefully adduced in illustration of the necessity and value of the principle of analogy. " In all reasonings concerning human life we are obliged to depend on analogy, if it were only from that uncertainty, and almost suspension of judgment, with which we must hold our conclusions. We can seldom obtain that number of instances which is requisite here to establish an inference indisputably. The conduct of persons or of parties may have been attended by certain antecedents and certain results in the examples before us ; still the state of the case may be owing, not so much to that conduct, as to other causes, which are shut out of our view, when our attention is fixed on the particular examples adduced for the purpose of the inference. We must thus be strictly on our guard against transferring to other cases anything merely contingent and peculiar to the instances on which our reasoning is founded. And this is what analogical reasoning requires and enables us to do. If rightly pursued it is employed at once, both in generalizing and discriminating; in the acute perception at once of points of agreement and points of difference. The acmé of the philosophical power is displayed in the perfect co-operation of these two opposite proceedings. We must study to combine in such a way as not to merge real differences; and so to distinguish as not to divert the eye from the real correspondence."*

It may be objected, that the minds of men are so differently constituted, and so much influenced by differences of experience and culture, that the same evidence may produce in different individuals very different degrees of belief; that one man may unhesitatingly believe an alleged fact, upon evidence which will not in any degree sway the mind of another. It must be admitted that moral certainty is not the same fixed and unvarying standard, alike in every individual; that scepticism and credulity are modifications of the same principle, and that to a certain extent this objection is grounded in fact; but nevertheless, the psychological considerations which it involves have but little alliance with the present subject: the argument, if pushed to its extreme, would go to introduce universal doubt and distrust, and to destroy all confidence in human judgment founded upon moral evidence. It is as impossible to reduce men's minds to the same standard, as it is to bring their bodies to the same dimensions; but in the one case, as well as in the other, there is a general agreement and similarity, any wide departure from which is instantly perceived to be eccentric

* Hampden's Lectures, *ut supra*, 178.

and extravagant. The question is, not what may be the *possible* effect of evidence upon minds *peculiarly* constructed, but what ought to be its fair result with men, such as the generality of civilized men are.

It is of no moment, in relation to criminal jurisprudence, that exact expression cannot be given to the inferior degrees of belief. The doctrine of chances, and nice calculations of probabilities, cannot, except in a few cases, and then only in a very general and abstract way, be applied to human actions, which are essentially unlike, and dependent upon peculiarities of persons and circumstances which render it impossible to assign to them a precise value, or to compare them with a common numeral standard ; nor are they capable in any degree, or under any circumstances, of being applied to actions which infer legal responsibility. In the common affairs of life men are frequently obliged, from necessity and duty, to act upon the lowest degree of belief; and, as Mr. Locke justly observes, " He that will not stir, till he infallibly knows the business he goes about will succeed, will have little else to do but to sit still and perish."* But in such cases our judgments commonly concern ourselves, and our own motives, duties, and interests ; while in the administration of penal justice, the magistrate is called upon to apply to the conduct of *others*, a rule of action applicable to a given state of facts, where external and sometimes ambiguous indicia alone constitute the grounds of judgment. In the application of every such rule, the certainty of the facts is presupposed, and is its only foundation and vindication ; and upon any lower degree of assurance, its application would be arbitrary and indefensible.

* Essay on the Human Understanding, b. iv. ch. xiv. s. 1.

CHAPTER II.

CIRCUMSTANTIAL EVIDENCE.

Section 1.

ESSENTIAL CHARACTERISTICS OF CIRCUMSTANTIAL EVIDENCE.

THE epithets DIRECT and INDIRECT or CIRCUMSTANTIAL, as applied to testimonial evidence, have been sanctioned by such long and general use, that it might appear presumptuous to question their accuracy, as it would perhaps be impracticable to substitute others more appropriate. But assuredly these terms have frequently been very indiscriminately applied, and the misuse of them has occasionally been the cause of lamentable results; it is therefore essential accurately to discriminate the proper application of them.

On a superficial view, direct and indirect or circumstantial, would appear to be *distinct* species of evidence; whereas, these words denote only the different modes in which those classes of evidentiary facts operate to produce conviction. Circumstantial evidence is of a nature identically the same with direct evidence; the distinction is, that by DIRECT EVIDENCE is intended evidence which applies directly to the fact which forms the subject of inquiry, the *factum probandum*; CIRCUMSTANTIAL EVIDENCE is equally direct in its nature, but, as its name imports, it is direct evidence of a minor fact or facts, incidental to or usually connected with some other fact as its accident, and from which such other fact is therefore inferred. A witness deposes that he saw A. inflict on B. a wound, of which he instantly died; this is a case of direct evidence. B. dies of poisoning; A. is proved to have had malice and uttered threats against him, and to have clandestinely purchased poison, wrapped in a particular paper, and of the same kind as that which has caused death; the paper is found in his secret drawer, and the poison gone. The *evidence* of these facts is *direct*; the facts themselves are *indirect* and *circumstantial*, as applicable to the inquiry whether a murder has been committed, and whether it was committed by A.

So rapid are our intellectual processes, that it is frequently difficult, and even impossible, to trace the connection between an act of the judgment, and the train of reasoning of which it is the result; and the one appears to succeed the other instantaneously, by a kind of necessity. This fact obtains most commonly in respect of matters which have been frequently the objects of mental association.

In matters of direct testimony, if credence be given to the relators, the act of hearing and the act of belief, though really not so, seem to be contemporaneous. But the case is very different when we have to determine upon circumstantial evidence, the judgment in respect of which is essentially *inferential*. There is no apparent necessary connection between the facts and the inference; the *facts* may be true and the *inference* erroneous, and it is only by comparison with the results of observation in similar or analogous circumstances, that we acquire confidence in the accuracy of our conclusions.

The term PRESUMPTIVE is frequently used as synonymous with CIRCUMSTANTIAL EVIDENCE; but it is not so
used with strict accuracy. The word 'presumption,' *ex
vi termini*, imports an *inference* from facts ; and the ad-
junct 'presumptive,' as applied to evidentiary facts, *implies*
the certainty of some *relation* between the facts and the
inference. Circumstances generally, but not necessarily,
lead to particular inferences; for the facts may be indis-
putable, and yet their relation to the principal fact may
be only apparent and not real; and even when the connection is real, the deduction may be erroneous. Circumstantial and presumptive evidence differ therefore as genus
and species.

The force and effect of circumstantial evidence depend
upon its incompatibility with, and incapability of, explanation or solution upon any other supposition than
that of the truth of the fact which it is adduced to prove;
the mode of argument resembling the method of demonstration by the *reductio ad absurdum*. But this is a part
of the subject which will more appropriately admit of
amplification in a future part of this essay.

Section 2.

PRESUMPTIONS.

IT is essential to a just view of our subject that our notions
of the nature of PRESUMPTIONS should be precise and distinct. A PRESUMPTION is a probable consequence, drawn
from facts (either certain, or proved by direct testimony),
as to the truth of a fact alleged, but of which there is no
direct proof. It follows, therefore, that a presumption of
any fact is an inference of that fact from others that are
known.* The word 'presumption,' therefore, inherently

† Per Abbott C. J. in Rex r. Burdett, 4 B. and Ald.161.

imports an act of reasoning,—a conclusion of the judgment; and it is applied to denote such facts or moral phenomena, as from experience we know to be invariably or commonly connected with some other related fact. A wounded and bleeding body is discovered; it has been plundered; wide and deep footmarks are found in a direction proceeding from the body; or a person is seen running from the spot. In the one case are observed marks of flight, in the other is seen the fugitive, and we know that guilt naturally endeavours to escape detection. These circumstances induce the presumption that crime has been committed; the presumption is a conclusion or consequence from the circumstances. The antecedent circumstances therefore are one thing, the presumption from them another and different one. Of presumptions afforded by moral phenomena, a memorable instance is recorded in the Judgment of Solomon, whose knowledge of the all-powerful force of maternal love supplied him with an infallible criterion of truth.* So, when Aristippus, who had been cast away on an unknown shore, saw certain geometrical figures traced in the sand, his inference that the country was inhabited by a people conversant with mathematics was a presumption of the same nature.† It is evident that this kind of reasoning is not peculiar to legal science, but is a logical process common to every subject of human investigation.

All presumptions connected with human conduct are inferences founded upon the observation of man's nature as a sentient being and a moral agent; and they are necessarily infinite in variety and number, differing according to the diversities of individual character, and to the

* Domat's Civil Law, b. iii. tit. 6.
† Gambier's Introduction to the Study of Moral Ev. 55.

innumerable and ever-changing situations and emergencies in which men are placed. Hence the importance of a knowledge of the instincts, affections, desires, and moral capabilities of our nature, to the correct deduction of such presumptions as are founded upon them, and which are therefore called NATURAL PRESUMPTIONS.*

LEGAL PRESUMPTIONS are founded upon natural presumptions, being such natural presumptions as are connected with human actions, so far as they are authoritatively constituted by the legislator or deduced by the magistrate.

The civilians divided legal presumptions into two classes, namely, *præsumptiones juris et de jure*, and *præsumptiones juris* simply.

Presumptions of the former class were such as were considered to be founded upon a connection and relation so intimate and certain between the fact known and the fact sought, that the latter was deemed to be an infallible consequence from the existence of the first. Such presumptions were called *præsumptiones juris*, because their force and authority were recognized by the law; and *de jure*, because they were made the foundation of certain specific legal consequences,† against which no argument or evidence was admissible; while *præsumptiones juris* simply, though deduced from facts characteristic of truth, were always subject to be overthrown by proof of facts leading to a contrary presumption.

In matters of property, the principal modifications of which are matters of positive institution, the laws of every country have created artificial legal presumptions, grounded upon reasons of policy and convenience, to pre-

* 3 Mascardus De Probationibus, Conclusio MCCXXVI.
† Menochius De Præsumptionibus, lib. i. q. 3.

vent social discord and to fortify private right. The justice and policy of such regulations have been thus eloquently enforced: " Civil cases regard property: now, although property itself is not, yet almost everything concerning property, and all its modifications, is of artificial contrivance. The rules concerning it become more positive, as connected with positive institutions. The legislator therefore always, the jurist frequently, may ordain certain methods, by which alone they will suffer such matters to be known and established; because their very essence, for the greater part, depends on the arbitrary conventions of men. Men act on them with all the power of a creator over his creatures. They make fictions of law and presumptions of law (*præsumptiones juris et de jure*) according to their ideas of utility—and against those fictions, and against presumptions so created, they do and may reject all evidence."*

But in penal jurisprudence, man as a physical being and a moral agent, such as he is by natural constitution and by the influences of social condition, is the subject of inquiry. Punitive justice is applied to injurious actions proceeding from malignity of purpose, and not to physical actions merely. It has been said with great force and accuracy, that " where the subject is of a physical nature, or of a moral nature, independent of their conventions, men have no other reasonable authority, than to register and digest the results of experience and observation;" and that " the presumptions which belong to criminal cases are those natural and popular presumptions which are only observations turned into maxims, like adages and apophthegms, and are admitted (when their grounds

* 2 Burke's Works, 623: ed. 1834, by Holdsworth and Ball; 3 Mascardus, *ut supra*, Conclusio MCCXXVIII.

are established) in the place of proof, where better is
wanting, but are to be always overturned by counter-
proof."[*]   Hence therefore a third class of presumptions,
which the civilians called *præsumptiones hominis*, because
they were inferred by the sagacity and discretion of the
judge from the facts judicially before him.   Such presumptions are in fact natural presumptions simply, de-
riving their force from that relation and connection which
are recognized and acknowledged by the unsophisticated
reason of all observing and reflecting men.

Presumptions of every kind, to be just, must be dic-
tated by nature and reason ; and, except under special
and peculiar circumstances, it is impossible, without a de-
reliction of every rational principle, to lay down positive
rules of presumption, where every case must of necessity
be connected with peculiarities of personal disposition and
of concomitant circumstances, and be therefore irreducible to any fixed principle.   In criminal jurisprudence,
therefore, arbitrary presumptions should be sparingly admitted; and even when they are so, they occasionally work
injustice.   On the conviction of the captain of a schooner
for having naval stores in his possession, Mr. Baron
Alderson, in passing sentence of six months' imprisonment, said that he was satisfied he had become possessed
of the stores in ignorance of the Act of Parliament, but
that it was of the greatest importance that its provisions
should be generally known, and expressed his hope that
his good character would operate to obtain a mitigation
of the sentence.[†]   It would be as unreasonable to subject human actions to unbending rules of presumption, as

* 2 Burke's Works, *ut supra*, 623 ; 3 Mascardus, *ut supra*, Conclusio
MCCXXVIII.

† Reg. *v.* Trannock, Liverpool Winter Ass. 1848.

to prescribe to the commander of a ship inflexible rules for his conduct, without any latitude of discretion in the unforeseen and innumerable accidents and contingencies of the tempest and the ocean. Where a peremptory presumption of legal guilt is not pernicious and unjust, it is in general at least unnecessary; for, if it be a fair conclusion of the reason, it will be adopted by the tribunals, without the mandate of the legislature. There may, no doubt, be cases, where the provisions of the law are peculiarly liable to be defeated or evaded by subtle contrivances and shifts most difficult of prevention. But, even in such cases, legal presumptions can only be justifiable where the proximate substituted fact of presumption is clearly of a guilty character and tendency *per se*, and would afford, even in the absence of legal enactment, a strong moral ground of presumption indicative of the particular act of criminality intended to be repressed;[*] and however explicit and exclusive may be the language of the legislature, the tribunals must by an inherent necessity give effect to all such surrounding circumstances as tend to repel or modify the particular presumption, or to create a counter-presumption of equal or superior weight.[†] It is impossible to recall without horror the sanguinary law[‡] which made the concealment of the death of an illegitimate child by its mother, conclusive evidence of murder, unless she could make proof, by one witness at least, that the child was born dead, and which too long disgraced our statute-book; whereas in truth it affords no ground to warrant such a conclusion, since it is more natural and more just to attribute the suppression to a desire to conceal female shame and to escape open dishonour.

* Traité des Preuves, par Bonnier. 702: 3rd ed.
† See *infra*, s. 8.   ‡ Stat. 21 Jac. I. c. 27.

As evidentiary circumstances and their combinations are infinitely varied, so also are the presumptions to which they lead; and a complete enumeration would in either case be impracticable. The writers on the civil law have made a comprehensive and instructive collection of facts and inferential conclusions, in relation to a vast number of actions connected with legal accountability. But many things advanced by those laborious and elaborate authors have relation to a state of society, and to legal institutions and modes of procedure, wholly dissimilar from our own. The law of England admits of no such thing as the *semiplena probatio*, founded on circumstances of conjecture and suspicion only, which in many countries governed by the Roman law, was held to warrant the infliction of torture with a view to compel admissions and complete imperfect proof. Hence the total inapplicability with us of the subdivisions of *indicia, signa, adminicula, conjecturæ, dubia,* and *suspiciones,* which are found in the writers of other countries whose jurisprudence is founded upon that of Rome—subdivisions which appear to be arbitrary, vague, and useless. But it is manifest that, under legal institutions which admitted of compulsory self-accusation, in order to complete proof insufficient and inconclusive in itself, and where the laws were administered by a single judge, without the salutary restraints of publicity and popular observation, an accurate and elaborate record of the multitudinous actions and occurrences which had been submitted to the criminal tribunals, operated as an important limitation upon the tyranny and inconstancy of judicial discretion.

It is calculated to excite surprise, that arbitrary technical rules should ever have been adopted, for estimating the force and effect of particular facts as leading to presumptions ; a matter purely one of reason and logic. It is probable, nevertheless, that the attempt originated in the desire to escape a still greater absurdity. " *Testis unus, testis nullus*," " *unus testis non est audiendus*," were fundamental maxims of the text-writers on the Civil and Canon Laws, and of most ancient codes,[*] as they still are of judicial procedure in many parts of Europe.[†] Since presumptions have not the same force as direct evidence, it was hence supposed to be required, as a logical sequence, that there should be a concurrence of three presumptions, as the imaginary equivalent for the testimony of two ocular witnesses, where such testimony was not to be had. It is discreditable to the state of moral and legal science that these absurd and antiquated notions, worthy of the darkest ages of society, should have been countenanced and perpetuated in the legislation of several of the nations of Europe even to the present day.[‡] It is obvious that a single presumption may be conclusive, and that an accumulation of many presumptions may be of but little weight. The simplest and most elementary dictates of common sense require that presumptions should not be numbered merely, but that they should be weighed according to the principles which are applied in estimating the effect of testimonial evidence.

The prevalence of these fallacious methods of judging of the force of evidence, explains the foundation of the practice, abhorrent to every principle of judicial integrity,

* Deut. xvii. 6, 7, xix. 15 ; Numb. xxxv. 30 ; 4 Michaelis on the Laws of Moses, by Smith, Art. cexcix.

† Code Hollandais, 1838 ; Code Pénal d'Autriche ; Code de Bavière, and many other German Codes.

‡ Code Criminel de Prusse, 1805 ; Code de Procédure Criminelle d'Autriche, 1853 ; ditto de Modène, 1855.

and which still extensively prevails, of condemning to a
minor punishment persons who may be innocent, but
against whom there may exist apparent grounds of strong
presumption, though not that exact kind and amount of
proof which the rules of evidence arbitrarily and unreasonably require; as if a middle term in criminal jurisprudence were not an absurdity and self-contradictory.[*]
An eminent foreign jurist well remarks, that, "Jamais il
n'y a eu plus de condamnations injustes que sous l'empire
d'une jurisprudence qui défendait de prononcer la peine
capitale sur de simples indices."[†]

The unreasonable stress, which in many countries
whose criminal procedure is derived from the Civil Law,
is laid upon the confession of the accused, and the unwarrantable means which are resorted to in order to obtain it, are the natural results of arbitrary and unphilosophical rules of evidence, which necessarily have the effect of closing many of the channels of truth; and frequently render it so difficult to obtain full legal proof of
crime, that a late eminent jurist and criminal judge declared, that unless a man chose to perpetrate his crimes
in public, or to confess them, he need not fear a conviction.[‡]

Attempts have been made by our own juridical writers,
but with no useful result, to classify presumptions in a

---

[*] See several such cases in Narratives of Remarkable Criminal Trials,
translated from the German of Feuerbach, by Lady Duff Gordon. At
Berne, in 1842, a man accused of murder by poisoning was sentenced to
six years' imprisonment, as *véhémentement suspect*.

[†] Bonnier, *ut supra*, 677.

[‡] Ed. Rev. lxxxii. 330; and see in Christison on Poisons, 61, ed. 2,
a case where the crime of murder by poisoning was considered as not
fully proved because the prisoner would not confess, but on account
of the probability of his guilt he was condemned to fifteen years' imprisonment.

more general way under terms expressive of their effect, as VIOLENT or NECESSARY, PROBABLE or GRAVE, and SLIGHT.* But this arrangement is specious and fanciful rather than practical and real; nor is it entirely accurate, since a presumption may be violent and yet not necessary.† A more precise and intelligible classification of presumptions is into, violent or strong, and slight. But it is impossible thus to classify more than a comparatively few of the infinite variety of circumstances connected with human actions and motives, or to lay down rules for distinguishing presumptions of one of these classes from those of another; and the terms of designation, from the inherent imperfections of language, although not wholly destitute of utility, are unavoidably defective in precision. We can therefore only usefully apply these epithets as relative terms; and the effect of particular facts must of necessity depend upon the reality and closeness of the connection between the principal and secondary facts, and upon a variety of considerations peculiar to each individual case, and can no more be predicated than the boundaries can be defined, of the separate colours which form the solar bow.

It is convenient, and may be advantageous even, in order to obtain a comprehensive view of the tendencies and effect of a number of circumstances, to group them together in their chronological relation to the *factum pro-bandum*, as ANTECEDENT, CONCOMITANT, and SUBSEQUENT; but to require the concurrence of these several kinds of presumption, as is the case in the new criminal code of

---

* Bentham's Rationale of Judicial Evidence, b. i. c. vi.: Coke on Litt. 6. b.; 4 Blackstone's Comm. 353.

† See Menochius, *ut supra* lib. 1. q. 3, nos. 1, 2, 3; Essai des Preuves, par Gabriel, 373; Best on Presumptions, 40.

Bavaria, is an outrage upon all legal and philosophical principle.*

By various statutes, many acts are made legal presumptions of guilt, and the onus of proving any matter of defence is expressly cast upon the party accused; but, with these exceptions, the truth of every accusation is determined by the voice of a jury, upon consideration of the intrinsic and independent merits of each particular case, acting upon those principles of reason and judgment by which mankind are governed in all other cases where the same intellectual process is called into exercise, unfettered by any obligatory and inflexible presumptions. The inexpediency and inefficacy of positive presumptions, as indications of the criminality of intention, in which alone consists the essence of legal guilt, have been thus exposed with equal force and elegance by the hand of a master:—"The connection of the intention and the circumstances, is plainly of such a nature, as more to depend on the sagacity of the observer than on the excellency of any rule. The pains taken by the civilians on that subject have not been very fruitful; and the English lawwriters have, perhaps as wisely, in a manner abandoned the pursuit. In truth, it seems a wild attempt to lay down any rule for the proof of intention by circumstantial evidence."†

Section 3.

RELATIVE VALUE OF DIRECT AND INDIRECT OR CIRCUMSTANTIAL EVIDENCE.

The foregoing observations naturally lead to a comparison of the relative value of Direct and Indirect or Circum-

* Bonnier, *ut supra*, 683; Traité de la Preuve, par Mittermaier (traduit par Alexandre), c. 61.   † 2 Burke's Works. *ut supra*, 623.

stantial Evidence; an inquiry which becomes the more necessary, on account of some novel and questionable doctrines which have received countenance even from the judgment-seat.

The best writers, ancient and modern, on the subject of evidence, have concurred in treating circumstantial as inferior in cogency and effect to direct evidence; a conclusion which seems to follow necessarily from the very nature of the different kinds of evidence. But language of a directly contrary import has been so often used by authorities of no mean note, as to have become almost proverbial, and to require examination.

It has been said that "circumstances are inflexible proofs; that witnesses may be mistaken or corrupted, but things can be neither."* "Circumstances," says Paley, "cannot lie."† It is astonishing that sophisms like these should have passed current without animadversion. The "circumstances" are assumed to be in every case established beyond the possibility of mistake; and it is implied, that a circumstance established to be true possesses some *mysterious force* peculiar to facts of a certain class. Now, a circumstance is neither more nor less than a minor fact, and it may be admitted of all facts, that they cannot lie; for a fact cannot at the same time exist and not exist: so that in truth, the doctrine is merely the expression of a truism, that a fact is a fact. It may also be admitted that "circumstances are inflexible proofs," but assuredly of nothing more than of their own existence: so that this assertion is only a repetition of the same truism in different terms. It seems also to have been overlooked, that circumstances and facts of every kind must be proved

* Burnett's C. L. of Scotland, 523.
† Principles of Moral and Political Philosophy, b. vi. c. ix.

by human testimony ; that although " circumstances cannot lie," the narrators of them may ; that, like witnesses
of all other facts, they may be biassed or mistaken, and
that the facts, even if indisputably true, may lead to erroneous inference. Thus far then, circumstantial possesses
no advantage over direct evidence.

A distinguished statesman and orator has advanced in
unqualified terms the proposition, supported, he alleges,
by the learned, that " when circumstantial proof is in its
greatest perfection, that is, when it is most abundant in
circumstances, it is much superior to positive proof."*
Paley has said, with more of caution, that " a concurrence
of well-authenticated circumstances composes a stronger
ground of assurance than positive testimony, unconfirmed
by circumstances, usually affords."†   Mr. Baron Legge,
upon a trial for murder, told the jury that where a " violent presumption *necessarily* arises from circumstances,
they are more convincing and satisfactory than any other
kind of evidence, *because facts cannot lie.*"‡   Mr. Justice
Buller, in his charge to the jury in Donellan's case, said
" that a presumption which *necessarily* arises from circumstances is very often more convincing and more satisfactory than any other kind of evidence, because it is not
within the reach and compass of human abilities to invent
a train of circumstances which shall be so connected together as to amount to a proof of guilt, without affording
opportunities of contradicting a great part if not all of
those circumstances."§

It is obvious that the doctrine laid down in these se-

* 2 Burke's Works, *ut supra*, 624.
† Moral and Political Philosophy, b. vi. c. ix.
‡ Rex *v.* Blandy, 18 State Trials, 1187.
§ Gurney's Report of the Trial of John Donellan, Esq., for murder, at
the Assize at Warwick, March 30th, 1781.

veral passages is propounded in language which not only does not accurately state the question, but implies a fallacy, and that extreme cases—the strongest ones of circumstantial, and the weakest of positive evidence—have been selected for the illustration and support of a general position. "A presumption which *necessarily* arises from circumstances" cannot admit of dispute, and requires no corroboration; but then it cannot in fairness be contrasted with and opposed to positive testimony, unless of a nature equally cogent and infallible. If evidence be so strong as *necessarily* to produce certainty and conviction, it matters not by what *kind* of evidence the effect is produced; and the intensity of the proof must be precisely the same, whether the evidence be direct or circumstantial. It is not intended to deny that circumstantial evidence affords a safe and satisfactory ground of assurance and belief; nor that in many individual instances it may be superior in proving power to other individual cases of proof by direct evidence. But a judgment based upon circumstantial evidence cannot, in any case, be more satisfactory than when the same result is produced by direct evidence, free from suspicion of bias or mistake.

Perhaps no single circumstance has been so often considered as certain and unequivocal in its effect, as the *anno-domini* water-mark usually contained in the fabric of writing-paper; and in many instances it has led to the exposure of fraud in the propounding of forged as genuine instruments. But it is beyond any doubt (and several instances of the kind have recently occurred) that issues of paper have taken place bearing the water-mark of the year succeeding that of its distribution,—a striking exemplification of the fallacy of some of the arguments which have been remarked upon. How often has it been iterated in such cases, that circumstances are inflexible facts, and that facts cannot lie!

The proper effect of circumstantial, as compared with direct evidence, was thus more accurately stated by Lord Chief Baron Macdonald. " When circumstances connect themselves closely with each other, when they form a large and a strong body, so as to carry conviction to the minds of a jury, it MAY BE proof of a more satisfactory sort than that which is direct. In some lamentable instances it has been known that a short story has been got by heart, by two or three witnesses; they have been consistent with themselves, they have been consistent with each other, swearing positively to a fact, which fact has turned out afterwards not to be true. It is almost impossible for a variety of witnesses, speaking to a variety of circumstances, so to concert a story, as to impose upon a jury by a fabrication of that sort, so that where it is cogent, strong, and powerful, where the witnesses do not contradict each other, or do not contradict themselves, it MAY BE evidence more satisfactory than even direct evidence; and there are more instances than one where that has been the case."*   In another case the same learned judge said, " Where the proof arises from the irresistible force of a number of circumstances, which we cannot conceive to be fraudulently brought together to bear upon one point, that is less fallible than under *some circumstances* direct evidence MAY BE."†

But, in truth, direct and circumstantial evidence ought not to be placed in contrast, since they are not mutually opposed; for evidence of a circumstantial and secondary

---

* Rex v. Patch, Surrey Spring Assizes, 1806.
† Rex v. Smith, for arson, Old Bailey, June 15, 1813, Short-hand Report by Gurney.

nature can never be justifiably resorted to, except where evidence of a direct and therefore of a superior nature is unattainable.

The argument founded upon the abundance of the circumstances, and the consequent opportunities of contradiction which they afford, belongs to another part of the subject. While each of these incidents adds greatly to the probative force of circumstantial evidence in *particular* cases, they have clearly no connection with an inquiry into the value of circumstantial evidence in the *abstract*. However numerous may be the independent circumstances to which the witnesses depose, the result cannot be of a different kind from, or superior to, that strong moral assurance which is the consequence of satisfactory proof by direct testimony, and for which, if such proof be attainable, every tribunal, every reasonable mind would reject any attempt to substitute indirect or circumstantial evidence, as inadmissible, and as affording the strongest reason for suspicion and disbelief.

It has been said, that " though in most cases of circumstantial evidence there be a *possibility* that the prisoner may be innocent, the same often holds in cases of direct proof, where witnesses may err as to identity of person, or corruptly falsify, for reasons that are at the time unknown."* This observation is unquestionably true. Even the testimony of the senses, though it affords the safest ground of moral assurance, cannot be implicitly depended upon, even where the veracity of the witnesses is above all suspicion. An eminent barrister, a gentleman of acute mind and strong understanding, swore positively to the persons of two men, whom he charged with robbing him in the open daylight. But it was proved by conclusive

* Burnet on the C. L. of Scotland, 524.

evidence, that the men on trial were, at the time of the robbery, at so remote a distance from the spot that the thing was impossible. The consequence was, that they were acquitted, and some time afterwards the robbers were taken, and the articles stolen found upon them. The prosecutor, on seeing these men, candidly acknowledged his mistake, and it is said gave a recompense to the persons he prosecuted, and who so narrowly escaped conviction.* It is probable that he was deceived by the broad glare of sunlight, but there can be no doubt of the sincerity of his impressions.

Many similar instances are upon record of the fallibility of human testimony, even as to matters supposed to be grounded upon the clearest evidence of the senses, and where the misconception has related to the substantive matters of judicial inquiry. It has been said with the strictest philosophical truth, that " proof is nothing more than a presumption of the highest order."† But these considerations, instead of establishing the superior efficacy of circumstantial evidence, seem irresistibly to lead to the conclusion that it is, *à fortiori*, more probable that similar misconception may take place as to *collateral* facts and incidents, to which perhaps particular attention may not have been excited.

There is another source of fallacy and danger, to which, as already intimated, circumstantial evidence is peculiarly liable, and of which it is necessary to be especially mindful. Where the evidence is direct, and the testimony credible, belief is the immediate and necessary result; whereas, in cases of circumstantial evidence, processes of inference and deduction are essentially involved,—fre-

* Rex v. Wood and Brown: 28 State Trials, 819; Ann. Reg. 1784.
† Per Lord Erskine in the Banbury Peerage Case.

quently of a most delicate and perplexing character,—
liable to numerous causes of fallacy, some of them inherent in the nature of the mind itself, which has been
profoundly compared to the distorting power of an un-
even mirror, imparting its own nature upon the true
nature of things.*   Mr. Baron Alderson, upon a trial
of this kind, said, " It was necessary to warn the jury
against the danger of being misled by a train of circumstantial evidence.   The mind was apt to take a pleasure in adapting circumstances to one another, and even
in straining them a little, if need be, to force them to
form parts of one connected whole ; and the more ingenious the mind of the individual, the more likely was it,
in considering such matters, to overreach and mislead
itself, to supply some little link that is wanting, to take
for granted some fact consistent with its previous theories
and necessary to render them complete."†

It may be objected that the foregoing observations tend
to create distrust in all human testimony.   While it must
be admitted that the senses cannot be implicitly depended
upon, it is certain that their liability to mistake may be
greatly diminished by habits of accurate observation and
relation.   The general conformity of our impressions to
truth and nature, and the universal opinion and practice
of mankind, establish the reasonableness and propriety
of our faith in testimonial evidence.   The interest to
which all controverted matters of fact give occasion, is
a manifestation of the preference in the human mind of
truth to falsehood ; and, finally, the number of mistaken
inferences from the testimony of the senses is inconceiv-

* Novum Organum, lib. i. Aph. 41, 45 ; Best. on Presumptions, 255 ;
and see 3 Bentham's Jud. Ev. b. v. c. xv. s. iv.

† Reg. v. Hodges, 2 Lewin's C. C. 227.

ably small, as compared with the almost infinite number of judgments which are correctly drawn from evidence of the kind in question.

Section 4.

OF THE SOURCES AND CLASSIFICATION OF CIRCUM-STANTIAL EVIDENCE.

In the present state of knowledge there can be little danger of mistake as to the legitimate subjects of human belief; but how melancholy is the degradation of the human intellect exhibited in the records of superstition, imposture, and delusion, of enthusiasm and credulity, of judicial darkness and cruelty, in the pages of our own history, as well as in those of every other nation!

A profound ignorance of the laws of nature, an inability to account for the origin of evil, and to reconcile its existence with the Divine attributes, and the impulse to avenge wrongs for which human institutions afforded no remedy, led to a universal belief in the supernatural interposition of the Supreme Being on behalf of his injured moral offspring. Of this persuasion, augury, divination, judicial combat, the various forms of trial by ordeal, the supposed intimations of truth conveyed by means of apparitions and dreams, the bleeding of a corpse in the presence of the murderer, and his reluctance to touch it,* were thought to be so many manifestations; while, with the wildest inconsistency, the belief was equally general in the existence and influence of witchcraft and other modes of demoniacal agency over the minds and actions of men. The history of all nations affords lamentable

* See Rex v. Standsfield, 11 St. Tr. 1403; and Rex v. Okeman, 14 ibid. 1324.

memorials of judicial murders, the natural consequences of such mistaken and degrading views. Without adverting to other reasons, it is conclusive against all departure by the Supreme Being from the ordinary course of his administration, that so many instances of erroneous conviction and execution have occurred in all ages and in all countries.

The course of external nature, and the mental and physical constitution of man, and his actions and moral and mechanical relations, are the only true sources of those facts which constitute circumstantial evidence.

In every inquiry into the truth of any alleged fact, as to which our means of judgment are secondary facts, there must exist relations and dependencies, inseparable from the principal fact, which will commonly be manifested by external appearances. No action of a rational being is indifferent or independent; and every such action must necessarily be connected with antecedent, concomitant, and subsequent conditions of mind, and with external circumstances, of the actual existence of which, though it may not invariably be apparent, there can be no doubt.

A crime, so far as it falls within the cognizance of human tribunals, is an *act* proceeding from a wicked *motive ;* it follows therefore that in every such act, there must have been one or more voluntary agents; that it must have had corresponding relations to some precise moment of time and portion of space; that there must have existed inducements to guilt, preparations for, and objects and instruments of crime; these,—the acts of disguise, flight, or concealment, the possession of plunder or other fruits of crime, and innumerable other particulars connected with individual conduct, and with moral, social, and physical relations, afford materials for the determination of the judgment. It would be impracticable to enumerate the infinite variety of circumstantial evidentiary facts, which of necessity are as various as the modifications and combinations of events in actual life. "All the acts of the party, all things that explain or throw light on these acts, all the acts of others relative to the affair, that come to his knowledge and may influence him; his friendships and enmities, his promises, his threats, the truth of his discourses, the falsehood of his apologies, pretences, and explanations; his looks, his speech, his silence where he was called to speak; everything which tends to establish the connection between all these particulars;—every circumstance, precedent, concomitant, and subsequent, become parts of circumstantial evidence. These are in their matter infinite, and cannot be comprehended within any rule, or brought under any classification."*

Evidentiary facts of a circumstantial nature are susceptible only of a very general arrangement, into two classes; namely, moral indications, afforded by the relations, and language and conduct of the party; and, secondly, facts which are apparently extrinsic and mechanical, and independent of moral conduct and demeanour: and each of these classes may be further considered, as such facts are inculpatory or exculpatory. But this division is grounded upon the apparent rather than the real qualities of actions, and cannot be regarded as strictly accurate; since all the actions of a rational agent are prompted by motives, and are therefore really moral indications, though it may not be always practicable to develope their moral relations.

* 2 Burke's Works, *ut supra*, 623.

CHAPTER III.

INCULPATORY MORAL INDICATIONS.

Although, for reasons which have been explained, a complete enumeration of facts as invariably conjoined with authoritative presumptions would be impracticable, it is important, in illustration of the general principles which determine the relevancy and effect of circumstantial evidence, to notice some particulars of moral conduct, of frequent occurrence in courts of criminal jurisdiction, which are popularly, and on that account judicially, considered as leading to important and well-grounded presumptions.

These circumstances may be considered under the heads of motives to crime, declarations or acts indicative of guilty consciousness or intention, preparations for the commission of crime, possession of the fruits of crime, refusal to account for appearances of suspicion, or unsatisfactory explanations of such appearances, evidence indirectly confessional, the suppression, destruction, simulation, and fabrication of evidence, statutory presumptions, and scientific testimony.

Section 1.

MOTIVES TO CRIME.

As there must pre-exist a motive to every voluntary action of a rational being, it is proper to comprise in the class of moral indications, such particulars of external relation as are usually observed to operate as inducements

to the commission of crime, as well as such indications
from language and conduct as more directly and unequi-
vocally manifest a connection between the deed and the
mind of the actor. In strictness the word 'motive,' though
popularly applied to denote the external objects poten-
tially calculated to act on the mind, ought to be limited
to the designation of such objects only as have actually
influenced the will, as the efficient causes of moral action.

The metaphorical origin of this word has given rise to
serious misconception as to the nature of moral and legal
responsibility, upon which it is essential that our concep-
tions should be accurate. From its primary application
to material force, an imaginary analogy has been supposed
between the action of moral and physical agencies. In
reality, however, there is no resemblance between the fatal
and irresistible constraint of mechanical power and the
influence of motives on the self-originating will of an
intelligent and free agent. MAN is not the passive subject of necessity or chance; nor are his moral judgments
merely the abstractions of logic : on the contrary, he is en-
dowed with instincts, passions, and affections, and above
all with reason, and the capacity of estimating the qualities and tendencies of his volitions and actions, and with
the power of choosing from among the various inducements, emotional and rational, which are presented to
him, the governing principles of his conduct.*

These considerations constitute the foundation of moral
and legal responsibility; and it follows from them, that in
all their important actions we naturally, reasonably, and
safely judge of men's motives by their conduct, as we
conclude from the nature of the stream the qualities of

* 6 Stewart's collected Works, 349 ; Cousin, Cours de l'Hist. de
Philosophie, prem. sér. tome 4, Leçon xxiv.

its source. It is indispensable, therefore, in the investigation of imputed guilt to look at all the surrounding circumstances which connect the actor with other persons and things, and may have operated as motives and influenced his actions.

The common inducements to crime are, the desire of revenging some real or fancied wrong; of getting rid of a rival or an obnoxious connection; of escaping from the pressure of pecuniary or other obligation or burden; of obtaining plunder or other coveted object; of preserving reputation, either that of general character or the conventional reputation of profession or sex; or of gratifying some other selfish or malignant passion. But it is of the essence of moral weakness that it forms a mistaken estimate of present good, and a want of proportion will therefore of necessity be found between the objects of desire and the means employed to obtain them. The assassin's dagger may be put in requisition for a few pieces of gold, and the difference between that and other inducements to crime is a difference only of degree. Indeed, tried by the strict rules of morality, there can be no such thing as an adequate motive to the commission of crime.

It is always a satisfactory circumstance of corroboration when, in connection with convincing facts of conduct, an apparent motive can be assigned; but, as the operations of the mind are invisible and intangible, it is impossible to go further; and it must be remembered that there may be motives which no human being but the party himself can divine. Nor must undue importance be attached to external circumstances supposed to be indicative of guilty motive, for there are few men to whom some or other of the forms of crime may not apparently prove advantageous. Neither ought the existence of such apparent inducements, to supersede the necessity for the same amount of proof as would be deemed necessary in the absence of all evidence of such a stimulus. Suspicion, too readily excited by the appearance of supposed inducement, is incompatible with that even and unprejudiced state of mind which is indispensable to the formation of correct and sober judgment. While true it is, that frequently "imputation and strong circumstances . . . lead directly to the door of truth," it is equally true that entirely to penetrate the mind of man is out of human power, and that circumstances which apparently have presented powerful motives, may never have acted as such. Who can say that some "uncleanly apprehension," some transient thought of sinister aspect, in the dimness of moral light momentarily mistaken for good, may not float unbidden across the purest mind? And how often is it that man has no control over circumstances of apparent power over his motives?

It follows from the foregoing remarks, that evidence of collateral facts which may appear to have presented a motive for a particular action deserves *per se* no weight. With motives merely, the legislator and the magistrate have nothing to do; ACTIONS, AS THE OBJECTS OR RESULTS OF MOTIVES, are the only legitimately cognizable subjects of human laws. *Actus non facit reum nisi mens sit rea*, is a maxim of reason and justice not less than of positive law.* Motives and their objects differ, it has been remarked, as the springs and wheels of a watch differ from the pointing of the hour, being mutually related in like manner.† But such evidence is most pertinent and important when clearly connected with declarations which demonstrate that the particular motive has passed into ac-

* 3 Inst. 107.   † Hampden's Lect. *ut supra*, 241.

tion, or with inculpatory moral facts which it tends to explain and co-ordinate, and which would otherwise be inexplicable.

The particulars of external relation and moral conduct will in general correctly indicate the character of the motive in which they have originated. On the other hand, the entire absence of surrounding circumstances, which on the ordinary principles of human nature may reasonably be supposed to have acted as an inducing cause, is justly regarded, whenever upon the general evidence the imputed guilt is doubtful, as affording a strong presumption of innocence.

It occasionally happens that actions of great enormity are committed, for which no apparent motive is discoverable. It must not be concluded however that no pre-existent motive has operated; and upon principles of reason and justice essential to common security, the actor is held to be legally accountable for his actions, unless it be clearly and indubitably shown that he is bereft of reason and moral power. A sense of injury, and long-cherished feelings of resentment, may ultimately induce a state of mind independent of self-restraint, and render their victim the sport of ungovernable impulses of passion;* but the distinction is evident and just between such actions as are the consequences of a voluntary abdication of moral control, and actions committed under the over-mastering power of a delusion of the imagination, which, though groundless, operates upon the mind with all the force of reality and necessity.†

On a late trial for murder, Lord Chief Justice Camp-

---

* Rex v. Earl Ferrers, 19 St. Tr. 885.

† Rex v. Hadfield, 27 St. Tr. 1281; Rex v. Martin, York Sp. Ass. 1831, Short-hand Rep. by Fraser; Rex v. Offord, 5 C. & P. 168.

bell thus summed up the doctrine under discussion. "With respect to the alleged motive, it is of great importance to see whether there was a motive for committing such a crime, or whether there was not; or whether there is an improbability of its having been committed so strong as not to be overpowered by positive evidence. But if there be any motive which can be assigned, I am bound to tell you that the adequacy of that motive is of little importance. We know, from the experience of criminal courts, that atrocious crimes of this sort have been committed from very slight motives; not merely from malice and revenge, but to gain a small pecuniary advantage, and to drive off for a time pressing difficulties."*

It is a general rule for the interpretation of conduct as indicative of motives, demanded by social security and founded in substantial justice, that every man shall be held to have intended, and therefore to be legally accountable for, the natural and probable consequences of his actions;† and no one can be permitted to speculate with impunity upon the precise extent to which he may securely carry his mischievous intentions, the reality and degree of which it is alike impossible to determine. If therefore the motive have been to commit, not the particular crime, but another of equal legal degree, then the maxim applies that *in criminalibus sufficit generalis malitia intentionis cum facto paris gradus,*‡ "All crimes," says Bacon, "have their conception in a corrupt intent, and have their consummation and issuing in some particular fact, which though it be not the fact at which the intention of the malefactor levelled, yet the law giveth

* Reg. *v.* Palmer, Short-hand Report, 308.
† Rex *v.* Farrington, R. & R. 209; Rex *v.* Harvey, 2 B. & C. 257; Rex *v.* Dixon, 2 M. & S. 11.   ‡ Bacon's Max. Reg. xv.

him no advantage of the error, if another particular occur
of as high a nature. Therefore if an empoisoned apple be
laid in a place to empoison J.S., and J. D. cometh by chance
and catcth of it, this is murder in the principal, that is
actor, and yet the malice *in individuo* was not against J.
D."* "In capital cases," declares the same high authority,
"*in favorem vitæ*, the law will not punish in so high a
degree, except the malice of the will and intention appear."† But nevertheless the rule under discussion has
been extended beyond all reasonable application, as where
two persons were convicted of lying in wait and slitting
the prosecutor's nose with intent to maim and disfigure,
an offence then capital by the statute 22 & 23 Car. II.,
c. 1, though the real intention was to commit murder, in
order to obtain an estate, an offence not capital, and
there was no such special intent as the statute required;‡
a case which, as extending a criminal law by equity, is
inconsistent with the general principles of jurisprudence,
and with the spirit of many later cases.§

SECTION 2.

DECLARATIONS AND ACTS INDICATIVE OF GUILTY CON-SCIOUSNESS OR INTENTION.

IT is very common with persons who have been engaged,
or are about to engage, in crime, to make obscure or
mysterious allusion to their criminal acts or purposes,
or to boast to others whose standard of moral conduct is the same as their own, of what they have done or

---

* Bacon's Max. Reg. xv.   † *Ib.* vii.

‡ Rex *v.* Coke and Woodburne, 16 St. Tr. 54.

§ 4 Lord Campbell's Lives of the L. Ch. 601; Rex *v.* Bell, Foster's
Discourses on Cr. Law, App.; Rex *v.* Carroll, 2 East's P. C. 400; Rex
v. Duffin, R. & R. 365.

will do, or to give vent to expressions of revengeful feelings or of malignant satisfaction at the accomplishment or anticipated occurrence of some serious mischief. Such declarations or allusions are of great moment when clearly connected by independent evidence with some anterior or subsequent criminal action.

When an act is of such a nature as not necessarily to imply a guilty intention, and such intention is the specific point in issue, then the evidence of declarations by the party, or of collateral circumstances, may be of the last importance, as explanatory of his motives and purposes. In regard to declarations referring to former and existing facts, Lord Chief Justice Eyre said that "Such declarations are the explanation and connection of those facts which serve to make them intelligible. What a prisoner has said respecting a particular fact is admissible evidence, not in the nature of a confession, but in evidence of the particular fact; and such declarations are therefore receivable in all cases whatever, in order to explain and to establish the state of any matter of fact which is in dispute, or the subject of inquiry before a jury."*

The just effect of such language in reference to future events is to show the existence of the *disposition*, from which criminal actions proceed, to render it less improbable that the person proved to have used it would commit the particular offence, and, if in itself ambiguous, to explain the real motive and object of the contemplated action. But evidence of such language cannot dispense with the obligation of sufficient proof of the criminal facts; for, though malignant feelings may possess the mind, and lead to intemperate and criminal expressions,

* See Rex v. Crossfield, 26 St. Tr. 215.

they nevertheless may exercise but a transient influence, without leading to action.* It must be borne in mind, too, as in regard to the proof of language in general, that declarations may be obscure in themselves, or imperfectly remembered, and that witnesses may speak without a strict and due regard to truth.† "Words," says Mr. Justice Foster, "are transient and fleeting as the wind; they are frequently the effect of sudden transport, easily misunderstood, and often misreported."‡ It has been well remarked that, "Mere threats often proceed from temporary irritation without deep-rooted hostility. They indicate a rash and unguarded rather than a determinedly malignant character; and the very utterance of them, as every one well knows, tends to defeat their execution. The man who has resolved on a crime, is more apt to keep his purpose to himself, or to confide it to an associate, under the seal of secrecy. Even the most wary, however, sometimes let their wicked purposes peep out accidentally in the freedom of companionship, or the weakness of drunken confidence. When such unguarded hints, dark and apparently unmeaning at the time, coincide with the subsequent tokens of guilt, they are strong cords in the net of criminating evidence."§

On the principle under consideration, all such relevant *acts* of the party as may reasonably be considered explanatory of his motives and purposes, even though they may severally constitute distinct felonies, are clearly admissible in evidence; of which our reports present many illustrations. Thus, where upon the trial of a man

* 3 Benth. Jud. Ev. b. 5. c. 4.
† Per Dallas, J., in Rex v. Turner, 30 St. Tr. 1132.
‡ Foster's Cr. L., *ut supra*. Disc. 1.
§ 1 Dickson's Law of Ev. in Scotland. 157.

for setting fire to a stack of straw it appeared that it had been set on fire by his having fired a gun very near to it, evidence was admitted that the stack had been set fire to the day before, and that the prisoner was very near to it with his gun at the same time;* and in a similar case, Mr. Justice Patteson admitted evidence of the prisoner's presence and demeanour at incendiary fires of other ricks, the property respectively of two other persons, which occurred the same night, although those fires were the subjects of other indictments against the prisoner; but the learned judge held that evidence could not be given of threats, statements, and particular acts pointing alone to such other charges, and not tending to explain the conduct of the prisoner in reference to the fire in question.† Mr. Justice Erle said, his experience had taught him that in cases of arson indications of guilt were often found in extremely minute circumstances, which were not the less cogent on that account; that it was to the words, whether true or false, by which a man accounted for himself at the critical time, to his conduct when the fire was in progress, to his manner of offering assistance, and other such particulars, that attention should be directed, and that in the absence of broad facts, such minute circumstances often afforded satisfactory evidence.‡ Upon a charge of maliciously shooting, where the question was whether the act proceeded from accident or design, evidence was admitted that the prisoner had intentionally shot at the same person about a quarter of an hour before.§   On a trial for murder by administering

---

* Reg. *v.* Dossett, 2 C. & K. 306, coram Maule, J.

† Reg. *v.* Taylor, 5 Cox's C. C. 138.

‡ Charge to the Grand Jury: Warwick Spring Ass. 1859.

§ Rex *v.* Coke, R. & R. 653.

prussic acid in porter, Mr. Baron Parke admitted evidence that the deceased had been taken ill several months before, after partaking of porter with the prisoner, and said, that although this was no direct proof of an attempt to poison, the evidence was nevertheless admissible, because anything tending to show antipathy in the party accused against the deceased was admissible.*

In like manner, upon a charge of uttering forged notes, the forged notes, either of the same or of a different bank, found on the prisoner's person, were allowed to be given in evidence to show guilty knowledge ;† and upon an indictment for uttering a forged Bank of England note, evidence was admitted that other notes of the same fabrication had been found on the files of the Bank, with the prisoner's handwriting on the back of them ;‡ but in a similar case, evidence of the subsequent uttering of another forged note was held to be inadmissible to prove guilty knowledge, unless the latter uttering was in some way connected with the uttering which was the subject of indictment, as by showing that all of the notes were of the same manufacture.§   So, the possession of a large quantity of counterfeit coin, many of each sort being of the same mould, and each piece of it being wrapped in a separate piece of paper, and the whole distributed in different pockets of the dress, was held to be evidence that the prisoner knew that the coin was counterfeit, and intended to utter it.‖ In a late case, on an indictment for uttering a counterfeit

* Reg. v. Tawell, *infra*.

† Rex v. Sunderland, 1 Lewin, 102 ; Rex v. Hodgson, *ib.* 103 ; Rex v. Kirkwood, *ib.* 103 ; Rex v. Martin, *ib.* 104; Rex v. Hall ; Rex v. Millward, R. & R. 245 ; Reg. v. Green, 3 C & K. 209.

‡ Rex v. Ball, 1 Campbell, 324 ; R. & R. 132.

§ Rex v. Taverner, 6 C & P. 413 ; and see Reg. v. Smith, *ib.*

‖ Reg. v. Jarvis, 25, L. J. M. C. 30 ; Rex v. Fuller, R. & R. 308.

crown-piece, knowing it to be counterfeit, evidence was admitted, in order to prove the guilty knowledge, that the prisoner on a day subsequent to such uttering uttered a counterfeit shilling ;* but this seems to have carried the principle very far.

Where, upon an indictment for receiving goods knowing them to have been stolen, it appeared that the articles had been stolen and had come into the possession of the prisoner at several distinct times, the judge, after compelling the prosecutor to elect upon which act of receiving he would proceed, told the jury that they might take into their consideration the circumstances of the prisoner having the various articles of stolen property in his possession and pledging or otherwise disposing of them at various times, as an ingredient in coming to a determination, whether when he received the articles for which the prosecutor elected to proceed, he knew them to have been stolen.† In like manner, upon an indictment against principal and receiver, where goods were found upon the receiver's premises, which had been taken from the prosecutor's premises, it was held that the prosecutor might give evidence of the finding of other goods at the house of the principal, notwithstanding there was no evidence to connect the receiver with them, and that he was not bound to elect.‡ On the same principle, evidence of the murder of one person may be given in evidence upon a trial for the murder of another, if such evidence tend to show that the prisoner might have had a motive arising out of the other murder for committing that with which he is charged.§

* Reg. v. Foster, 6 Cox's C. C. 521, 24 L. J. M. C. 134.

† Rex v. Dunn, 1 Moody's C. C. 150 ; and see Reg. v. Bleasdale, 2 C. & K. 765.   ‡ Reg. v. Hinley, 1 Cox's C. C. 12.

§ Rex v. Clewes, 4 C. & P. 221 ; and see Reg. v. Geering, *infra.*

On the principle of these cases, it is provided by statute, that the prosecutor may give evidence of any number of distinct acts of embezzlement, not exceeding three, committed against the same master,* or of larceny committed against the same person† respectively within six calendar months from the first to the last of such acts; and by St. 2 Wm. IV. c. 34, s. 7, any person uttering counterfeit coin, and having in his possession at the same time one or more pieces of counterfeit coin, or who either on the day of such uttering or within ten days shall utter other counterfeit coin, is made guilty of a much more aggravated offence than that of simply uttering base coin.

But it is not permitted in explanation of a party's motive to give evidence of a distinct and different offence committed against another person, unconnected with and unrelated to the particular act in question. Therefore it was held, that it was not competent for the prosecutor, in proof of the guilty knowledge of the prisoner, to give in evidence, that, at a time previous to the receipt of the prosecutor's goods, he had in his possession other goods of the same sort as those mentioned in the indictment, but belonging to a different owner, and that such goods had been stolen from such owner.‡   Lord Chief Justice Campbell said that "the law of England does not allow one crime to be proved in order to raise a probability that another crime has been committed by the perpetrator of the first. The evidence did not tend to show that the prisoner knew that the particular goods were stolen at the time he received them. The rule," he added, "which has prevailed in the case of indictment for uttering forged notes, of allowing evidence to be given of the

* 7 & 8 Geo. IV. c. 29, s. 48.   † 14 & 15 Vict. c. 100, s. 16.
‡ Reg. v. Oddy, 20 L. J. M. C. 198, and 5 Cox's C. C. 210.

uttering of other forged notes to different persons, has gone great lengths, and I should be unwilling to see that rule applied generally in the administration of the criminal law."*

SECTION 3.

PREPARATIONS AND OPPORTUNITY FOR THE COMMISSION OF CRIME.

PREMEDITATED crime must necessarily be preceded not only by impelling motives, but by appropriate preparations. Possession of the instruments or means of crime, under circumstances of suspicion—as of poison, coining instruments, combustible matters, picklocks, housebreaking instruments, dark-lanterns, or other destructive or criminal or suspicious weapons, materials, or instruments, and many other acts of apparent preparation—are important facts in the judicial investigation of imputed crime. Where a man had in his possession a large quantity of counterfeit coin unaccounted for, and there was no evidence that he was the maker, it was held to raise a presumption that he had procured it with intent to utter it.† But the personal character for probity, and the civil station of the party, are highly material in connection with facts of this kind. A medical man, for instance, in the ordinary course of his profession, has legitimate occasion for the possession of poisons, a locksmith for the use of picklocks. In many cases the possession of such materials or instruments, and other acts indicative of purpose to commit crime, are made by statute *primá facie* presumptions of guilt, and in some even substantive offences.‡

* Reg. *v.* Butler, 2 C. & K. 221.   † Rex *v.* Fuller, R. & R. 308.
‡ See *infra*, Sect. 8.

Facts of the kind referred to become more powerful indications of guilty purpose, if false reasons are assigned to account for them; as in the case of possessing poison, that it was procured to destroy vermin, which is the excuse commonly resorted to in such cases.

The bare possession of the means of crime, or other mere acts of preparation, without more conclusive evidence, are not in general of great weight, because the intended guilt may not have been consummated; and until that takes place there is the *locus pœnitentiæ*. But as preparations must necessarily precede the commission of premeditated crime, some traces of them may generally be expected to be discovered; and if there be not clear and decisive proof of guilt, the absence of any evidence of such preliminary measures is a circumstance strongly presumptive of innocence.

In the foregoing remarks it is of course assumed that the party possessed the *opportunity* of committing the imputed act, without which neither the existence of motives, nor the manifestation of criminal intention by threats or otherwise, followed even by preparations for its commission, can be of any weight.

Section 4.

RECENT POSSESSION OF THE FRUITS OF CRIME.

Since the desire of dishonest gain is the impelling motive to theft and robbery, it naturally follows that the possession of the fruits of crime recently after it has been committed, affords a strong and reasonable ground for the presumption that the party in whose possession they are found, was the real offender, unless he can account for such possession in some way consistently with his innocence.* The force of this presumption has been recognized from the earliest times; and it is founded on the obvious consideration, that if such possession have been lawfully acquired, the party would be able, at least shortly after its acquisition, to give an account of the manner in which it was obtained; and his unwillingness or inability to afford such explanation is justly regarded as amounting to strong self-condemnatory evidence. But it has been ruled, that if the party give a reasonable account of the way in which he came possessed of the property, as by stating the name of the person from whom he obtained it, and such party is known to be a real person, and capable of being easily referred to, it is then incumbent on the prosecutor to show that such account is false. Therefore, where a man was indicted for stealing a piece of wood, which was found in his shop five days after the theft, and he stated that he had bought it from a person whom he named, who lived about two miles off, it was held that the prosecutor was bound to show that the account was false.† But if the account given be unreasonable or improbable on the face of it, or if the party have given different accounts of the same transaction, then he will not be relieved from the pressure of the general rule of presumption.‡

In such cases it is a question for the jury, whether there is a sufficiently reasonable account given by the prisoner to enable the prosecutor to find the party named.§ But these refinements are not strictly followed in prac-

* Rex v. Burdett, 4 B. & Ald. 149; Burnett on the C. L. of Scotl. 555; 2 Mascardus De Prob. *ut supra*, Concl. DCCCXXXIV; 1 Hume's Comm. on the C. L. of Scotl. 111; Best on Pres. 44.

† Reg. v. Smith, 2 C. & K. 217.

‡ Reg. v. Crowhurst, 1 C. & K. 370; Reg. v. Harmer, 3 Cox's C. C. 487; Reg. v. Debley, 2 C. & K. 818.

§ Reg. v. Hughes, Cox's C. C. 176.

tice, and are indeed not always easily capable of application. Thus, where a prisoner was convicted of stealing some articles of dress, and the evidence was that he was in possession of the stolen property recently after it had been stolen, that he sold it openly in a public-house, and on his arrest stated to the constable that C. and D. brought the things to his house, and that W., who was at his house, would say that it was true; and C., D., and W. were known to the constable, and might have been produced as witnesses, but were not called, and inquiries were made of W., but the result of the inquiry was not given in evidence; it was held that the conviction was good, and that it was not incumbent on the prosecutor to call the persons to whom the prisoner had referred, to disprove his statement.*

1. It is manifest that the force of this rule of presumption depends upon the recency of the possession as related to the crime, and that if the interval of time is considerable, the presumption is much weakened, and more especially if the goods are of such a nature as in the ordinary course of things frequently to change hands. From the nature of the case, it is not possible to fix any precise period within which the effect of this rule of presumption can be limited; it must depend not only upon the mere lapse of time, but upon the nature of the property, and the concomitant circumstances of each particular case. Where two pieces of woollen cloth in an unfinished state, consisting of about twenty yards each, were found in the possession of the prisoner two months after being missed, and still in the same state, it was held that this was a possession sufficiently recent to call upon him to show how he came by the property.†   In another

* Reg. v. Wilson, 26 L. J. M. C. 45. and 7 Cox's C. C. 310.
† Reg. v. Partridge. 7 C. & P. 551.

case, Mr. Justice Bayley directed an acquittal, because the only evidence against the prisoner was, that the goods were found in his possession after a lapse of sixteen months from the time of their loss;[*] and where a shovel was found, six months after the theft, in the house of the prisoner, who was not then at home, Mr. Baron Gurney held that on this evidence alone the prisoner ought not to be called upon for his defence.[†]   Where the evidence against a prisoner, charged with the larceny of a saw and mattock, was, that the stolen articles were found in his possession three months after they were missed, it was held that this was not such a recent possession as *per se* to put him upon showing how he came by them;[‡] and where a stolen horse was found in the prisoner's possession six months after it was lost, Mr. Justice Maule held that this was no case to go to the jury.[§]   But in another case, where three sheets were found upon the prisoner's bed in his house three months after they had been stolen, Mr. Justice Wightman held that the case must go to the jury, on the ground that it was impossible to lay down any rule as to the precise time which was too great to call upon the prisoner to account for the possession;[||] and where seventy sheep were put upon a common on the 18th of June, but not missed until November, and the prisoner was proved to have had possession of four of them in October, and of nineteen more on the 23rd of November, the judge allowed evidence of the possession of both to be given.[**]

2. It is obviously essential to the just application of this rule of presumption, that the house or other place

---

[*] Anon. 7 Monthly Law Mag. 58.

[†] Rex v. Cruttenden, Best on Pres. 306; 6 Jurist, 267.

[‡] Rex v. Adams, 3 C. & P. 600.   § Reg. v. Cooper, 3 C. & K. 318.

[||] Rex v. Hewlett, 2 Russell on Cr., by Greaves, 728.

[**] Rex v. Dewhirst, 2 Stark. 614.

in which the stolen property is found should be in the *exclusive* possession of the prisoner. Where it is found in the apartments of a lodger, for instance, the presumption may be stronger or weaker, according as the evidence does or does not show an exclusive possession. As a general rule, where stolen goods are found in the house of a married man, they must be considered in his possession, and not in the possession of his wife, unless there be evidence of something specially to implicate her, such as statements made, or acts done by her, in which case it must be left to the jury to decide in whose possession they were.* Therefore, where a wife was indicted with her husband for receiving stolen property, and it appeared that she had destroyed the property, it was held to be a question for the jury whether she had so dealt with it, to aid her husband in turning it to profit, or merely to conceal his guilt, or screen him from the consequences.† And where a constable went with a warrant to search the prisoner's premises for stolen iron, and almost immediately after he was taken away from the premises, at the conclusion of the search, his wife carried some tin under her cloak from a warehouse on the premises, Mr. Justice Coleridge, on the trial of the prisoner for receiving stolen brass and tin, held that it was for the jury to consider whether her possession was not the prisoner's, she being upon the premises, and all the circumstances being taken into consideration, and that it was not like the case where the wife is in possession of stolen property at a distance from the premises of her husband.‡

* Reg. *v.* Banks, 1 Cox's C. C. 238.
† Reg. *v.* M'Clarens, 3 Cox's C. C. 425; and see also Reg. *v.* Brook, 6 *ib.* 151.   ‡ Reg. *v.* Mansfield, 1 C. & M. 112.

3. The force of this presumption is greatly increased if the fruits of a plurality or of a series of thefts be found in the prisoner's possession, or if the property stolen consist of a number of miscellaneous articles, or be of an uncommon kind, or from its value or other circumstances be inconsistent with or unsuited to the station of the party. On the trial of two men at Aberdeen autumn circuit, 1824, it appeared that a carpenter's workshop at Aberdeen was broken open on a particular night, and some tools carried off, and that on the same night the counting-houses of Messrs. Davidson and of Messrs. Catto and Co., in different parts of that city, were broken into, and goods and money to a considerable extent stolen. The prisoners were met at seven on the following morning in one of the streets of Aberdeen, at a distance from either of the places of depredation, by two of the police Upon seeing the officers they began to run ; and being pursued and taken, there was found in the possession of each a considerable quantity of the articles taken from Catto and Co., but none of the things taken from the carpenter's shop or Davidson's. But in Catto and Co.'s warehouse were found a brown coat and other articles got from Davidson's, which had not been there the preceding evening when the shop was locked up; and in Davidson's were found the tools which had been abstracted from the carpenter's. Thus, the recent possession of the articles stolen from Catto and Co.'s proved that the prisoners were the depredators in that warehouse; while the fact of the articles taken from Davidson's having been left there, connected them with that prior housebreaking; while again, the chisels belonging to the carpenter's shop, found in Davidson's, identified the persons who broke into that last house with those who committed the origi-

nal theft at the carpenter's. The prisoners were convicted of all the thefts.* A still stronger case of the same kind occurred at Aberdeen, in April, 1826, on the trial of a man, who was accused of no fewer than nine different acts of theft by housebreaking, committed in and around that place at various times during the summer of 1825 and the following winter. No suspicion had been awakened against the prisoner, who was a carter, living an industrious and apparently regular life, until one occasion, when some of the stolen articles having been detected in a broker's shop, and traced to his custody, a search was made, and some articles from all the houses broken open found amongst an immense mass of other goods, evidently stolen, in a large chest, and about various parts of the prisoner's house. Their number and variety, and the place where they were found, were quite sufficient to convict him of receiving the stolen property; but as they were discovered at the distance of many months from the times when the various thefts had been committed, the difficulty was how to connect him with the actual theft. The charges selected for trial were five in number, and as nearly connected with each other in point of time as possible. In none of them was the prisoner identified as the person who had broken into the houses, although the thief had been seen, and more than once fired at ; but in all the first four houses which had been broken into, were discovered some of the articles taken from the others, and in the prisoner's custody were found some articles taken from them all, which sufficiently proved that all the depredations had been committed by one person ; and the mark of an iron instrument was found on three of

* Rex *v.* Downie and Milne; Alison's Princ. 313 ; 2 Mascardus, *ut supra*, Concl. DCCCXXXI.

the windows broken open, which coincided exactly with a chisel left in the last house.   Two days after the house-breaking of that house, an old watch, part of the stolen property was shown by the prisoner to a shopkeeper, to whom he soon afterwards sold it, and by him delivered up to the officers.   Upon this evidence the prisoner was convicted of all the charges of housebreaking.*

4. The recent possession of stolen property may some-times be referable not to the crime of theft, but to that of having received it with a guilty knowledge of its having been stolen.   Four persons were found guilty of housebreaking on proof of the recent possession of the goods, and narrowly escaped execution, the offence at that time being capital, but it was afterwards ascertained that one of them, who had long been known as a receiver of stolen goods, knew nothing of the robbery until after it had been committed, and had purchased the goods from the real thieves the day after the robbery.†   The difficulty of referring the act of possession specifically to one of those crimes frequently led to the failure of jus-tice; thus, where stolen goods were found shortly after the theft concealed in an old engine-house, and the place being watched, the prisoners were seen to go there and take them away, but, being indicted as receivers, they were acquitted; Mr. Justice Patteson being of opinion that this seemed to be evidence rather of a stealing than a receiving.‡   But these distinctions are now abolished by St. 11 & 12 Vict. c. 46, s. 3, which provides that in every indictment for feloniously stealing, a count may be added for feloniously receiving, the same property know-

* Rex v. Bowman, Alison's Princ. 314.

† Rex v. Ellis, Sessions Papers & A. R. 1831.

‡ Reg. v. Dursley, 6 C. & P. 899 ; and see Rex v. Dyer, 2 East, P. C. 767 ; and Rex v. Howell, ib. 768.

ing it to have been stolen, and that in an indictment for feloniously receiving, a count may be added for feloniously stealing the same property.

It is not necessary that the receiver of stolen property should have obtained a guilty knowledge by direct information; it is sufficient if the circumstances under which it was received were such as must have satisfied any reasonable mind that it must have been dishonestly obtained; as, if he purchased it at an undue value,* at suspicious and unseasonable times, or from persons who in the ordinary course of things could not fairly be considered as the unsuspected owners of property of the particular description, or has secreted or endeavoured to secrete it, or attempted to explain the manner of acquisition by falsehood or prevarication.†

5. The possession of stolen goods recently after the loss of them, may be indicative not merely of the offence of larceny, or of receiving with guilty knowledge, but of any other more aggravated crime which has been connected with theft. Upon an indictment for arson, proof that property which was in the house at the time it was burnt, was soon afterwards found in the possession of the prisoner, was held to raise a presumption that he was present and concerned in the offence.‡ This particular fact of presumption commonly forms also a material element of evidence in cases of murder; which special application of it has often been emphatically recognized. It is upon the same principle that a sudden and otherwise inexplicable transition from a state of indigence and a consequent change of habits, or a profuse or unwonted

---

* Hale's P. C. 619.   † See Alison's Prin. 330.

‡ 2 Rex v. Rickman, East's P. C. 1035; and see Rex v. Fuller, R. and R. 308.

expenditure inconsistent with the position in life of the party, is sometimes a circumstance extremely unfavourable to the supposition of innocence.*

But the rule must be applied with discrimination, for the bare possession of stolen property, though recent, uncorroborated by other evidence, is sometimes fallacious and dangerous as a criterion of guilt. Sir Matthew Hale lays it down, that "if a horse be stolen from A., and the same day B. be found upon him, it is a strong presumption that B. stole him; yet," adds that excellent lawyer, "I do remember before a learned and very wary judge, in such an instance B. was condemned and executed at Oxford Assizes, and yet within two assizes after, C., being apprehended for another robbery, and convicted, upon his judgment and execution confessed he was the man that stole the horse, and being closely pursued, desired B., a stranger, to walk his horse for him, while he turned aside upon a necessary occasion, and escaped; and B. was apprehended with the horse and died innocently."† A very similar case occurred at the Surrey Summer Assizes, 1827, where a young man was convicted of stealing two oxen. The prisoner, having finished his apprenticeship to a butcher at Monkwearmouth, went to visit an uncle at Portsmouth, from whence he set out to return to London. On the road between Guildford and London, about three o'clock in the morning, he overtook a man riding upon a pony and driving two oxen, who finding that he was going to London, offered him five shillings to drive them for him to London, which he agreed to do, the man engaging to meet him at Westminster Bridge. At Wandsworth he was apprehended by the prosecutor's son, and

* Rex v. Burdock, Bristol Summ. Ass. 1835; Rex v. Varnham and others, *infra*.   † 2 Hale's P. C. ch. 39.

charged with stealing the oxen.   On his apprehension he assumed a false name, under which he was tried, to conceal his situation from his friends, and convicted, but on a representation of the circumstances he received a pardon, when on the point of being transported for life :* he had been the dupe of the real thief, who, finding himself closely pursued, had thus contrived to rid himself of the possession of the cattle.

7. The rule under discussion is occasionally attended with uncertainty in its application, from the difficulty attendant upon the positive identification of articles of property alleged to have been stolen; and it clearly ought never to be applied, where there is reasonable ground to conclude that the witnesses may be mistaken, or where from any other cause identity is not satisfactorily established.   But the rule is nevertheless fairly and properly applied in circumstances where, though positive identification is impossible, the possession of the property cannot without violence to every reasonable hypothesis but be considered of a guilty character; as in the case of persons employed in carrying tea, sugar, tobacco, and other like articles from ships and wharfs. Cases have frequently occurred of convictions of larceny, in such circumstances, upon evidence that the parties were detected with property of the same kind upon them recently after coming from such places, although the identity of the property as belonging to any particular person could no otherwise be proved.†   On this principle two men were convicted of larceny upon evidence that the prosecutor's soap-manufactory, near Glasgow, had been broken into in the night and robbed of about 120lbs. of yellow soap,

* Rex v. Gill, Sessions Papers and A. R. 1827.
† 2 East's P. C. 1035.

and that the prisoners were met on the same night, about eleven o'clock, by the watchman, near the centre of the city, from whom they attempted to escape, one bearing on his back forty pounds of soap of the same size, shape, and make as that stolen from the prosecutor's premises, and the other with his clothes soiled over with the same substance, though the property could not be more distinctly identified.† It is seldom however that juries are required to determine upon the effect of evidence of the mere recent possession of stolen property ; from the very nature of the case, the fact is generally accompanied by other corroborative or explanatory circumstances of presumption. If the party have secreted the property,— if he deny that it is in his possession, and such denial be discovered to be false,—if he cannot show how he became possessed of it,—if he give false, incredible, or inconsistent accounts of the manner in which he acquired it, as that he found it, or that it had been given or sold to him by a stranger, or left at his house,—if he have disposed of or attempted to dispose of it, at an unreasonably low price.—if he have absconded or endeavoured to escape from justice,—if other stolen property, or housebreaking tools, or other instruments of crime be found in his possession,—if he were seen near the spot at or about the time when the act was committed,—or if any article belonging to him be found at or near the place where the theft was committed, at or about the time of the commission of the offence,—if the impressions of his shoes or other articles of apparel correspond with marks left by the thieves,—if he have attempted to obliterate from the articles in question marks of identity, or to tamper with the parties or the officers of justice,—these,

* Rex v. M'Kechnie and Tolmie, Alison's Princ. 322.

and all like circumstances, are justly considered as throwing light upon and explaining the fact of possession, and render it morally certain that such possession can be referable only to a criminal origin, and cannot otherwise be rationally accounted for.

SECTION 5.

UNEXPLAINED APPEARANCES OF SUSPICION, AND ATTEMPTS TO ACCOUNT FOR THEM BY FALSE REPRESENTATIONS.

As a general rule, to which the exceptions can be but rare, it is a reasonable conclusion, that an innocent party can explain suspicious or unusual appearances, connected with his person, dress, or conduct; and that the desire of self-preservation, if not a regard for truth, will prompt him to do so. The ingenuous and satisfactory explanation of circumstances of apparent suspicion always operates powerfully in favour of the accused, and obtains for him more ready credence when the explanation may not be easily verified. On the other hand, the force of suspicious circumstances is augmented, whenever the party attempts no explanation of facts which he may reasonably be presumed to be able and interested to explain. An old man on his way home from market, where he had stayed late, was attacked, thrown down and robbed by three men, one of whom he wounded in the struggle with a clasp-knife. Upon the apprehension of one of the robbers at the house of his mother, he was dressed in a new pair of trousers, and the constable found in a room upstairs, between the bed and the mattrass, a pair of trousers with two long cuts in one thigh, one of which had penetrated through the lining, and was stained with blood at that spot; and the holes had been sewed with

F

thread which was not discoloured, showing that the blood must have been applied to the cloth previous to the repair, and a corresponding cut bound over with plaisters was found on the prisoner's thigh.   He refused to give any explanation of the wound or of the cuts in the garments, and was convicted and transported.*

But circumstances of suspicion merely, without more conclusive evidence, are not sufficient to justify conviction, even though the party offer no explanation of them. Two women were indicted for colouring a counterfeit shilling and sixpence, and a man as counselling them; and the evidence against him was that he visited the women once or twice a week, that the rattling of copper money was heard while he was with them, that once he was counting something just after he came out, that on going to the room just after their apprehension, he resisted being stopped, and jumped over a wall to escape, and that there were found upon him a bad three-shilling-piece and five bad sixpences : upon a case reserved, the judges thought the evidence too slight to convict him.†

So natural and forcible is this rule of presumption, that the guilty are instinctively compelled to endeavour to evade its application, by giving some explanation or interpretation of adverse facts, consistent, if true, with innocence ; but its force is commonly aggravated by the improbability, or absurdity even, of such explanations, or the inconsistency of them with admitted or incontrovertible facts.   All such false, incredible, or contradictory statements, if disproved or disbelieved, are not simply neutralized, but become of a substantive inculpatory effect. But even in such circumstances, however, guilt cannot be

* Rex v. Dawtrey, York Sp. Ass. 1841.
† Rex v. Isaacs, 2 Russell, by Greaves, 729.

safely inferred, unless there has been laid such a sub-
stratum of evidence, direct or circumstantial, as creates
a strong independent *primâ facie* case against the prisoner.* On a trial for the murder of a female by poison,
whom the prisoner alleged to have died from the effects
of a draught taken by her in anger during an altercation between them, Mr. Baron Parke told the jury that
it was for them to say whether the falsehoods the prisoner had told, did not show that he was conscious that
he had been guilty of some act that required concealment; that it was very true he might not wish it to be
known he had been visiting a woman who, there was
good reason to believe, had formerly been his mistress;
but that, if he was an innocent man, and had been present at the death, one would have supposed he would
have disclosed it immediately and called in some assistance. They had here two untruths, that he meant to
dine at the west-end of the town and did not; and his
denial that he had been out of London that evening;
these, he said, were very material matters for their inquiry, bearing in mind that upon the evidence there was
a very ample case for grave consideration, to show that
the deceased died of prussic acid, and that the prisoner
was present in the house at the moment of that death.
His Lordship added, that if the prisoner's representation
had been true, that the deceased had poisoned herself, one
would have supposed that he would have taken the first
opportunity, having been present at the time this occurred,
of exonerating himself from it, by making this declaration to the first person he met; one would expect, if he
had been a man of the least cordial feeling, he would

* Per Mr. Justice Littledale in Rex *v.* Clark, Warwick Summ. Ass.
1831.

have waited to see whether it was true or not that she had taken this poison, and called for assistance, instead of which, he is proved to have gone in a short time to London, and when he got to London he is proved to have denied altogether that he had been there. You must judge, said the learned Baron, of the truth of the case against a person by all his conduct taken together.*

Allowance must nevertheless be made for the weakness of human nature, and for the difficulties which may attend the proof of circumstances of exculpation ;† and care must be taken that circumstances are not erroneously assumed to be suspicious without sufficient reason.‡

Section 6.

INDIRECT CONFESSIONAL EVIDENCE.

ALTHOUGH the subject of direct confession does not fall within the province of this essay, it is necessary to advert to some of the principal rules which relate to that important head of moral evidence; because they are of great moment in their application to such particulars of circumstantial evidence as are only indirectly in the nature of confessional evidence.

A voluntary confession of guilt, if it be full, consistent, and probable, is justly regarded as evidence of the highest and most satisfactory nature.§ Self-love, the mainspring of human conduct, will usually prevent a rational being from making admissions prejudicial to his interest and safety, unless when caused by the promptings of truth and conscience.

* Reg. v. Tawell, Aylesbury Sp. Ass. 1845.
† See Rex v. Gill, *ut supra*, 62, and 2 Hale's P. C. ch. 39.
‡ See Rex v. Looker, and Rex v. Thornton, *infra*.
§ 3 Mascardus *ut supra*, Concl. xv., xvi.; Rex v. Warrickshall, 1 Leach's C. C. 299; Greenleaf's L. of Ev. § 219.

By the law of England, a voluntary and unsuspected confession is clearly sufficient to warrant conviction, wherever there is independent proof of the *corpus delicti*. According to some authorities, confession alone is a sufficient ground for conviction, even in the absence of any such independent evidence; but the contrary opinion is most in accordance with the general principles of reason and justice, the opinions of the best writers on criminal jurisprudence, and the practice of other enlightened nations.* Nor are the cases adduced in support of the doctrine in question very decisive, since in all of them there appears to have been some evidence, though slight, of confirmatory circumstances, independently of the confession.†

Judicial history presents innumerable warnings of the danger of placing implicit dependence upon this kind of self-condemnatory evidence, even where it is exempt from all suspicion of coercion, physical or moral, or other sinister influence. How greatly then must such danger be aggravated, where confession constitutes the only evidence of the fact of a *corpus delicti;* and how incalculably greater in such cases is the necessity for the most rigorous scrutiny of all collateral circumstances, which may actuate the party to make a false confession ! The agonies of torture, the dread of their infliction, the hope of escaping the rigours of slavery or the hardships of military service, a weariness of existence, self-delusion, the desire to shield a guilty relative or friend from the penalties of justice,‡ the impulses of despair from the

* Best on Pres. 330, and the cases cited ; 1 Greenleaf's L. of Ev. § 217 ; Allison's Princ. 325 ; Code Pénal d'Autriche, partie 1, § 2, ch. x.

† Rex *v.* Fisher, 1 Leach, 286; Rex. *v.* Eldridge, R. & R. 441 ; Rex *v.* Faulkner, ib. 481 ; Rex *v.* White, ib. 508 ; Rex *v.* Tippett, ib. 509 ; 1 Greenleaf's L. of Ev. § 217.

‡ 1 Chitty's Crim. L. 85.

pressure of strong and apparently incontrovertible presumptions of guilt, the dread of unmerited punishment and disgrace, the hope of pardon—these and numerous other inducements have not unfrequently operated to produce unfounded confessions of guilt.

Innumerable are the instances on record of confession, extracted "by the deceitful and dangerous experiment of the criminal question,"[*] of offences which were never committed, or not committed by the persons making confession.[†] Nor have such instances been wanting in other parts of Europe even in the present century.

When Felton, upon his examination at the Council Board, declared, as he had always done, that no man living had instigated him to the murder of the Duke of Buckingham, the Bishop of London said to him, "If you will not confess, you must go to the rack." The man replied, "If it must be so, I know not whom I may accuse In the extremity of the torture,—Bishop Laud perhaps, or any lord at this Board."[‡] "Sound sense," observed the excellent Sir Michael Foster, " in the mouth of an enthusiast and a ruffian."[§]

Not less repugnant to policy, justice, and humanity is the moral torture to which in some (perhaps in most) of the nations of Europe, persons suspected of crime are subjected, by means of searching, rigorous, and insidious examinations, conducted by skilful adepts in judicial tactics, and accompanied sometimes even by dramatic circumstances of terror and intimidation.[‖]

---

* 3 Gibbon's Decline and Fall, ch. xvii.

† Jardine on the Use of Torture in the C. L. of England, 3, 6; and see Fortescue De Laudibus Legum Angliæ, ch. 22.

‡ 1 Rushworth's Collections, 688.   § Foster's C. L. 244, 3rd ed.

‖ See the case of Riembaur, a Bavarian priest, charged with murder, in Narratives of Remarkable Criminal Trials, by Feuerbach, *ut supra*.

Lord Clarendon gives a circumstantial account of the confession of a Frenchman named Hubert, after the fire of London, that he had set the first house on fire, and had been hired in Paris a year before to do it. " Though," says he, " the Lord Chief Justice told the King that 'all his discourse was so disjointed he did not believe him guilty,' yet upon his own confession the jury found him guilty, and he was executed accordingly :" the historian adds, " though no man could imagine any reason why a man should so desperately throw away his life, which he might have saved though he had been guilty, since he was accused only upon his own confession, yet neither the judges nor any present at the trial did believe him guilty, but that he was a poor distracted wretch, weary of life and chose to part with it this way."*

A very remarkable case of this nature was that of the two Boorns, convicted in the Supreme Court of Vermont in September term, 1819, of the murder of Russell Colvin, May 10, 1812. It appeared that Colvin, who was the brother-in-law of the prisoners, was a person of a weak and not perfectly sound mind; that he was considered burdensome to the family of the prisoners, who were obliged to support him ; that on the day of his disappearance, being in a distant field, where the prisoners were at work, a violent quarrel broke out between them, and that one of them struck him a violent blow on the back of the head, with a club, which felled him to the ground. Some suspicions arose, at that time, that he was murdered : which were increased by the finding of his hat, in the same field, a few months afterwards. These

* 3 Life and Continuation, etc., 94, (Clarendon, ed. 1824) ; and see 2 Mem. of Romilly, 182, where it is stated that an innocent man was executed erroneously by the sentence of a court-martial, on a charge of mutiny.

suspicions in process of time subsided ; but in 1819, one
of the neighbours having repeatedly dreamed of the murder, with great minuteness of circumstance, both in regard to his death and the concealment of his remains,
the prisoners were vehemently accused, and generally
believed guilty of the murder. Upon strict search, the
pocket-knife of Colvin, and a button of his clothes, were
found in an old open cellar in the same field ; and in a
hollow stump not many rods from it, were discovered two
nails and a number of bones believed to be those of a
man. Upon this evidence, together with the deliberate
confession of murder and concealment of the body in
those places, they were convicted and sentenced to die.
On the same day they applied to the legislature for a
commutation of the sentence of death, to that of perpe-
tual imprisonment ; which as to one only of them was
granted. The confession being now withdrawn and contradicted, and a reward offered for the discovery of the
missing man, he was found in New Jersey, and returned
home in time to prevent the execution. He had fled for
fear that they would kill him. The bones were those of
an animal. The prisoners had been advised by some
misjudging friends, that, as they would certainly be convicted, upon the circumstances proved, their only chance
for life was by a commutation of punishment, and that
this depended on their making a penitential confession,
and thereupon obtaining a recommendation to mercy.*

The State Trials contain numerous confessions of witchcraft, and abound with absurd and incredible details of
communications with evil spirits, which only show that the
parties were either impostors, or the involuntary victims

---

* 1 Greenleaf's L. of Ev. § 214 ; and see the case of the Perrys,
infra. and an American case in Wharton's C. L. of the U. S. 315.

of invincible self-delusion. One kind of false confession, that namely of being a deserter, is so common, as to have been made the subject of penal repression by rendering the offender liable to be treated as a rogue and vagabond, and to be imprisoned for any period not exceeding three months.*

A distinguished foreign lawyer well observes, that "whilst such anomalous cases ought to render courts and juries at all times extremely watchful of every fact attendant on confessions of guilt, the cases should never be invoked or so urged by the accused's counsel as to invalidate indiscriminately all confessions put to the jury, thus repudiating those salutary distinctions which the Court, in the judicious exercise of its duty, shall be enabled to make. Such a use of these anomalies, which should be regarded as mere exceptions, and which should speak only in the voice of warning, is no less unprofessional than impolitic, and should be regarded as offensive to the intelligence both of the Court and jury."†

It is essential to justice, that a confessional statement, if it be consistent, probable, and uncontradicted, should be taken together, and not distorted, or but partially adopted. "It is a rule of law," said Lord Ellenborough, "that when evidence is given of what a party has said or sworn, all of it is evidence (subject to the consideration of the jury, however, as to its truth), coming, as it does, in one entire form before them ; but you may still judge to what parts of the whole you can give credit ; and also whether that part which appears to confirm and fix the charge does not outweigh that which contains the exculpation."‡ On the trial of a man for a murder committed

* Stat. 20 Vict. 13, c. 49.
† 1 Hoffman's Course of Legal Study. 367.
‡ Rex v. Lord Cochrane and others, Gurney's Rep. 479.

twenty-four years before, the principal inculpatory evidence consisted of his confession, which stated in substance that he was present at the murder, but went to the spot without any previous knowledge that a murder was intended, and took no part in it.   It was urged that the prisoner's concurrence must be presumed from his presence at the murder, but Mr. Justice Littledale held that the statement must be taken as a whole; and that so qualified, it did not in fairness amount to an admission of the guilt of murder;[*] and where the prisoner's declaration, in which she asserted her innocence, was given in evidence, and there was evidence of other statements confessing guilt, the judge left the whole of the conflicting statements to the jury for their consideration.   But where there is, in the whole case, no evidence but what is compatible with the assertion of innocence, adduced in evidence for the prosecution, the judge will direct an acquittal.[†]   In the case of Strahan and Paul, it was unsuccessfully contended, that the admission made by the prisoner Strahan must be taken to the whole extent to which it was made, and that it would then fairly and reasonably lead to the conclusion that he had known nothing of the fraudulent transactions in which the other prisoner was the leading actor in March 1854; but Mr. Baron Alderson told the jury that they were not bound to believe either the whole or any part of the statement made by the prisoner Strahan, and that they must take it with this consideration as one of the circumstances of the case and no more.[‡]

Of the credit and effect due to a confessional statement the jury are the sole judges, and if it is inconsistent, im-

* Rex v. Clowes, 4 C. & P. 221, and Short-hand Rep.
† Rex v. Jones, 2 C. & P. 629.   ‡ C. C. C. Oct. 1855.

probable, or incredible, or is contradicted or discredited by
other evidence, or is the emanation of a weak or excited
state of mind, the jury may exercise their discretion in re-
jecting it, either wholly or in part, whether the rejected part
make for or against the prisoner.* On the trial of a man
for setting fire to a stack of hay, it appeared that between
two and three o'clock in the morning, a police constable
attracted by the cry of fire went to the spot, close to which
he met the prisoner, who told him that a haystack was
on fire, and that he was going to London ; the policeman
asked him to give information of the fire to any other policeman he might meet, and request him to come and assist.
Shortly afterwards, on his way towards London, the prisoner met a serjeant of police whom he informed of the
fire, stating that he was the man who set the stack on
fire, upon which he was taken into custody. The serjeant
of police, on cross-examination by the prisoner, stated
that the magistrates entertained an opinion that he was
insane, and directed inquiries to be made, from which it
appeared that he had before been charged with some
offence and acquitted on the ground of insanity. When
apprehended, the prisoner appeared under great excitement ; and upon his trial he alleged that he had been
confined two years in a lunatic asylum, and had been
liberated only about a year ago ; that his mind had been
wandering for some time ; and that passing by the place
at the time of the fire, he was induced, in a moment of
delirium, to make this groundless charge against himself.
He begged the Court to explain to the jury the different
result that would follow from his being acquitted on the
ground of insanity and an unconditional acquittal ; and

* Rex v. Higgins, 3 C. & P. 603 ; Rex v. Steptoe, 4 C. & P. 397 ;
1 Greenleaf's L. of Ev. § 218.

said that rather than the former verdict should be returned, which would probably have the effect of immuring him in a lunatic asylum for the rest of his life, he would retract his plea of not guilty, and plead guilty to the charge. Mr. Justice Williams in summing up remarked, that there did not appear to be the least evidence against the prisoner except his own statement ; and that it was for the jury to say under all the circumstances whether they believed that statement was founded in fact, or whether it was, as the prisoner alleged, merely the effect of an excited imagination and weak mind. The prisoner was acquitted.*

It is obvious that every caution observed in the reception of evidence of a direct confession, ought to be more especially applied in the admission and estimation of the analogous evidence of statements which are only indirectly in the nature of confessional evidence ; since such statements, from the nature of the case, must be ambiguous, or relate but obscurely to the *corpus delicti*. "Hasty confessions," says Sir Michael Foster, " made to persons having no authority to examine, are the weakest and most suspicious of all evidence. Proof may be too easily procured, words are often misreported,—whether through ignorance, inattention, or malice, it mattereth not to the defendant, he is equally affected in either case ; and they are extremely liable to misconstruction, and withal this evidence is not in the ordinary course of things to be disproved by that sort of negative evidence by which the proof of plain facts may be and often is confronted."†

* Reg. *v.* Wilson, Maidstone Wint. Ass. 1844. The same doctrine was held by L. C. J. Wilde, in a case of arson at Maidstone Spring Assizes, 1847, where the prisoner to conceal his disgrace refused to give his name.

† Foster's C. L. 243; and see 1 Greenleaf's L. of Ev. § 214.

" How easy is it," it has been admirably said, " for the hearer to take a word in a sense not intended by the speaker, and for want of an exact representation of the tone of voice, emphasis, countenance, eye, manner and action of the one who made the confession, how almost impossible it is to make third persons understand the exact state of his mind and meaning ! For these reasons such evidence is received with great distrust and under apprehension for the wrong it may do."[*]

Upon the trial of a man for the murder of a woman, who had been brutally assaulted by three men, and died from the injuries she received, it appeared that one of the offenders, at the time of the commission of the outrage, called another of them by the prisoner's name, from which circumstance suspicion attached to him. A person deposed that he met the prisoner at a public-house, and asked him if he knew the woman who had been so cruelly treated, and that he answered, " Yes, what of that ?" The witness said, that he then asked him if he was not one of the parties concerned in that affair; to which he answered, according to one account, " Yes, I was ; and what then ?" or, as another account states, " If I was, what then ?" It appeared that the prisoner was intoxicated, and that the questions were put with a view of ensnaring him ; but, influenced by this imprudent language, the jury convicted him, and he was executed. The real offenders were discovered about two years afterwards, and two of them were executed for this very offence, and fully admitted their guilt; the third having been admitted to give evidence for the Crown.[†]

* In Resp. v. Fields, Peck's Rep. 140, quoted in 1 Taylor's L. of Ev. 689, 2nd ed.

† Rex v. Coleman, Kingston Spring Ass. 1748-9 ; and 1 Remarkable Trials, 162, 172 ; Rex v. Jones and Welch, 4 Celebrated Trials, 314.

But in the most debased persons there is an involuntary tendency to truth and consistency, except when the mind is on its guard, and studiously bent upon concealment; and this law of our nature sometimes gives rise to minute and unpremeditated acts of great weight. In the memorable case of Eugene Aram, who was tried in 1759 for the murder of Daniel Clark, an apparently slight circumstance in the conduct of his accomplice, led to his conviction and execution. About thirteen years after the time of Clark's being missing, a labourer, employed in digging for stone to supply a limekiln near Knaresborough, discovered a human skeleton near the edge of the cliff. It soon became suspected that the body was that of Clark, and the coroner held an inquest. Aram and Houseman were the persons who had last been seen with Clark, on the night before he was missing. The latter was summoned to attend the inquest, and discovered signs of uneasiness: at the request of the coroner he took up one of the bones, and in his confusion dropped this unguarded expression, "This is no more Daniel Clark's bone than it is mine;" from which it was concluded, that if he was so certain that the bones before him were not those of Clark, he could give some account of him. He was pressed with this observation, and, after various evasive accounts, he made a full confession of the crime; and upon search, pursuant to his statement, the skeleton of Clark was found in St. Robert's Cave, buried precisely as he had described it.*

A remarkable fact of the same kind occurred in the case of one of three men convicted, in February 1807, of a murder on Hounslow heath. In consequence of dis-

* Life and Trial of Eugene Aram; and see Biog. Brit., article Eugene Aram.

closures made by an accomplice, a police-officer apprehended the prisoner four years after the murder on board the 'Shannon' frigate, in which he was serving as a marine. The officer asked him in the presence of his captain where he had been about three years before; to which he answered that he was employed in London as a day-labourer. He then asked him where he had been employed that time four years : the man immediately turned pale, and would have fainted away had not water been administered to him. These marks of emotion derived their weight from the latency of the allusion—no express reference having been made to the offence with which the prisoner was charged—and from the probability that there must have been some secret reason for his emotion connected with the event so obscurely referred to, particularly as he had evinced no such feeling upon the first question, which referred to a later period.*

To this head may be referred the acts of concealment, disguise, flight, and other indications of mental emotion usually found in connection with guilt.† By the common law, flight was considered so strong a presumption of guilt, that in cases of treason and felony it carried the forfeiture of the party's goods, whether he were found guilty or acquitted ;‡ and the officer always, until the abolition of the practice by statute,§ called upon the jury, after verdict of acquittal, to state whether the party had fled on account of the charge. These several acts in all their modifications are indications of fear ; but it would be harsh and unreasonable invariably to interpret them as indications of guilty consciousness, and greater weight

* Rex v. Haggerty and others, 6 Celebrated Trials, 19 ; and Sessions Papers, 1807.

† See Rex v. Crossfield, 26 St. Tr. 216 *et seq.* ; and Rex v. O'Coigley, 27 ib. 133.

‡ Co. Litt. 375.   § 7 & 8 Geo. IV. cap. 28, § 5.

has sometimes been attached to them than they have fairly warranted. ,Doubtless the manly carriage of integrity always commands the respect of mankind, and all tribunals do homage to the great principles from which consistency springs ; but it does not follow, because the moral courage and consistency which generally accompany the consciousness of uprightness raise a presumption of innocence, that the converse is always true. Men are differently constituted as respects both animal and moral courage, and fear may spring from causes very different from that of conscious guilt; and every man is therefore entitled to a candid construction of his words and actions, particularly if placed in circumstances of great and unexpected difficulty.* Mr. Justice Abbott on a trial for murder where evidence was given of flight, observed in his charge to the jury, that " a person, however conscious of innocence, might not have courage to stand a trial ; but might, although innocent, think it necessary to consult his safety by flight." " It may be," added the learned judge, " a conscious anticipation of punishment for guilt, as the guilty will always anticipate the consequences ; but at the same time it may possibly be, according to the frame of mind, merely an inclination to consult his safety by flight rather than stand his trial on a charge so heinous and scandalous as this is."† The learned judge in Professor Webster's case, said, " Such are the various temperaments of men, and so rare the occurrence of the sudden arrest of a person upon the charge of a crime so heinous, that who of us can say how an innocent or a guilty man ought or would be likely to act in such a case ? or that he was too much or too little moved for an innocent man ? Have you any

* Per Mr. Baron Gurney, in Reg. *v.* Belaney; *infra.*
† Rex *v.* Donnall, *infra.*

experience that an innocent man, stunned under the mere imputation of such a charge, will always appear calm and collected? or that a guilty man, who by knowledge of his danger might be somewhat braced up for the consequences, would always appear agitated or the reverse."*

It is not possible to lay down any express test by which these various indications may be infallibly referred to any more specific origin than the operation of fear. Whether that fear proceeds from the consciousness of guilt, or from the apprehension of undeserved disgrace and punishment, and from deficiency of moral courage, is a question which can be judged of only by reference to concomitant circumstances. Prejudice is often epidemic, and there have been periods and occasions when public indignation has been so much and so unjustly aroused, as reasonably to deter the boldest mind from voluntary submission to the ordeal of a trial. The consciousness that appearances have been suspicious, even where suspicion has been unwarrantable, has sometimes led to acts of conduct apparently incompatible with innocence, and drawn down the unmerited infliction of the highest legal penalty. The inconclusiveness of these circumstances is strikingly exemplified by a case mentioned in a preceding page, where the magistrate was so fully convinced of the prisoner's innocence, that he allowed him to go at large on bail to appear at the assizes. The coroner's inquest having brought in a verdict of ' guilty' against him, he endeavoured to escape from the danger of a trial in the excited state of public feeling by flight; but was subsequently apprehended, convicted, and executed on a charge of murder, of which he was unquestionably guiltless.†

* Bemis's Rep. 486.

† Rex v. Coleman, ante, 77 ; and see the case of Green and others,

In the endeavour to discover truth, no evidence should
be excluded; but a case must be scanty of evidence
which demands that importance should be attached to
circumstances so fallacious as the acts in question.   It
has been observed, that if the evidence without them is
sufficient, this species of evidence is unnecessary, and
that if not, then the inferences from language, conduct,
and behaviour, seems not of sufficient weight to give any
conclusive effect to the other proofs.*

Section 7.

THE SUPPRESSION, DESTRUCTION, FABRICATION, AND SIMULATION OF EVIDENCE.

It is a maxim of law, that *omnia præsumuntur contra
spoliatorem*, and the suppression or destruction of pertinent evidence is always therefore deemed a prejudicial
circumstance of great weight; for as no action of a rational being is performed without a motive, it naturally
leads to the inference that such evidence, if it were produced, would operate unfavourably to the party in whose
power it is to produce it, and who withholds it or has wil-
fully deprived himself of the power of producing it.†

A chimney-sweeper having found a jewel, took it to a
jeweller to ascertain its value; who, having removed it
from the socket, gave him three-halfpence, and refused
to return it.   The friends of the finder encouraged him
to bring an action against the jeweller; and the Lord

14 St. Tr. 1369, where several persons, one of whom had voluntarily sur-
rendered, were convicted in Scotland and executed, at a period of great
excitement against Englishmen, upon a groundless charge of piracy and
murder.

  * Per Shaw C. J. in Prof. Webster's case, Rep. *ut supra*, 487.

  † 1 Starkie's L. of Ev. 437.

Chief Justice Pratt directed the jury, that unless the defendant produced the jewel, and showed it not to be of the finest water, they should presume the strongest against him, and make the value of the best jewels the measure of their damages.* In an action of trover for a diamond necklace which had been unlawfully taken out of the owner's possession, and some of the diamonds were seen shortly afterwards in the defendant's possession, and he could give no satisfactory account how he came by them, the jury were directed to presume that the whole set of diamonds had come to the defendant's hands, and that the full value of the whole was the proper measure of damages.† On an ejectment involving the title to large estates in Ireland, the question being whether the plaintiff was the legitimate son of Lord Altham, and therefore prior in right to the defendant, who was his brother, it was proved that the defendant had procured the plaintiff, when a boy, to be kidnapped and sent to America, and on his return, fifteen years afterwards, on occasion of an accidental homicide, had assisted in an unjust prosecution against him for murder: it was held that these circumstances raised a violent presumption of the defendant's knowledge of title in the plaintiff; and the jury were directed that the suppressor and the destroyer were to be considered in the same light as the law considers a spoliator, as having destroyed the proper evidence; that against him, defective proof, so far as he had occasioned such defect, must be received, and everything presumed to make it effectual ; and that if they thought the plaintiff had given probable evidence of his being the legitimate son of Lord Altham, the proof might be turned on

* Armorie v. Delamirie, 1 Strange. 505 ; and see Rex v. Lord Melville, 29 St. Tr. 1457.   † Mortimer v. Craddock. 12 L. J. N. S. 166.

the defendant, and that they might expect satisfaction from him that his brother died without issue.* On a bill filed against a defendant who had destroyed a deed by which the plaintiff claimed under certain limitations a real estate, secondary evidence was given of the limitations in the deed; but the evidence, as the witnesses gave it, was of limitations which could not legally take effect, being of a term of years after an indefinite failure of issue,—Sir Joseph Jekyll, the Master of the Rolls, said that as against the man who had destroyed the instrument which would have shown what the rights of the plaintiff were, he would presume even what the plaintiff had not proved, that the limitation was to take place after the failure of issue in the life-time of a person then in being.†

The foregoing illustrations of the rule of evidence under consideration, are among the most remarkable recorded cases of its application; nor are they the less pertinent because they arose in civil cases, since the rules of evidence are the same in all cases, whether civil or criminal; and no inconsiderable proportion of the criminal trials which occur, present examples of its practical bearing and effect.‡

Amongst the most forcible of presumptive indications may be mentioned, all attempts to pollute or disturb the current of truth and justice, or to prevent a fair and impartial trial, by endeavours to intimidate, suborn,

---

* Craig on dem. of Annesley v. Earl of Anglesea, 17 St. Tr. 1416; and see the Tracy Peerage, 11 C. & F. 154; Clunnes v. Pezzey, 1 Campb. Rep. 8 ; Lawton v. Sweeney, 8 Jurist. 964; 1 Greenleaf's L. of Ev. § 37 ; and see the observations of Campbell L. C. J. in Reg. v. the Midland Railway Company, 20 L. Mag. M. C. 145.

† Dalston v. Cotsworth, 1 P. Wms. 731.

‡ Rex v. De la Motte, 21 St. Tr. 810; Rex v. Burdett, *ut supra*.

bribe, or otherwise tamper with the prosecutor, or the witnesses, or the officers or ministers of justice, the concealment, suppression, destruction, or alteration of any article of real evidence ; any of which acts, clearly brought home to the prisoner, or his agents, are of a most prejudicial effect, as denoting on his part a consciousness of guilt, and a desire to evade the pressure of facts tending to establish it.*   Perhaps in no case have circumstances of this kind held with such fatal effect as in that of Donellan, who was convicted of the murder of Sir Theodosius Boughton by poison.   The prisoner, after having administered the fatal draught in the form of medicine, rinsed out the phial which had contained it, and when that fact was stated before the coroner, he was observed to check the witness by pulling her sleeve.   In his charge to the jury, Mr. Justice Buller laid great stress upon that circumstance.   " Was there anything so likely," said the learned judge, " to lead to a discovery as the remains, however small they might have been, of medicine in the bottle? But that is destroyed by the prisoner.   In the moment he is doing it, he is found fault with.   What does he do next? He takes the second bottle, puts water into that, and rinses it also.   He is checked by Lady Boughton, and asked what he meant by it—why he meddled with the bottles. His answer is, he did it to taste it ; but did he taste the first bottle?   Lady Boughton swears he did not.   The next thing he does, is to get all the things sent out of the room ; for when the servant comes up, he orders her to take away the bottles, the basin, and the dirty things. He puts the bottles into her hand, and she was going to carry them away, but Lady Boughton stopped her. Why

* Rex _c._ Crossfield, 26 St. Tr. 217 ; Rex _c._ Donellan ; Rex _v._ Donnall ; Reg. _v._ Palmer, _infra_.

were all these things to be removed? Why was it necessary for the prisoner, who was fully advertised of the
consequence by Lady Boughton, to insist upon having
everything removed? Why should he be so solicitous
to remove everything that might lead to a discovery?"*
As to the conduct of the prisoner before the coroner,
Lady Boughton had mentioned the circumstance of the
prisoner's rinsing out the bottle, one of the coroner's jury
swears that he saw him pull her by the sleeve. Why
did he do that? If he was innocent, would it not be
his wish and anxious desire, as he expresses in his letter,
that all possible inquiry should be made? What passes
afterwards? When they got home, the prisoner tells his
wife that Lady Boughton had given this evidence unne-
cessarily; that she was not obliged to say anything but
in answer to questions that were put to her, and that the
question about rinsing out the bottles was not asked her.
Did the prisoner mean that she should suppress the truth?
that she should endeavour to avoid a discovery as much
as she could by barely saying Yes or No to the questions
that were asked her, and not disclose the whole truth?
If he was innocent, how could the truth affect him? but
at that time the circumstance of rinsing out the bottles
appeared even to him to be so decisive that he stopped
her on the instant, and blamed her afterwards for having
mentioned it. All these, said the learned judge, "are very
strong facts to show what was passing in the prisoner's
own mind." A boatman was convicted of stealing rum
which had been delivered to his master, a carrier by canal,
for conveyance from Liverpool to Birmingham. The carrier's agent at Liverpool had taken a sample of the spirit
and tested its strength; and upon delivery at its place of

* Gurney's Report, *ut supra.*

destination, the spirit was found to be under proof, and the portion abstracted had been replaced with water. The carrier's clerk, on the complaint of the consignee, went to the boat where the prisoner was, to require explanation; but as soon as he had stepped into it, the prisoner pushed him back upon the wharf, and forced the boat into the middle of the canal, where he broke three jars and emptied their contents, which by the smell were proved to be rum, into the canal.*

Other facts of the same kind are the common cases of the obliteration, effacing, or otherwise removing marks of ownership or identity from plate, linen, or other articles of property, or of stains of blood or other matter from the person or dress of the accused, or the suggestion or insinuation of false, groundless, or deceptive hypotheses, or explanations in order to neutralize or account for adverse facts or appearances. It is on the principle of these cases that, by statute, if any person on board a vessel which is chased by an officer of the preventive service, shall throw overboard, stave, or destroy any part of the freight, the vessel is declared to be forfeited; and that goods liable to duty concealed on board any vessel are also declared to be forfeited;† and that other similar statutable presumptions have been created; and that whenever absent witnesses are so mixed up with transactions before the court as to give rise to comments on their not being present, it is the common practice to prove the cause of their non-attendance, as, for instance, death, illness, or their having quitted the country.‡

Another fact of this kind is the attempt to prevent

---

* Rex *v.* Thomas, Warwick Spring Ass. 1836. coram Mr. Justice Bosanquet.　　　† 8 & 9 Vict. c. 87. ss. 5 d. 6, & 29.

‡ Per Pollock L.C.B., in Cowper *v.* French. Exch. N.P. July 10, 1850.

post mortem examination by the premature interment of human remains, under the pretext that it is rendered necessary by the state of the body, since it cannot but be known that such examination will always furnish important, and generally conclusive, evidentiary matter as to the cause of death.* So also is the concealment of death by the destruction or attempted destruction of human remains;† but in this case the presumption of criminality results from the act of concealment rather than from the nature of the means employed, however revolting, which must be regarded only as incidental to the fact of concealment and not as aggravating the character and tendency of the act itself. Where a prisoner tried for murder admitted that he had cut off the head and legs from the trunk of a female, and concealed the remains in several places, but alleged that her death had taken place by accident while she was in his company, and that in the alarm of the moment, and to prevent suspicion, he had determined to conceal the death, Lord Chief Justice Tindal told the jury that the concealment of death under such circumstances, had always been considered to be a point of the greatest suspicion, but that this evidence must be received with a certain degree of modification, and especially in a case where the feelings might be excited by the singular means of concealment adopted by the prisoner; that this point of evidence was therefore for the consideration of the jury, and that it was for them to judge how far it was a proof of the prisoner's guilt; but the mere general fact of the concealment, added the learned judge, is to

---

* Rex *v.* Donellan, Rex *v.* Donnall, Rex *v.* Palmer, *infra.*

† Rex *v.* Gardelle, 4 Celebrated Trials, 400; Rex *v.* Cook, *infra;* Reg. *v.* Good, Sess. Pap. May 1842.

be considered, and not the circumstances under which it took place.*

Other such facts are the officious affectation of grief and concern as an artifice to prevent or avert suspicion,† false representations as to the state of a party's health, or the utterance of obscure or mysterious predictions or allusions, the pretence of supernatural dreams, noises, or other omens or intimations, calculated to prepare the connections for the event of sudden death, and to diminish the surprise and alarm which naturally follow such an event. A woman who was convicted of murder, about a month before the catastrophe told the mother of an infant child whom she poisoned, as well as her own husband and child, that she had had her fortune told, and that within six weeks three funerals would go from her door, those of her husband and son and the child of the person she was addressing.‡

The fabrication of simulated facts and appearances calculated to create alarm, or otherwise to give a delusive tendency and interpretation to inculpatory facts, is an artifice frequently resorted to, for the avoidance, neutralization, or explanation of circumstances naturally presumptive of guilt; the resort to which is of the most prejudicial criminative tendency, inasmuch as it necessarily implies an admission of their truth, and a consciousness of the inculpatory effect if uncontradicted, or unexplained, of the facts which it thus seeks to divest of their natural significancy. As instances of such simulated facts may be mentioned the pretence of having partaken of a

* Rex v. Greenacre, C. C. Court, April, 1837, *infra*; and see Professor Webster's case, Bemis's Report, *ut supra*.

† Rex v. Blandy, *ut supra*; Rex v. Patch, *infra*.

‡ Rex v. Holroyd, 4 Cel. Tr. 167; and see Rex v. Donellan and Rex v. Donnall, *infra*.

poisonous draught which has caused death ;* the self-infliction of slight wounds to raise the inference that the offender had himself been the object of deadly attack ;† the attempt to fix guilt or suspicion upon others by the groundless suggestion of malicious feelings ;‡ the placing of a razor, pistol, or other weapon in the hand of or near to a dead body to lead to the notion of suicide, and many other such acts.   But cunning is " a sinister or crooked wisdom," and not unfrequently the very means employed to prevent suspicion, lead to the discovery of the real truth. A murderer, to simulate the appearance of suicide, placed a razor in the left hand of a right-handed woman. § A man was found shot, and his own pistol lying near him ; but, although no person had been seen to leave the house, the suspicion of suicide was negatived by the fact that the ball was too large to have entered the pistol. ‖

A very remarkable case of this kind is recorded in the State Trials, which was tried at Hertford Assizes, 4 Car. I., before Mr. Justice Harvey. A woman was found dead in her bed, with her throat cut, and a knife sticking in the floor. Several persons of the family who slept in the adjoining room deposed that the deceased went to bed with her child, her husband being absent, that the prisoners slept in the adjoining room, and that no person afterwards came into the house. The coroner's jury were inclined to return a verdict of *felo de se*, but suspicion being excited against these individuals, the jury, whose verdict was not yet drawn up in form, desired that the

* Rex *v.* Nairn and Ogilby, 19 St.Tr. 1284 ; Rex *v.* Wescombe, Exeter Sum. Ass. 1839.

† Reg. *v.* Bolam, Durham Summer Ass. 1839.

‡ Rex *v.* Patch, *ut supra.*

§ Rex *v.* Fitter. Warwick Sum. Ass. 1834, *coram* Mr. Justice Taunton.

‖ 3 P. & F. Med. J. 34.

remains of the deceased might be taken up, and accordingly, thirty days after her death, they were taken up, and the jury charged the prisoners with the murder. Upon their trial they were acquitted, but so much against the evidence, that the judge let fall his opinion that it were better an appeal were brought than so foul a murder should escape unpunished. Accordingly an appeal was brought by the child against his father, grandmother, and aunt, and her husband. On the trial of the appeal before Chief Justice Hyde, the evidence adduced was, that the deceased lay in a composed manner in her bed, with the bedclothes undisturbed, that her child lay by her side, that her neck was broken, and that her throat was cut from ear to ear. There was no blood in the bed, except a tincture on the bolster where her head lay. From the bed's head there was a stream of blood on the floor, which ran along till it pounded in the bendings of the floor, and there was also another stream of blood on the floor at the bed's foot, which pounded also on the floor to a very great quantity; but there was no communication of blood between these two places, nor upon the bed. A bloody knife was found in the morning sticking in the floor, at some distance from the bed; but the point of the knife, as it stuck, was towards the bed, and the handle from the bed; and there was the print of the thumb and fingers of a left-hand. It was beyond all question, from the circumstances, that the deceased had been murdered, for if she had committed suicide by cutting her own throat, she could not by any possibility have broken her own neck in bed. The father, grandfather, and aunt were convicted and executed.*

Two persons were convicted of murder; and it ap-

* Rex *v.* Okeman and others; comp. 10 Harg. St. Tr. app. 2, 29, and 14 St. Tr. 1324.

peared that the deceased was murdered in the night, and that the prisoners, one of whom was his niece, and the other, his servant man, had given an alarm from within the house; whereas the undisturbed state of the dew on the grass on the outside rendered it certain that the parties implicated were domestics.*

An unsuccessful attempt to establish an *alibi* is always a circumstance of the greatest weight against the prisoner, because the resort to that kind of defence implies an admission of the truth and relevancy of the facts alleged, and the correctness of the inference drawn from them if they remain uncontradicted. This defence is frequently fabricated, and is liable to many sources of fallacy, which will be more appropriately considered in a subsequent part of this essay; and a learned judge has said, that if the defence turns out to be untrue, it amounts to a conviction.† But it must not be overlooked that, such is the weakness of human nature, there have been cases where innocence, under the alarm of menacing appearances, has fatally committed itself, by the simulation of facts for the purpose of evading the force of circumstances of apparent suspicion. When the defence of an alibi fails, it is generally on the ground that the witnesses are disbelieved and the story considered to be a fabrication; and from the facility with which it may be fabricated, it is commonly entertained with suspicion, and sometimes, perhaps, unjustly so. ‡

Circumstances such as those which have been enumerated, are justly considered to be incompatible with integrity and innocence, and referable to a consciousness of

* Rex *v.* Jeffreys and Swan, 18 St. Tr. 1194; Mascardus, *ut supra* Concl. CCLXXIII. n. 20.

† Per Mr. Justice Daly, in Rex *v.* Killan, 20 St. Tr. 1085.

‡ See Rex *v.* Robinson, *infra.*

guilt and to a desire to evade the force of facts indicative of it; and they consequently subject the party guilty of them to very unfavourable and injurious inferences.

SECTION 8.

STATUTORY PRESUMPTIONS.

UPON the principle of the rule of presumption against persons in whose possession the fruits of crime are discovered recently after its commission, many acts have been constituted legal presumptions of guilt by statute, so as to throw the onus of rebutting or displacing such presumptions upon the party accused; such, for example, among many others, as the making or possessing, or buying or selling coining tools or instruments;* the possession of forged bank-notes, knowing the same to be forged, without lawful excuse;† the possession of marine stores marked with the king's mark,‡ the acting or behaving as the master or mistress of a disorderly house,§ the finding of instruments in any places suspected to be used as a common gaming-house,‖ and the being found by night in possession, without lawful excuse, of any picklock, key, crow, jack, bit, or other instrument of housebreaking.** The revenue laws abound with similar instances of presumptions created for the purpose of protecting the public against infractions of those laws.

By a remarkable anomaly, probably grounded upon some supposed analogy to the rule alluded to, the sale by

---

* St. 2 W. IV. c. 30. s, 10.
† St. 11 G. IV. and 1 W. IV. c. 66, s. 12–19. and 28.
‡ St. 9 & 10 W. III. c. 41; and 39 & 40 G. III. c. 89.
§ St. 21 G. III. c. 49.   ‖ St. 8 & 9 Vic. c. 109.
** St. 14 & 15 Vict. c. 19, s. 1; and see Reg. v. Oldham, 5 Cox's C. C. 551, and 3 C. & K. 249.

a shopman of a book or newspaper containing libellous matter, was formerly held to constitute a conclusive presumption of publication by the authority of the master, from the consequences of which he could not protect himself by showing that such sale was not only unauthorized, but even without his knowledge.* This carried the doctrine of agency to an unwarrantable extent. A late statute has now brought this part of our law into harmony with the other parts of the system, by providing that whensoever, upon any trial for the publication of a libel, evidence shall have been given which shall establish a presumptive case of publication against the defendant by the act of any other person by his authority, it shall be competent to him to prove that such publication was made without his authority, consent, or knowledge, and that it did not arise from want of due care on his part.†

Of statutory presumptions this general notice is sufficient, as it is the object of this essay to consider the natural connection between facts and the presumptions to which they naturally lead, and not to enumerate the presumptions created by positive law.‡

It is evident that all such arbitrary presumptions depend for their reasonable force and authority upon the obnoxious character *per se* of the particular acts thus constituted legal presumptions, upon their strict connection and relation, as pregnant evidence either of some specific legal offence, or of the intention to commit such offence, and upon the facility of proof by the accused of matter of legal excuse where such matter exists.

* Rex *v.* Almon, 20 St. Tr. 803; Rex *v.* Cuthell, 27, ib. 641.

† St. 6 & 7 Vic. c. 96, s. 7.

‡ See a copious collection of such presumptions in 1 Taylor's L. of Ev. 65, 96, 103, 269.

In the interpretation of laws which create positive presumptions of guilt, it is essential to distinguish between the letter and the spirit of the enactment ; to such laws the maxim is specially pertinent, " *scire leges, non est, earum verba tenere, sed vim ac potestatem.*"* It is not practicable to predicate all the cases which may fall within the language of the rule, or to anticipate the necessary exceptions which a proper regard to the intention of the legislature would exclude from its operation, and which it is reasonable to conclude that the legislature would have expressly excluded if they had been foreseen. However peremptory and apparently conclusive, therefore, the language of such enactments may be, it is not allowed to exclude or control the just force and operation of such concomitant circumstances as tend to repel the presumption of the *malus animus* arising from the bare facts which constitute the presumption.† The following cases illustrate the necessity of thus controlling the application of positive presumptions, by such qualifying considerations as must be supposed to have been within the contemplation of the legislature though it has not expressed them in words.

A widow woman was indicted before Mr. Justice Foster on the 9th & 10th Wm. III. c. 41, for having in her custody divers pieces of canvas marked with the king's mark, she not being employed by the Commissioners of the Navy to make the same for the king's use. The canvas was marked as charged in the indictment, and was clearly proved to be such as was made for the use of the navy, and to have been found in the defendant's custody. She did not attempt to show that she was within any exception of the act, as being a person employed to

* L. 47. § De Legibus.   † Puffendorf, lib. v. c. 12 ; .2 East's P. C. 765.

make canvas for the navy ; nor did she offer to produce
any certificate from any officer of the crown, touching the
occasion of such canvas coming into her possession. Her
defence was, that when there happened to be in his Majesty's stores a considerable quantity of old sails, no longer
fit for that use, it had been customary for the persons entrusted with the stores to make a public sale of them in
lots larger or smaller, as best suited the purpose of the
buyers ; and that the canvas produced in evidence, which
had been made up long since, some for table-linen and
some for sheeting, had been in common use in the defendant's family a considerable time before her husband's
death ; and upon his death came to the defendant, and
had been used in the same open manner by her to the
time of prosecution.   The counsel for the crown insisted
that as the act allows of but one excuse, the defendant,
unless she could avail herself of that, could not resort to
any other ; that, if the canvas were really bought of the
commissioners, or of persons acting under them, there
ought to have been a certificate taken at the time of the
purchase, and that the second section admits of no other
excuse.   But the learned judge was of opinion, that
though the clause of the statute which directs the sale of
these things had not pointed out any other way of indem-
nifying the buyer than the certificate, and though the
second section seemed to exclude any other excuse for
those in whose custody they should be found, yet still
the circumstances attending every case which might
seem to fall within the act, ought to be taken into consideration ; otherwise a law calculated for wise purposes,
might, by a too rigid construction of it, be made a handle
for oppression.   There was no room to say that this canvas came into the possession of the defendant by any act

of her own ; it was brought into family use in the lifetime of her husband, and continued so to the time of his death; and by act of law it came to her. Things of that kind had frequently been exposed to public sale ; and though the act pointed out an expedient for the indemnity of buyers, yet probably few buyers, especially where small quantities had been purchased at one sale, had used the caution suggested by the act. And if the defendant's husband really bought the linen at a public sale, but neglected to take a certificate, or did not preserve it, it would be contrary to natural justice, after such a length of time, to punish her for his neglect. He therefore thought the evidence given by the defendant proper to be left to the jury ; and directed them, that if upon the whole evidence they were of opinion that the defendant came to the possession of the linen without any fraud or misbehaviour on her part, they would acquit her ; and she was accordingly acquitted.[*]

In a similar case Lord Kenyon said, that though in prosecutions under the statutes 9 & 10 Wm. III. c. 41, and 17 Geo. II. c. 40, s. 10, it was sufficient for the crown to prove the finding of the stores with the king's mark in the defendant's possession, to call upon him to account for that possession, so as to throw upon him the onus of proving that he had legally become possessed of them, yet that he had other means of showing that he had lawfully become possessed of them than by the production of the certificate from the Navy Board ; as for example, he might show that he had bought them from another person who was in the practice of buying stores at the navy sales, and who therefore might fairly be presumed to have had the regular certificate, but who, when

* Foster's C. L. App. 439.

he sold part to the defendant, could not consistently with his own safety, part with the certificate he had obtained of his having been the purchaser of the whole lot.* Where a defendant, charged with the unlawful possession of two lots of marked metal stores, produced in his defence two certificates in respect of several lots, signed respectively by the Commodore Superintendent of the Woolwich Dockyard and the Secretary to the Board of Ordnance, the former having been granted to the person from whom he purchased, the latter to the defendant himself, it was held that these certificates, though not strictly in accordance with the statute 9 & 10 Wm. III. c. 41, were nevertheless an answer to the charge; Mr. Justice Coltman said, that, although the certificates were not strictly in conformity with the act, the Government ought not to dispute their validity.†   It must also appear that the goods were on the defendant's premises with his knowledge, and he is not responsible if they were improperly received by his servants without his knowledge.‡

Upon an indictment on the statute 5 & 6 Wm. IV. c. 19, which makes it a misdemeanour in the master of a vessel to leave a seaman behind, and enacts that the only defence which he can set up is the production of the certificate of the consul or other party mentioned in the statute, it was held nevertheless that a defendant might show that it was impracticable to obtain such certificate,§ and this qualification has been introduced into the subsequent statute, 7 & 8 Vict. c. 112, s. 48.

In like manner, although the repealed statute 21 Jac. I. c. 27, made the concealment of the death of an illegiti-

* Rex *v.* Banks, 1 Esp. 144.   † Reg. *v.* Wilmet, 3 Cox's C. C., 281.
‡ Reg. *v.* Wilmet, *ib.*   § Reg. *v.* Dunnett. 1 C. & K. 425.

mate child conclusive evidence of murder by the mother, except she could prove by one witness at least that it was actually born dead, nevertheless in the construction of that law it was usual to require that some sort of presumptive evidence should be given that the child was born alive, before the other constrained presumption, that the child whose death was concealed was therefore killed by its parent, was admitted to convict the prisoner.[*]

SECTION 9.

SCIENTIFIC TESTIMONY.

THE testimony of skilled or scientific witnesses constitutes a very important source of circumstantial evidence, especially in regard to the proof of the *corpus delicti* in cases of suspected homicide, and in questions concerning the *doli capax*. Such evidence in its details belongs to other departments of science; but as the principles which govern its reception and application fall exclusively within the province of jurisprudence, some general observations upon it are therefore necessary.

If it be true, that proof is nothing more than a presumption of the highest order,[†] *a fortiori* is such the case with respect to the testimony of skilled or scientific witnesses, which not unfrequently presents a sequence of presumptions grounded upon conflicting opinions, even with regard to the actual state of science. Such testimony is therefore of a nature *sui generis*, and, according to the attainments and means of knowledge of the witness, may be of little moment, or deserving of entire and undoubting confidence.

Science moreover is never final; and new facts are every

* 4 Bl. Comm. (by Stephen) b. iv. c. xii.   † *Ut supra*, p. 32.

day found to disturb or modify long-established convictions. Thus Reinsch's test, which had long been confidently employed for the separation of arsenic, has lately been discovered to be fallacious when applied to chlorate of potass, and the arsenic which was found in the particular mixture had been set free from the copper employed in the experiment.[*]

In many countries this kind of testimony, technically termed *expertise*, is invested with a sort of semi-official authority, and special rules are laid down for the estimation of its proving force.[†] By the law of England, however, no peculiar authority is given to the testimony of witnesses of this description; its value is estimated by the same general principles as are applied in estimating the capacity, credit, and weight of all other witnesses,[‡] and the courts have wisely repelled all attempts to depart from the established and ordinary rules of evidence and judgment. On a trial for murder, before Lord Chief Justice Tindal, several medical witnesses, who had been present during the trial and heard the whole of the evidence, but had no other means of forming an opinion on the question, were admitted to testify that in their judgment the prisoner was insane. But the propriety of admitting such evidence having been made the subject of discussion in the House of Lords, the question was submitted to the Judges, who were of opinion that a medical witness could not in strictness be asked his opinion as to the state of the prisoner's mind at the time of the commission of the alleged crime, or whether he was conscious at the time of doing the act, that he was acting contrary to law,

* Reg. *v.* Smethurst, C. C. C. Aug. 1859, Sess. Papers.
† Mittermaier, *ut supra, c.* 126, *et seq.*
‡ See Best's Prin. of Ev. 385 *et seq.*

or whether he was labouring under any and what delusions, because each of those questions involves the determination of the truth of the facts deposed to, which it is for the jury to decide, and the questions are not mere questions upon a matter of science; in which case such evidence is admissible; but that where the facts are admitted, or not disputed, and the question becomes substantially one of science only, it may be convenient to allow the question to be put in that general form, though the same cannot be insisted on as matter of right.*

On a subsequent occasion, Mr. Baron Alderson, with the concurrence of Mr. Justice Cresswell, refused to allow a witness to be asked whether, from all the evidence he had heard, both for the prosecution and defence, he was of opinion that the prisoner at the time he committed the act was of unsound mind, and said that the proper mode is to ask what are the symptoms of insanity, or to take particular facts, and, assuming them to be true, to ask whether they indicate insanity on the part of the prisoner; but to take the course suggested, he said, was really to substitute the witness for the jury, and to allow him to decide upon the whole case; that the jury must have the facts before them, and that they alone must interpret them by the general opinions of scientific men.† Upon a trial for murder, where the death was alleged to have been caused by suffocation, a physician who had attended in court and heard the evidence, was asked his opinion as to the cause of death; but Mr. Justice Patteson expressed himself very strongly upon the unsatisfactory nature of such evidence, the witness not having seen the body, and his opinion being founded on the facts stated by other

* Reg. c. M'Naghten, 10 Cl. & F. 200; 1 C. & K. 138; 8 Scott, N. R. 595.   † Reg. v. Francis, 4 Cox's C. C. 57.

witnesses.* These cases have been followed by a series of determinations in which such evidence has been held to be inadmissible.†

The reasonable principle appears to be, that scientific witnesses shall be permitted to testify only to such matters of fact as have come within their own cognizance, or as they have acquired a knowledge of by their reading, and to such inferences from them, or from other facts provisionally assumed to be proved, as their particular studies and pursuits especially qualify them to draw ; so that the jury may thus be furnished with the necessary scientific *criteria* for testing the accuracy of their conclusions, and enabled to form their own independent judgment by the application of those *criteria* to the facts established in evidence before them.

But where the witnesses are men of unquestionable character and ability, it can hardly be material whether the question is asked in a more or less direct form ; especially as there can be no difficulty in so shaping the question as to mask while it substantially involves the precise objection; and in several late cases medical witnesses have been permitted without objection to give their opinions as to the sanity of parties charged with crime, as grounded upon the evidence that had been adduced both for the prosecution and the defence ; though, if made, the objection must of course prevail.‡

It is scarcely necessary to add, that scientific evidence being generally matter of opinion, can seldom be impli-

* Reg. v. Newton, Shrewsbury Spring Ass. 1850, *infra.*
† Reg. v. Pate, C. C. C. 12 July, 1850 ; Doe d. Bainbridge v. Bainbridge, *coram* Campbell, L. C. J., Stafford Summer Ass. 1850 ; 4 Cox's C. C. 454 ; Reg. v. Leyton, *ib.* 149, *coram* Rolfe B.
‡ Reg. v. Baranelli, C. C. C. Ap. 1855 ; Reg. v. Westron, C. C. C. Feb. 1856 ; Starkie's L. of Ev., 4th ed. 175.

citly adopted. Lord Cottenham said, he had seen enough of professional opinions to be aware that in matters of doubt, upon which the best constructed and best informed minds may differ, there is no difficulty in procuring opinions on either side.*

A learned writer on the Law of Scotland observes, that "there is perhaps no kind of testimony more subject to bias in favour of the adducer than that of skilled witnesses; for many men, who would not willingly misstate a simple fact, can accommodate their opinions to the wishes of their employers, and the connection between them tends to warp the judgment of the witnesses without their being conscious of it; and hence skilled witnesses, in questions of handwriting, can usually be got in equal numbers on either side; and engineers are more frequently like counsel for their employers than like witnesses giving their real opinions on oath."† Nor is it possible, after the discreditable exhibitions which have lately taken place in our courts of justice, to restrict the foregoing reproaches to witnesses taken from the particular professions which have been enumerated. Happily, however, such cases are but exceptional; and true scientific knowledge, under the government of high principle, is of the greatest value, as subsidiary to the ends of justice.‡

Some valuable remarks upon this kind of evidence were made by Lord Chief Justice Cockburn, upon a trial for murder, at Taunton Spring Assizes, 1857. The murder was effected by cutting the throat. A knife was found

---

* Dyce Sombre's case, 1 M·N. & Gord. 128.

† 2 Dickson on the L. of Ev. *ut supra*, 996; and see the language of Lord Campbell in the Tracey Peerage, 10 C. & F. 191.

‡ On the subject of scientific evidence in cases of poisoning, see *infra* Ch. VII. s. 4; and of infanticide, *ib.* s. 5.

on the person of the prisoner, with stains of blood upon it ; and it was contended that the murder had been effected with this weapon, while it was alleged on the part of the prisoner that it had been used for cutting raw beef. A professional analyst called on the part of the prosecution stated that the blood had not coagulated till it was on the knife, that the knife had been immersed in *living* blood up to the hilt, and that it was not the blood of an ox, a sheep, or a pig. His opinion was grounded upon the relative sizes of the globules of blood in man and other animals, that of man being stated to be 1-3400th of an inch, of the ox 1-5300th, of the sheep 1-5200th, and of the pig 1-4500th, the relative sizes being as 53 to 34 in the ox, 52 to 34 in the sheep, and 45 to 34 in the pig. The learned Judge said, " The witness had said the blood on the knife could not be the blood of an animal as stated by the prisoner, and took upon himself to say that it was not the blood of a dead animal ; that it was living blood, and that it was human blood, and he had shown them the marvellous powers of the modern microscope. At the same time, admitting the great advantages of science, they were coming to great niceties indeed when they speculated upon things almost beyond perception, and he would advise the jury not to convict on this scientific speculation alone." The case was conclusive on the general evidence.*

The following cases are remarkable as exemplifying the inconclusiveness of scientific evidence, when uncorroborated by conclusive facts, physical or moral.

A young man was tried for the murder of his brother, who resided with their father, and overlooked his farm. The prisoner, who lived about twenty miles from his father's house, went on a visit to him, and on the day after

---

* Reg. *v.* Nation, Taylor's Med. Jour. 279.

his arrival his brother was found dead in the stable, not far from a vicious mare, with her traces upon his arm and shoulders; two other horses were in the stable, but they had their traces on. Suspicion fell upon the prisoner, who was on ill terms with his brother, and the question was whether the deceased had been killed with a spade, or by kicks from the mare? The spade was bloody, but it had been inadvertently used by a boy in cleaning the stable; and the cause of death could only be determined by the character of the wounds. There were two straight incised wounds on the left side of the head, one about five and the other about two inches long, which had apparently been inflicted by an obtuse instrument. On the right side of the head there were three irregular wounds, two of them about four inches in length, partaking of the appearance both of lacerated and incised wounds. There was also a wound on the back part of the head, about two inches and a half long. There was no tumefaction around any of the wounds, the integuments adhering firmly to the bones; and, except where the wounds were inflicted, the fracture of the skull was general throughout the right side, and extended along the back of the head toward the left side, and a small part of the temporal bone came away. The deceased was found with his hat on, which was bruised, but not cut, and there were no wounds on any other part of the body. Two surgeons expressed a positive opinion that the wounds could not have been inflicted by kicks from a horse, grounding that opinion principally on the distinctness of the wounds, the absence of contusion, the firm adherence of the integuments, and the straight lateral direction and the similarity of the wounds; whereas, as they stated, the deceased would have fallen from the first blow if he had been standing, and if lying down, the wounds would have been perpendicular ; and moreover they were of opinion that the wounds could not have been inflicted if the hat had been on the deceased's head without cutting the hat, and that he could not have put on his hat after receiving any of the wounds. The learned Judge however stated that he remembered a trial at the Old Bailey where it had been proved that a cut and a fracture had been received without having cut the hat ; and evidence was adduced of the infliction of a similar wound by a kick without cutting the hat. The prisoner was acquitted.*

A woman who was tried for the murder of her mother, had lived for nine or ten years as housekeeper to an elderly gentleman, who was paralyzed and helpless; the only other inmate being another female servant, who slept on a sofa in his bedroom to attend upon him. The deceased occasionally visited her daughter at her master's house, and sometimes stopped all night, sleeping on a sofa in the kitchen. She came to see her daughter about eight o'clock one night, in December, 1848 ; the other servant retired to bed about half-past nine, leaving the prisoner and her mother in the kitchen, and she afterwards heard the prisoner close the door at the foot of the stairs, which was usually left open that they might hear their master if he wanted assistance. About two o'clock in the morning she was aroused by the smell of fire, and a sense of suffocation, and found the bedroom full of smoke ; upon which she ran downstairs, the door at the bottom of which was still closed. As she went downstairs she saw a light in the yard, and she found the kitchen full of smoke, and very wet, particularly near the fireplace, as also was

* Rex *v.* Booth, Warwick Spring Assizes, 1808, *coram* Mr. Baron Wood.

the sofa, but there was very little fire in the grate. She then unfastened the front door, and ran out to fetch her master's nephew, who lived near, and who, after ascertaining that his uncle was safe, went into the kitchen, and threw some water on the sofa, which was on fire. The prisoner then drank to intoxication from a bottle of rum, and laid herself down on the sofa. The pillows and entire back part of the sofa-cover were burnt to the breadth of the shoulders. The remains of the deceased were found lying across the steps of the brewhouse, and on the back of the head lay a piece of the sofa-cover, and near the body was a cotton bag, besmeared with oil, which had been used indiscriminately as a bag or pillow. Near the feet of the body there were four pairs of sheets, which had been in the kitchen the night before, wet and almost entirely consumed. The prisoner's clothes were on a chair in the kitchen, and it appeared from the state of the bed-clothes that she had not been in bed. A butter-boat, which had been full of dripping, and a pint bottle, which had been nearly full of lamp-oil, and left near the fire overnight, were both empty, and there were spots of grease and oil on the pillow-case, sheets, and sofa. A stocking had been hung up to cover a crevice in the window-shutter, through which any person outside might have seen into the kitchen. The door-post of the kitchen leading into the yard was much burnt about three feet high from the ground; and there was a mark of burning on the door-post of the brewhouse. The surface of the body was completely charred, the tongue was livid and swollen, and one of the toes was much bruised, as if it had been trodden on. There was a small blister on the inner side of the right leg, far below where the great burning commenced, which contained straw-coloured *serum*, but there was no other blister on any part of the body, nor any marks of redness around the blister, or at the parts where the injured and uninjured tissues joined. The nose, which had been a very prominent organ during life, was flattened down so as not to rise more than the eighth of an inch above the level of the face, and as it never recovered its original appearance, it was stated that it must have been so flattened for some time before death. The lungs and brain were much congested, and a quantity of black blood was found in the right auricle of the heart. From these facts the medical witnesses examined in support of the prosecution concluded, that the deceased had been first suffocated by pressing something over her mouth and nostrils so forcibly as to break and flatten the nose in the way described; but they had made no examination of the larynx and trachea, and other parts of the body. A physician, who had heard the evidence but not seen the deceased, gave his opinion that the appearances described by the other witnesses were signs of death by suffocation; that the absence of vesication, and of the line of redness were certain signs that the body had been burnt after death; but he added that, as there were no marks of external injury, an examination should have been made of the parts of the body above mentioned, in order to arrive at a satisfactory conclusion. Another medical witness thought it possible that suffocation might have been produced by the flames preventing the access of air to the lungs, while others again thought it impossible that such could have been the case, as no screams had been heard in the night, and they were also of opinion that if alive the deceased must have been in such intense agony that she could not, if she had been strong enough to walk from the kitchen to the brewhouse, have refrained from screaming. One of these witnesses stated that he did not think it possible that the deceased, if alive, could have fallen in the position in which she was found, as her first impulse would have been to stretch out her arms to prevent a fall; but, on the other hand, it was urged that it was not possible to judge of the acts of a person in the last agonies of death by the conduct of one in full life. Under the will of her grandfather the prisoner was entitled in expectancy on the demise of her mother to the sum of £200, and to the interest of the sum of £300, for her life. She had frequently cruelly beaten the old woman, threatened to shorten her days, bitterly reproached her for keeping her out of her property by living so long, and declared that she should never be happy so long as she was above-ground, and she had once attempted to choke her by forcing a handkerchief down her throat, but was prevented from doing so by the other servant. The magistrates had been frequently appealed to, but they could only remonstrate, as the old woman would not appear against her unnatural daughter. The case set up on behalf of the prisoner was, that she was in bed and, perceiving a smell of fire, came downstairs, and finding the sofa on fire, fetched water and extinguished it, and that she knew nothing of her mother's death until she heard of it from others. It appeared that the old woman was generally very chilly, and in the habit of getting near the fire; that on two former occasions she had burned portions of her dress; that on another she had burned the corner of the sofa-cushion; that she used to smoke in bed, and light her pipe with lucifer matches, which she carried in a basket; and that on the night in question she had brought her pipe which was found on

the following morning in her basket. It was urged as
the probable explanation of the position in which the
body was found, that, finding herself on fire, she must
have proceeded to the brewhouse, where she knew there
was water, and leaned in her way there against the door-
post, and that, feeling cold in the night, she had wrapped
the sheets around her, and did not throw them off until
she reached the yard. The prisoner, though accustomed
to sleep up-stairs, was in the habit of undressing in the
kitchen, which was stated to be the reason why the
stocking had been so placed as to prevent any person
from seeing into the kitchen. Mr. Justice Patteson, in
his charge to the jury, characterized the evidence of the
medical practitioners who had examined the body as extremely unsatisfactory in consequence of the incomplete-
ness of their examination ; the opinion of the physician
who had not seen the body was also, he said, very unsatisfactory as substituting him for the jury; that he had
only expressed his opinion as founded upon the facts
stated by the other witnesses ; that if he had seen the
body himself, his views might have been materially
different; that the other witnesses might have omitted
to mention particulars which he might deem of the
greatest importance, but on which they looked as of no
significance; that therefore opinions expressed on such
partial statements ought to be received with the greatest
reluctance and suspicion ; that he had always had a strong
opinion against such evidence, as tending to encroach
upon the proper duty of juries ; and he recommended
them to exercise their own judgment upon the other evidence in the case, without yielding it implicitly to the authority of this witness. The jury acquitted the prisoner ;
and indeed it would have been contrary to all principle

to do otherwise, in the midst of so much uncertainty as to
the *corpus delicti.**

* Reg. *v.* Newton, Salop Spring Ass. 1850.   Two former juries, at
the assizes in the preceding year, had been unable to agree, and had
been discharged, a circumstance unparalleled, it is believed, in English
jurisprudence.

CHAPTER IV.

EXTRINSIC AND MECHANICAL INCULPATORY INDI-CATIONS.

INCULPATORY circumstances of an extrinsic and mecha-nical nature, are such as are derived from the physical peculiarities and characteristics of persons and things,—from facts and objects which bear a relation to our cor-poreal nature, and are apparently independent of moral indications. Such facts are intimately related to, and as it were dovetail with the *corpus delicti;* and they are the links which establish the connection between the guilty act and its invisible moral origin. It is impossible even to classify, and still less to attempt an enumeration of, evi-dentiary facts of the kind in question, except in a very general way; but it may be interesting and instructive, by way of illustration, to advert to some of the principal heads of such evidence, and to some remarkable cases which have occurred in the records of our criminal juris-prudence. One important and admonitory result of such an enumeration will be to show that all such facts are unavoidably associated with attendant sources of error and fallacy.

The principal facts of circumstantial evidence, of an ex-ternal character, relate to questions of identity,—of per-son ; of things ; of hand-writing ; and of time ; but there must necessarily be a number of isolated facts which ad-mit of no specific classification.

Section 1.

IDENTIFICATION OF PERSON.

In the investigation of every allegation of legal crime, it is fundamentally requisite to establish, by direct or circumstantial evidence, the identity of the individual accused as the party who committed the imputed offence. It might be concluded, by persons not conversant with judicial proceedings, that identification is seldom attended with serious difficulty, but such is not the case. Illustrations are numerous to show that what are supposed to be the clearest intimations of the senses, are sometimes fallacious and deceptive, and some extraordinary cases have occurred of mistaken personal identity.* Hence the particularity, and as unreflecting persons too hastily conclude, the frivolous minuteness of inquiry, by professional advocates as to the *causa scientiæ*, in cases of controverted identity, whether of persons or of things.

Two men were convicted before Mr. Justice Grose of a murder, and executed; and the identity of the prisoners was positively sworn to by a lady who was in company with the deceased at the time of the robbery and murder; but several years afterwards two men, who suffered for other crimes, confessed at the scaffold the commission of the murder for which these persons were executed.†

A young man was tried at the Old Bailey, July 1824, on five indictments for different acts of theft. It ap-

---

* Rex *v.* Wood and Brown, *ut supra.* 33; Rex *v.* Coleman, *ut supra*, 68, 82; Reg. *v.* Markham, sentenced to four years' penal servitude for uttering a forged cheque, O. B. 1856, but subsequently pardoned on the conviction of the real offender.

† Rex *v.* Clinch and Mackley, 3 P. & F. 144, and Sess. Pap. 1797.

peared that a person resembling the prisoner in size and general appearance had called at various shops in the metropolis for the purpose of looking at books, jewellery, and other articles, with the pretended intention of making purchases, but made off with the property placed before him while the shopkeepers were engaged in looking out other articles. In each of these cases the prisoner was positively identified by several persons, while in the majority of them an *alibi* was as clearly and positively established, and the young man was proved to be of orderly habits and irreproachable character, and under no temptation from want of money to resort to acts of dishonesty. Similar depredations on other tradesmen had been committed by a person resembling the prisoner, and those persons deposed that, though there was a considerable resemblance to the prisoner, he was not the person who had robbed them. He was convicted upon one indictment, but acquitted on all the others ; and the judge and jurors who tried the last three cases expressed their conviction that the witnesses had been mistaken, and that the prosecutor had been robbed by another person resembling the prisoner. A pardon was immediately procured in respect of that charge on which the conviction had taken place.*

A few months before the last-mentioned case, a respectable young man was tried for a highway robbery committed at Bethnal Green, in which neighbourhood both he and the prosecutor resided. The prosecutor swore positively that the prisoner was the man who robbed him of his watch. A young woman, to whom the prisoner paid his addresses, gave evidence which proved a complete *alibi*. The prosecutor was then ordered out of court,

* Rex *v.* Robinson, Old Bailey, Sessions Papers, 1824.

and in the interval another young man, who awaited his trial on a capital charge, was introduced and placed by the side of the prisoner. The prosecutor was again put into the witness-box, and addressed by the prisoner's counsel thus : " Remember, the life of this young man depends upon your reply to the question I am about to put, Will you swear again that the young man at the bar is the person who assaulted and robbed you?" The witness turned his head toward the dock, when beholding two men so nearly alike, he dropped his hat, became speechless with astonishment for a time, and at length declined swearing to either. The prisoner was of course acquitted. The other young man was tried for another offence and executed ; and before his death acknowledged that he had committed the robbery in question.* Upon a trial for burglary, where there was conflicting evidence as to the identity of the prisoner, Mr. Baron Bolland, after remarking upon the risk incurred in pronouncing on evidence of identity exposed to such doubt, said that when at the bar, he had prosecuted a woman for child-stealing, tracing her by eleven witnesses, buying ribbons and other articles at various places in London, and at last into a coach at Bishopsgate, whose evidence was contradicted by a host of other witnesses, and she was acquitted ; and that he had afterwards prosecuted the very woman who really stole the child, and traced her by thirteen witnesses. " These contradictions," said the learned Judge, " make one tremble at the consequences of relying on evidence of this nature, unsupported by other proof."†

As incidental to the establishment of identity, the quantity of light necessary to enable a witness to form a

* 3 P. & F. 143 ; Amos's Great Oyer of Poisoning, 265.
† Rex v. Sawyer, Reading Ass.

satisfactory opinion has occasionally become the subject of discussion. A man was tried in January, 1799, for shooting at three Bow-street officers, who, in consequence of several robberies having been committed near Hounslow, were employed to scour that neighbourhood. They were attacked in a post-chaise by two persons on horseback, one of whom stationed himself at the head of the horses, and the other went to the side of the chaise. One of the officers stated that the night was dark, but that from the flash of the pistols he could distinctly see that one of the robbers rode a dark-brown horse, between thirteen and fourteen hands high, of a very remarkable shape, having a square head and thick shoulders, that he could select him out of fifty horses, and had seen him since at a stable in Long Acre ; and that he also perceived that the person at the side glass had on a rough shag great-coat.* Similar evidence was given on a trial for high-treason; † and in a case of burglary before the Special Commission at York, January 1813, a witness stated that a man came into his room in the night, and caused a light by striking on the stone floor with something like a sword, which produced a flash near his face, and enabled him to observe that his forehead and cheeks were blacked over in streaks, that he had on a dark-coloured top coat and a dark-coloured handkerchief, and was a large man, from which circumstances and from his voice, he believed the prisoner to be the same man.‡   In an-

* Rex v. Haines, 3 P. & F. 144.   † Rex v. Byrne, 18 St. Tr. 819.

‡ Rex v. Brook, 31 St. Tr. 1135, 1137; but see ‘Traité de la Preuve.’ par Desquiron, 274, where it is stated that after the condemnation of a man for murder, on the testimony of two witnesses, who deposed that they recognized him by the light from the discharge of a gun, experiments were made, from which it appeared that such recognition was impossible.

other case a gentleman who was shot at while driving home in his gig, and wounded in the elbow, stated that when he observed the flash of the gun, he saw that it was levelled towards him, and that the light enabled him to recognize at once the features of the accused. On cross-examination he stated that he was quite sure he could see him, and that he was not mistaken as to his identity : but the prisoner was acquitted.*

The liability to mistake must necessarily be greater where the question of identity is matter of deduction and inference, than where it is the subject of direct evidence. The circumstances from which identity may be thus inferred are innumerable, and admit of only a very general classification, of which the following are perhaps the most remarkable heads.

Family likeness has often been insisted upon as a reason for inferring parentage and identity. In the Douglas case Lord Mansfield said : " I have always considered likeness as an argument of a child's being the son of a parent ; and the rather as the distinction between individuals in the human species is more discernible than in other animals ; a man may survey ten thousand people before he sees two faces perfectly alike, and in an army of a hundred thousand men every one may be known from another. If there should be a likeness of feature, there may be a discriminancy of voice, a difference in the gestures, the smile, and various other things ; whereas a family likeness runs generally through all these, for in everything there is a resemblance, as of features, size, attitude, and action."†   But in a case in Scotland, where

---

* Reg. *v.* White, Croydon Summ. Ass. 1839; Taylor's Med. J. 331 (4th ed.).

† 2 Collectanea Juridica, 402 ; Beck's Med. Jur. 371; and see Report of the case of Doe dem. of Day *v.* Day, Huntingdon Assizes, July, 1793.

the question was who was the father of a certain woman, an allegation that she had a strong resemblance in the features of the face to one of the tenants of the alleged father, was held not to be relevant, as being too much a matter of fancy and loose opinion to form a material article of evidence;[*] and in another Scotch case, a trial for child-murder, it was permitted—after proof that the child had six toes—to ask a witness whether any members of the prisoner's family had supernumerary fingers and toes ; though the inference to be deduced was evidently only matter of opinion.[†]

A case of capital conviction occurred a few years ago where the prisoner had given his portrait to a youth, which enabled the police, after watching a month in London, to recognize and apprehend him;[‡] and photographic likenesses now frequently lead to the identification of offenders. It is well known that shepherds readily identify their sheep, however intermingled with others ;[§] and offenders are not unfrequently recognized by the voice.[||] Circumstances frequently contribute to identification, by confining suspicion and limiting the range of inquiry to a class of persons ; as where crimes have been committed by left-handed persons;[**] or where, notwithstanding simulated appearances of external violence and infraction, the offenders must have been domestics ; as in the case mentioned on a former page, of two persons convicted of murder, who created an

---

* Rutledge *v.* Carruthers, Tait's L. of Ev. 443.
† 1 Dickson's L. of Ev. *ut supra*, 14.
‡ Rex. *v.* Arden, 8 London Med. Gaz. 36.
§ Rex *v.* Oliver, 1 Syme's Justiciary Rep. 224.
|| Rex *v.* Brook, 31 St. Tr. 1135.
** Rex *v.* Okeman and others, *ut supra*, 91; Rex *v.* Richardson, Rex *v.* Patch, *infra*.

alarm from within the house; but upon whom nevertheless suspicion fell, from the circumstance that the dew on the grass surrounding the house had not been disturbed on the morning of the murder, which must have been the case had it been committed by any other than inmates.* On the trial of a gentleman's valet for the murder of his master, it appeared that there were marks on the back door of the house, as if it had been broken into, but the force had been applied from within, and the only way by which this door could be approached from the back, was over a wall, covered with dust which lay undisturbed; and over some tiling, so old and perished that it would not have borne the weight of a man; so that the appearances of burglarious entry must have been contrived by a domestic, and other facts conclusively fixed the prisoner as the murderer.†

Identification is often satisfactorily inferred from the correspondence of fragments of garments, or of written or printed papers, or of other articles belonging to or found in the possession of parties charged with crime, with other portions or fragments discovered at or near the scene of crime, or otherwise related to the *corpus delicti*;‡ or by means of wounds or marks inflicted upon the person of the offender. A woman who was tried for setting the prosecutor's ricks on fire, had been met near the ricks, about two hours after midnight, and a tinder-box was found near the spot containing some unburnt cotton rag, as also a piece of a woman's neckerchief in one of the ricks where the fire had been extinguished. The piece of cotton in the tinder-box was examined with a lens, and

---

* Rex *v.* Jefferys and Swan, *ut supra;* Rex *v.* Scofield, 31 St. Tr. 1061; and see Mascardus, *ut supra,* Concl. CCLXXII.

† Reg. *v.* Courvoisier, *infra.*　　‡ See Mascardus, *ut supra,* Concl. DCCCXXXI.

the witness deposed that it was of the same fabric and pattern as a gown and some pieces of cotton print taken from the prisoner's box at her lodgings ; that a neckerchief taken from a bundle belonging to the prisoner, found in her lodgings, corresponded with the colour, pattern, and fabric of the piece found in the rick, and that they had both belonged to the same square ; and from the breadth of the hemming, and the distance of the stitches on both pieces, as well as from the circumstance that both pieces were hemmed with black sewing-silk of the same quality (whereas articles of that description were generally sewed with cotton), he clearly inferred that they were the work of the same person. The prisoner was capitally convicted, but there being reason to believe that she was of unsound mind, she was reprieved.*

A man was connected with the robbery of a bank, by the fragment of a key found in the lock of one of the safes, which an ironmonger proved that he had shortly before made for the prisoner ;† and a servant-man was identified with the larceny of a number of sovereigns, by the discovery, in the lock of a bureau which had been broken open, of a small piece of steel which had formed part of the blade of a knife belonging to him.‡   An attempt to murder, by sending to the prosecutor a parcel, consisting of a tin case containing several pounds of gunpowder, so packed as to explode by the ignition of detonating powder, enclosed between two pieces of paper, connected with a match fastened to the lid and bottom of the box,

---

* Rex v. Hodges, Warwick Spring Assizes, 1818, *coram* Mr. Baron Garrow.

† Rex v. Heath, Alison's Prin. *ut supra*, 318.

‡ Reg. v. Crump, Stafford Sum. Ass. 1851, *coram* Mr. Justice Erle.

was brought home to the prisoner by the circumstance
that underneath the outer covering of brown paper was
found a portion of the 'Leeds Intelligencer' of the 5th
of July, 1832, the remaining portion of which identical
paper was found in his house.* In other cases identification has been established by the correspondence of the
wadding of a pistol, which stuck in a wound, and was
part of a ballad, which corresponded with another part
found in the prisoner's possession ;† and by the like correspondence of the wadding of firearms with part of a
newspaper of which the remainder was found in the possession of the prisoner.‡

A Spaniard was convicted of having occasioned a grievous injury to an officer of the post-office, by means of
several packets containing fulminating powder, put by
him into the post-office, one of which exploded in the act
of stamping. The letters, which were in Spanish, and one
of them subscribed with the prisoner's name, were addressed to persons at Havannah and Matanzas, who appeared to be the objects of the writer's malignant intentions. There was no proof that the letters were in the
prisoner's handwriting, but he was proved to have landed
at Liverpool on the 20th of September, and to have put
several letters into the post-office on the evening of
the 22nd, the explosion having occurred on the 24th;
and there was found upon his person a seal which
corresponded with the impression upon the letters, which
circumstance (though there were other strong facts)
was considered as conclusive of his guilt, and he was
accordingly convicted and sentenced to two years' impri-

* Rex *v.* Mountford, Stafford Sum. Ass. 1835, 1 Moody's C. C. 441.
† *Ex relatione* Lord Eldon, in 3 Hans. Parl. Deb. 1740, 3rd ser.
‡ Reg. *v.* Courtnage, and others, *infra.*

sonment.* On a trial for the forgery of a document, the impression of a seal attached to it corresponded with another impression upon a packet of papers produced in evidence by the prisoner, and both impressions were taken from a seal in the possession of a member of his family.†

The impressions of shoes, or of shoe-nails, or of other articles of apparel, or of patches, abrasions, or other peculiarities therein, discovered in the soil or clay, or snow, at or near the scene of crime, recently after its commission, frequently lead to the identification and conviction of the guilty parties.‡ The presumption founded on these circumstances has been appealed to by mankind in all ages, and in inquiries of every kind, and is so obviously the dictate of reason, if not of instinct, that it would be superfluous to dwell upon its importance. The following remarkable cases illustrate the pertinency and weight of such mechanical facts, especially when connected with other concurring circumstances leading to the same result.

A farm labourer was tried for the murder of a young woman, a domestic servant living in the same service. A little before seven in the evening she went on an errand to take some barm to a neighbouring house, about 200 yards distant, but it not being wanted, she did not leave it, and set out about seven o'clock on her way back. Being about to leave her situation that evening, she had requested the prisoner to carry her box to the gardener's house, about a quarter of a mile distant. Soon after she set out on her errand, the prisoner followed her carry-

* Rex v. Palayo, Liverpool Mids. Quarter Sess. 1836.

† Rex v. Humphreys, *infra*.

‡ Menochius, *ut supra*, lib. v. præs. 31 ; Mascardus, *ut supra*, Concl. dcccxx., pl. 11 ; Traité de la Preuve, par Mittermaier, *ut supra*, c. 57.

ing her box, but did not reach the gardener's cottage until after eight. On the following morning she was found, lying on her back, drowned in a shallow pit near a footpath leading from her master's house to the gardener's cottage. There were marks of violence on her person, and one of her shoes and the jug in which she had carried the barm were found near the pit. Barm was also found spilt near the spot, and there were marks of much trampling; and chaff and grains of wheat were scattered about, which were material facts, the prisoner having been engaged the day before in threshing wheat. Impressions were found in the soil, which was stiff and retentive, of the knee of a man who had worn breeches made of striped corduroy, and patched with the same material, but the patch was not set on straight, the ribs of the patch meeting the hollows of the garment into which it had been inserted; which circumstances exactly corresponded with the prisoner's dress. The prisoner denied that he had seen the deceased after she left the house on her errand, and stated that he had been in the interval before his arrival at the gardener's house in company with an acquaintance whom he had met with on the road; but it was proved that the person referred to, at the time in question, was at work thirty miles off. He was convicted and executed.*

A man was tried at Stafford Summer Assizes, 1844, for the murder of an elderly woman, the housekeeper of an old gentleman at Wednesbury, who, with a man-servant, were the only other inmates. Her master went from home on a Saturday morning, about half-past nine o'clock, as he was accustomed to do on that day of the week, leaving the deceased in the house alone. Upon

* Rex v. Brindley, Warwick Spring Ass. 1816.

his return, a quarter before two, he found her dead body in the brewhouse, her throat having been cut and the house robbed. The murder had probably been committed about a quarter past ten o'clock, as the butcher called at that time and was unable to obtain admittance, and about the same time a scream was heard. Traces were found of a man's right and left footsteps leading from a stable in a small plantation near the front of the house, from which any person leaving the house by the front door could be seen; and similar footsteps were found at the back of the house leading from thence across a ploughed field for a considerable distance in a sequestered direction, until they reached a canal bank, where they were lost on the hard ground. From the distance between the steps at the back of the house and in the ploughed field, the person whose footsteps they were must have been running; the impressions were those of right and left boots, and were very distinct, there having been snow and rain, and the ground being very moist. The right footprints had the mark of a tip round the heel; and the left footprints had the impression of a patch fastened to the sole with nails different in size from those on the sole itself; and altogether there were four different sorts of nails on the patch and soles, and in some places the nails were missing. Suspicion fell upon the prisoner, who had formerly lived as fellow-servant with the deceased, and who had been seen by several persons in the vicinity of the house a little before ten o'clock. Upon his apprehension on the following morning, his boots, trousers, shirt, and other garments were found to be stained with blood, and the trousers had been rubbed or scraped, as if to obliterate stains. The prisoner wore right and left boots, which were carefully compared with the foot-prints;

by making impressions of the soles in the soil about six inches from the original footmarks; which exactly corresponded as to the patch, the tip, and the number, shape, sizes, and arrangement of the nails. The boots were then placed lightly upon the original impressions, and here again the correspondence was exact. There could therefore be no doubt that the impressions of all these footsteps had been made by the prisoner's boots. He had been seen about a quarter before eleven on the morning of the murder with something bulky under his coat, near the place where the foot-steps were lost on the hard ground, and proceeding thence towards the town of Wednesbury. At about eleven o'clock he called at the 'Pack Horse' in that place, not far from the house, where he took something to drink and immediately left, and at a little after twelve he called at another public-house, which was also near the scene of the murder, where he staid some time smoking and drinking. In the interval between the times when the prisoner had called at these public-houses, he was seen at some distance from them, near an old whimsey; and he was subsequently seen returning in the opposite direction towards Wednesbury. Five days afterwards, upon further search, the same footprints were discovered on a footpath leading in a direction from the 'Pack Horse' towards the whimsey, where two bricks appeared to have been placed to stand upon, close to which was found an impression of a right foot corresponding with the impressions which had been before discovered; and in the flue was concealed a handkerchief in which were tied up a pair of trousers and waistcoat, part of the property stolen from the house. The prisoner must have availed himself of the interval between the times when he was seen at the two public-houses, to secrete the stolen garments in the whimsey, and thus to divest himself of the bulky articles which had been observed under his coat on his arrival at the 'Pack Horse.' The jury, after deliberating several hours, returned a verdict of guilty, and he was executed pursuant to his sentence, having previously made a confession of his guilt.*

In an American case, a prisoner charged with arson had turned his horse's shoes round after arriving at the house, so as to create the appearance of two persons having proceeded to and from it; but the artifice was the means of detection, since the removal of the shoes was indicated by the recent marks of nails on the horse's foot, and afforded one of the most emphatic of the indications by which the prisoner's guilt was established.†

To guard against error, it is manifest that the recency of the discovery and comparison of the impressions, relatively to the time of the occurrence of the *corpus delicti*, and before other persons may have resorted to the spot, is of the highest importance. So, the accuracy of the comparison is obviously all-important, and therefore as a further means of guarding against mistake, it must be shown that the shoes were compared with the footmarks before they were put on them ;‡ and where the comparison had not been previously made, Mr. Justice Park desired the jury to reject the whole inquiry relating to the identification by shoe-marks.§ Nor must it be overlooked, that, even where the identity of footmarks has been established beyond all doubt, they may have been fabri-

* Reg. *v.* Beards, *coram* Mr. Serjeant Atcherley; and see other cases of this kind, Rex *v.* Richardson, Rex *v.* Smith and others, *infra ;* Rex *v.* Spiggott and others, 4 Col. Tr. 446.

† Spooner's case, 2 Chandler's American Crim. Tr.

‡ Rex *v.* Heaton, 1 Lewin's C. C. 116.   § Rex *v.* Shaw, *ib.*

cated with the intention of diverting suspicion from the
real offender, and fixing it upon an innocent party ;[*]
and that in other respects this kind of evidence may lead
to erroneous interpretation and inference.[†]

The identification of human remains is attended with
peculiar difficulties consequent upon the changes produced by death, which will be considered in a subsequent part of this essay.

SECTION 2.

IDENTIFICATION OF ARTICLES OF PROPERTY.

THE identification of articles of property, like that of
the human person, is capable of being established, not
only by direct evidence, but by means of numberless
circumstances which it is not possible to enumerate.
Most of the cases of identification which have been enumerated in the preceding Section, are in fact cases of
identification of articles of property, applied inferentially
to the establishment of personal identity, and sufficiently
illustrate the difficulties which attend investigations of
this kind. The following cases, as well as others which
have been already mentioned, show how liable even well-
intentioned witnesses, who speak to facts of this particular kind, are to error and misconception.

At the spring assizes, at Bury St. Edmunds, 1830, a respectable farmer, occupying twelve hundred acres of land,
was tried for a burglary and stealing a variety of articles.
Amongst the articles alleged to have been stolen were
a pair of sheets and a cask, which were found in the

* See the remarkable case of François Mayenc, Gabriel, *ut supra*,
403.

† Rex *v.* Thornton ; Rex *v.* Isaac Looker, *infra*.

possession of the prisoner, and were positively sworn to by the witnesses for the prosecution to be those which had been stolen.   The sheets were identified by a particular stain, and the cask by the mark " P. C. 84." enclosed in a circle at one end of it.   On the other hand, a number of witnesses swore to the sheets being the prisoner's, by the same mark by which they had been identified by the witnesses on the other side as being the prosecutor's. With respect to the cask, it was proved by numerous witnesses, whose respectability left no doubt of the truth of their testimony, that the prisoner was in the habit of using cranberries in his establishment, and that they came in casks, of which the cask in question was one.   In addition to this, it was proved that the prisoner purchased his cranberries from a tradesman in Norwich, whose casks were all marked " P. C. 84." enclosed in a circle, precisely as the prisoner's were, the letters P. C. being the initials of his name, and that the cask in question was one of them.   In summing up, the learned judge remarked, that this was one of the most extraordinary cases ever tried, and that it certainly appeared that the witnesses for the prosecution were mistaken. The prisoner was acquitted.*

A man was tried in Scotland for housebreaking and theft.   The girl whose chest had been broken open, and whose clothes had been carried off, swore to the only article found in the prisoner's possession, and produced, namely, a white gown, as being her property.   She had previously described the colour, quality and fashion of the gown, and they all seemed to correspond with the article produced. The housebreaking being clearly proved, and the goods, as it was thought, clearly traced, the case

* A. R. 1820, 50; the report was supplied by a barrister of eminence.

was about to be closed by the prosecutor, when it occurred to one of the jury to cause the girl to put on the gown. To the surprise of every one present, it turned out that the gown which the girl had sworn to as belonging to her,—which corresponded with her description, and which she said she had worn only a short time before,—would not fit her person. She then examined it more minutely, and at length said it was not her gown, though almost in every respect resembling it. The prisoner was, of course, acquitted; and it turned out that the gown produced belonged to another woman, whose house had been broken into about the same period, by the same person, but of which no evidence had at that time been produced.*

On the trial of a young woman for child-murder, it appeared that the body of a newly-born female child was found in a pond about a hundred yards from her master's house, dressed in a shirt and cap, and a female witness deposed that the stay or tie which was pinned to the cap, and made of spotted linen, was made of the same stuff as a cap found in the prisoner's box ; but a mercer declared that the two pieces were not only unlike in pattern, but different in quality.†

A youth was convicted of stealing a pocket-book containing five one-pound notes, under very extraordinary circumstances. The prosecutrix left home to go to market in a neighbouring town, and having stooped down to look at some vegetables exposed to sale, she felt a hand resting upon her shoulder, which on rising up she found to be the prisoner's. Having afterwards purchased some

* Rex v. Webster, Burnett's C. L. of Scot. 558 ; 19 St. Tr. 491.
† Rex v. Bate, Warwick Autumn Ass. 1809, before Mr. Justice Lo Blanc.

K

articles at a grocer's shop, on searching for her pocket-book in order to pay for them, she found it gone. Her suspicion fell upon the prisoner, who was apprehended, and upon his person was found a black pocket-book, which she identified by a particular mark, as that which she had lost, but it contained no money. Several witnesses deposed that the prisoner had long possessed the identical pocket-book, speaking also to particular marks by which they were enabled to identify it; but some discrepancies in their evidence having led to the suspicion that the defence was a fabricated one, the jury returned a verdict of guilty, and the prisoner was sentenced to be transported. During the continuance of the assizes, two men who were mowing a field of oats through which the path lay by which the prosecutrix had gone to market, found in the oats close to the path a black pocket-book containing five one-pound notes. The men took the notes and pocket-book to the prosecutrix, who immediately recognized them; and the committing magistrate despatched a messenger with the articles found, and her affidavit of identity to the judge at the assize town, who directed the prisoner to be placed at the bar, publicly stated the circumstances so singularly brought to light, and directed his immediate discharge. The prosecutrix must have dropped her pocket-book, or drawn it from her pocket with her handkerchief, and had clearly been mistaken as to the identity of the pocket-book produced upon the trial.*

It is not, however, necessary that the identity of stolen property should be invariably established by positive evidence. In many such cases identification is impracti-

* Rex *v.* Gould, *coram* Mr. Baron Garrow, Stafford Summer Ass. 1820.

cable; and yet the circumstances may render it impossible to doubt the identity of the property, or to account for the possession of it by the party accused upon any reasonable hypothesis consistent with his innocence; as in the case of labourers employed in docks, warehouses, or other such establishments, found in possession of tea, sugar, tobacco, pepper, or other like articles, concealed about the person, in which cases the similarity or general resemblance of the article stolen is sufficient.*   Two men were convicted of stealing a quantity of soap from a soap manufactory near Glasgow, which was broken into on a Saturday night by boring a hole in the wall, and 120 lbs. of yellow soap abstracted.   On the same night, at eleven o'clock, the prisoners were met by a watchman near the centre of the city, one of them having 40lbs. of yellow soap on his back, and the other with his clothes greased all over with the same substance. The prisoners, on seeing the watchman, attempted to escape, but were seized.   The owner declared that the soap was exactly of the same kind, size, and shape, with that abstracted from his manufactory; but, as it had no private mark, he could not identify it more distinctly. One of the prisoners had formerly been a servant about the premises, and both of them alleged that they got the soap in a public-house from a man whom they did not know.†   A servant-man was seen to come from a part of his master's premises where he had no right to go, and where a large quantity of pepper was stored in bulk, and on being stopped, a quantity of pepper of the same

* 2 East's P. C. 637 ; 2 Russell on Crimes (by Greaves), 107 ; Rex v. White, R. & R. 508; Rex v. Dredge, 1 Cox's C. C. 235.

† Rex v. M'Kechnie and Tolmie, Glasgow Spring Circuit, 1828, Alison's Princ., *ut supra*, 322.

kind was found on his person : it was held by the Criminal Court of Appeal that though the pepper could not be positively identified, he had been properly convicted of larceny.*

SECTION 3.

PROOF OF HANDWRITING.

THE usual mode of proving handwriting is, by the direct testimony of some witness, who has either seen the party write, or acquired a knowledge of his handwriting from having corresponded with him, and had transactions in business with him, on the faith that letters purporting to have been written or signed by him were genuine. In either case, the witness is supposed to have received into his mind an exemplar of the general character of the handwriting of the party, impressed on it as the involuntary and unconscious result of constitution, habit, or other permanent cause, and which is therefore itself permanent; and he is called on to speak to the writing in question by reference to the standard so formed in his mind.*

It is necessary to recall these leading principles of proof of handwriting by direct, as introductory to the consideration of the various methods of proof by indirect evidence.

Evidence of similitude of handwriting by the comparison of controverted writing with the admitted or proved writing of the party, made by a witness who has never

* Rex v. Burton, 23, L. J. M. C. 52; 6 Cox's C. C. 293; and see Reg. v. Hooper, 1 F. & F. 85.

† *Per* Coleridge, J., in Doe d. Mudd v. Suckermore, 5 A. & E. 705, and 2 N. & P. 16.

seen the party write, nor has any knowledge of his hand-writing, and who arrives at the inference that it is his handwriting because it is like some other which is so,* is a mode of proof which has been much lauded by writers on the civil law, and is commonly admitted in those countries whose jurisprudence is founded on that system; the comparison being made by professional *experts* appointed by the Court or agreed upon by the parties, under many restrictions for securing the genuineness of the writings which are to form the standard of comparison. Comparison of handwriting appears also to be a recognized mode of proof in some of the American States, whose judicial systems are generally founded on our own.† Such evidence is in general inadmissible in this country, though the leaning of text-writers of authority appears to have been rather in favour of the principle of its admissibility; the only admitted exceptions are, where the writing acknowledged to be genuine is already in evidence in the cause, or the disputed writing is an ancient writing.‡ In these excepted cases, the evidence is admitted, it is said, of necessity,—in the former case because it is not possible to prevent the jury from making such comparison, and therefore it is best, as was remarked by Lord Denman,§ for the Court to enter with the jury into that inquiry, and do the best it can under circum-

---

* Benth. Jud. Ev. b. iii. c. 7; Rex v. De la Motte, 21 St. Tr. 810.

† See in Bemis's Rep. of the Tr. of Professor Webster, some curious evidence of this kind.

‡ Allport v. Meek, 4 C. & P. 267; Bromage v. Rice, 7 ib. 548; Waddington v. Cousins, ib. 595; Griffith v. Williams, 1 C. & J. 47; Doe d. Perry v. Newton, 1 N. & P. 1; and 5 A. & E. 514; Solita v. Yarrow, 1 M. & R. 133; Griffits v. Ivery, 11 A. & E. 222.

§ In Doe d. Perry v. Newton, *ut supra;* Walter Peerage, 10 C & F. 193; Doe d. Jenkins v. Davies, 10 Q. B. 314; 16 L. J Q. B. 228; and see Reg. v. Taylor, 6 Cox's C. C. 58.

stances which cannot be helped ;—in the latter, because from the lapse of time no living person can have any knowledge of the handwriting from his own observation,* and because in ancient documents it often becomes a pure question of skill, the character of the handwriting varying with the age, and the discrimination of it being materially assisted by antiquarian researches.†

The evidence of persons accustomed to the critical examination of handwriting, as engravers and inspectors of franks, who, without any previous knowledge of a person's handwriting, profess to be able to determine by comparison of the disputed with the genuine writing, whether a signature be genuine or not, and also from the general character and appearance of writing, whether it is written in a natural or feigned hand, appears to have been formerly considered another exception to the rule ;‡ but such evidence is now considered to be of so little weight, and attempts to introduce it are so much discountenanced, that, in the language of Lord Denman,§ this chapter may be considered as expunged from the book of evidence. It has been justly remarked that besides being subject to the same defects as the opinions of persons speaking from previous familiar knowledge, it arises from a forced acquaintance with the hand-writing of a few, often from selected specimens, while the examination is made solely with a view to giving evidence in favour of the party to whom the witness looks for

* *Per* Patteson, J., in Doe d. Mudd v. Suckermore, *ut supra.*

† *Per* Coleridge, J., *ib.*

‡ Goodtitle v. Revett, 4 T. R. 497 ; Rex v. Cator, 4 Esp. 117 ; Rex v. Johnson, 29 St. Tr. 81.

§ Doe d. Mudd v. Suckermore, *ut supra ;* and see Gurney v. Langlands, 5 B. & Ald. 330 ; Constable v. Steibel, 1 Hagg. 56 ; Young v. Brown, *ib.* 569 ; Fitzwalter Peerage, 10 C. & F. 193 ; Tracy Peerage, *ib.* 154.

remuneration ;* so that, in the words of an eminent Scotch Judge, "in almost all countries, the evidence of persons of skill on this subject is almost totally abandoned."†

An attempt has lately been made to introduce a new mode of proof, by satisfying the witness by some information or evidence, that certain papers are in the handwriting of the party, and then desiring him to study those papers, so as to acquire a knowledge of the handwriting, and fix an exemplar in his mind, and afterwards putting into his hand the writing in question and asking his belief respecting it ; or by merely putting certain papers into the witness's hand without telling him who wrote them, and desiring him to study them, and acquire a knowledge of the handwriting, and afterwards showing him the writing in question and asking his belief, whether they are written by the same person, and calling evidence to prove to the jury that the former are the handwriting of the party.‡   The question in the cause was the due execution of a will.   On the first day of the trial the defendant called an attesting witness, who swore that the attestation was his.   On his cross-examination, two signatures to depositions respecting the same will in an ecclesiastical court, and several other signatures were shown to him (none of them being in evidence for any other purpose of the cause), and he stated that he believed them to be his.   On the following day the plaintiff tendered a witness to prove the attestation not to be genuine. The witness was a Bank-inspector, who had no know-

* Dickson's L. of Ev. *ut supra.*
† *Per* Lord Mackenzie, quoted *ib.*
‡ *Per* Mr. Justice Patteson, in Doe dem. Mudd *v.* Suckermore, *ut supra.*

ledge of the handwriting of the supposed attesting witness, except from having previous to the trial, and again
between the two days, examined the signatures admitted
by the attesting witness, which admission he had heard
made in court.   Mr. Justice Vaughan rejected the evidence; and upon a motion for a new trial, on the ground
of its improper rejection, the judges of the Court of
Queen's Bench were equally divided in opinion.*   By
a recent statute† comparison of a disputed writing with
any writing proved to the satisfaction of the judge to
be genuine, shall in civil cases be permitted to be
made by witnesses, and such writings, and the evidence
of witnesses respecting the same, may be submitted to
the court and jury as evidence of the genuineness or
otherwise of the writing in dispute; but it seems to be
an anomaly that a different rule should govern the. admissibility of evidence in civil and criminal cases.

Evidence to handwriting is subject to many sources
of fallacy and error, among which may be enumerated
tuition by the same preceptor, employment with other persons in the same place of business, as well as designed
imitation or disguise, all of which are frequently causes
of great similarity in writing.   Men in certain businesses
or professions sometimes adopt peculiarities of character,
though less frequently than formerly; and there are characteristic peculiarities indicative of age, infirmity, and
sex.‡

Handwriting is sometimes most successfully imitated.
On a trial for forgery of bank-notes, a banker's clerk

---

* *Ibid.;* and see Hughes *v.* Rogers, 8 M.& W. 123; Young *v.* Horner,
2 M. & R. 573, and 1 C. & K. 51.

† 17 & 18 Vict., c. 125, s. 27.

‡ See Rex *v.* Johnson, *ut supra.*

whose name was on one of the notes swore distinctly that it was his handwriting, while he spoke hesitatingly with respect to his genuine subscription.* Lord Eldon mentioned a very remarkable instance of the uncertainty of this kind of evidence. A deed was produced at a trial on which much doubt was thrown as a discreditable transaction. The solicitor was a very respectable man, and was confident in the character of his attesting witnesses. One of them purported to be Lord Eldon himself, and the solicitor, who had referred to his signature to pleadings, had no doubt of its authenticity, yet Lord Eldon declared that he had never attested a deed in his life.†

In a case in Doctors' Commons the learned judge repudiated the common objection of painting or touching, as a reason for inferring fraud, saying that there could scarcely be a less certain criterion, and peremptorily declined the use of a glass of high powers, said to have been used by the professional witnesses, observing, in substance, that glasses of high powers, however fitly applied to the inspection of *natural* subjects, rather tend to distort and misrepresent than to place *such* objects in their *true* light; especially when used (their ordinary application in the hands of prejudiced persons) to confirm some theory or preconceived opinion.‡ But it is the daily practice of Courts of Common Law to admit the artificial aid of glasses and lamps; and on an indictment for forgery, the question being whether a paper had originally contained certain pencil-marks which were alleged to have been rubbed out, and ink-writing written in their stead, the opinion of an engraver, who was in the habit of looking at minute lines on paper, and had examined

---

* Rex v. Carsewell, Burnett's C. L. of Scotl 502.
† Eagleton v. Kingston, 8 Ves. 473. ‡ Robson v. Rocke, 2 Addams, 79.

the document with a mirror, was held to be receivable, although of no weight unless confirmed.*

The following extract from a learned judgment of Sir John Nicholl embodies many instructive observations upon this kind of evidence: "This court has often had occasion to observe, that evidence to handwriting is at best, in its own nature, very inconclusive; affirmative, from the exactness with which handwriting may be imitated; and negative, from the dissimilarity which is often discoverable in the handwriting of the same person under different circumstances. Without knowing very precisely the state and condition of the writer at the time, and exercising a very discriminating judgment upon these, persons deposing, especially, to a mere *signature* not being that of such or such a person, from its dissimilarity— howsoever ascertained or supposed to be—to his usual handwriting, are so likely to err, that negative evidence to a mere subscription, or signature, can seldom, if ever, under ordinary circumstances, avail in proof, against the final authenticity of the instrument to which that subscription, or signature, is attached. But such evidence is peculiarly fallacious, where the dissimilarity relied upon is not that of general character, but merely particular letters; for the slightest peculiarities of circumstance or position,—as, for instance, the writer sitting up or reclining, or the paper being placed upon a harder or softer substance, or on a plane more or less inclined,—nay, the materials, as pen, ink, etc., being different at different times,—are amply sufficient to account for the same *letters* being made variously at the different times by the same individual. Independent however of anything of this sort, few individuals, it is apprehended, write so

* Reg. v. Williams, 8 C. & P. 434.

uniformly that dissimilar formations of particular letters are grounds for concluding them not to have been made by the same person."*

The difficulty of proving handwriting is greatly increased where it is studiously disguised; but such is the power of habit, that though persons may succeed to a certain extent in disguising their writing, they commonly fall into their natural manner and characteristic peculiarities of writing;† such peculiarities being most commonly manifested in the formation of particular letters, or in the mode of spelling particular words.‡

A tailor, of the name of Alexander, having learned that a person of the same name had died, leaving considerable property without any apparent heirs existing, obtained access to a garret in the family mansion; and it was said found there a collection of old letters about the family. These he carried off, and with their aid fabricated a mass of similar productions, which, it was said, clearly proved his connection with the family of the deceased, and the Lord Ordinary decided the cause in his favour; the case however was carried to the Inner House. When it came into court, certain circumstances led Lord Meadowbank, then a young man at the bar, to doubt the authenticity of the documents. One circumstance was, that there were a number of words in the letters, purporting to be from different individuals, spelt, or rather misspelt, in the same way, and some of them so peculiar, that on examining them minutely, there was no doubt that they were all written by the same hand. The case attracted the attention of the Inner House. The party was brought to the

* Robson v. Rocke, 2 Addams, 79.

† *Per* Macdonald C. B. in Rex v. Bingham, Horsham Spring Ass. 1811, Short-hand Rep. 106.   ‡ See Rex v. Johnson, *ut supra*.

clerk's table, and was examined in the presence of the court. He was desired to write to dictation of the Lord Justice Clerk, and he misspelt all the words that were misspelt in the letters in precisely the same way; and this and other circumstances proved that he had fabricated all of them himself. He then confessed the truth of his having written the letters on old paper, which he had found in the garret; and this result was arrived at in the teeth of the testimony of half-a-dozen engravers, all saying that they thought the letters were written by different hands.[*]

It is even still more difficult to depose with confidence to the identity of a disguised writing, if the disguise is applied to printed characters, and Mr. Baron Rolfe spoke of such evidence as of no value.[†]

SECTION 4.

VERIFICATION OF DATES AND TIME.

AMONGST the numerous physical and mechanical circumstances which occasionally lead to the detection of forgery and fraud, a discrepancy between the date of a writing and the *anno Domini* water-mark in the fabric of the paper is one of the most striking;[‡] but inasmuch as prospective issues of paper, bearing the water-mark of a succeeding year, are occasionally made, this circumstance is not always a safe ground of presumption;[§] and it is not uncommon among manufacturers both to post-date and

* Related by Lord Meadowbank in Reg. *v.* Humphreys, *infra;* and see Short-hand Report of the case of Smith *v.* Earl Ferrers, 1840.

† Reg. *v.* Rush, Norwich Spring Ass. 1849; Webster's case, Bemis's Report, *ut supra.*   ‡ Crisp. *v.* Walpole, 2 Hagg. 521.

§ A Commissioner of the Insolvent Debtors' Court sitting at Wakefield in 1836, discovered that the paper he was then using, which had been issued by the government stationer, bore the water-mark of 1837.

to ante-date their paper-moulds. A witness examined in 1834 stated that he was then making moulds with the date of 1828, under a special order.* In an old case a criminal design was detected by the circumstance that a letter, purporting to come from Venice, was written upon paper made in England.†

The critical examination of the internal contents of written instruments, perhaps of all others, affords the most satisfactory means of disproving their genuineness and authenticity, especially if they profess to be the productions of an anterior age. It is scarcely possible that a forger, however artful in the execution of his design, should be able to frame a spurious composition without betraying its fraudulent origin by peculiarities of writing or orthography characteristic of a different age or period, or by the employment of words of later introduction, or by the use of them in a sense or meaning which they did not then bear, or by some statement or allusion not in harmony with the known character, opinions, and feelings of the pretended writer, or with events or circumstances which must have been known to him, or by a reference to facts, or modes of thought characteristic of a later or a different age from that to which the writing relates. A writer, eminent alike for his critical sagacity and for his imaginative genius, declared that he had met in his researches with only one poem which, if it had been produced as ancient, could not have been detected on internal evidence.‡ Judicial history presents innumerable examples in illustration of the soundness of these prin-

* Rodger *v.* Kay, 12 Cases in Court of Session, 317; Miller *v.* Fraser, 4 *ib.* 55; 4 Murray's Cases in Jury Court, 118.
† Best on Presumptions, 56; referring to Moore, 817.
‡ 2 Lockhart's Life of Scott, c. ix.

ciples of judgment, of which the following are not the least interesting.

A deed was offered in evidence, bearing date the 13th of November in the second and third years of the reign of Philip and Mary, in which they were called "*king* and *queen* of Spain and both Sicilies, and *dukes* of Burgundy, Milan, and Brabant," whereas at that time they were formally styled "*princes* of Spain and Sicily," and Burgundy was never put before Milan, and they did not assume the title of king and queen of Spain and the two Sicilies until Trinity Term following.[*]

A most curious and instructive case of this kind was that of Alexander Humphreys, before the High Court of Justiciary at Edinburgh, April, 1839, for forging and uttering several documents in support of a claim advanced by him to the earldom of Stirling and extensive estates. One of those documents purported to be an excerpt from a charter of Novodamus of King Charles I., bearing date the 7th of December, 1639, in favour of William the first Earl of Stirling, and making the honours and estates of that nobleman, which under previous grants were inheritable only by heirs *male*, descendable in default of heirs male to his eldest heirs female, without division, of the last of such heirs male, and to the heirs male of the body of such heirs female respectively. This excerpt purported in the *testatum* clause to be witnessed by Archbishop Spottiswood "our chancellor," whereas he died on the 26th of November, 1639, and it was proved by the register of the Privy Council that he resigned the office of chancellor, and that the Great Seal was delivered to the custody of James, Marquess of Hamilton, on the 13th of November, 1638, more than a year before the date of the

* Mossom *v.* Ivy, 10 St. Tr. 616 ; and *vide* Coke's First Inst. 7 *b.*

pretended charter, and that there was an interregnum in the office of chancellor until the appointment of Lord Loudon on the 30th of September, 1641. A genuine charter, dated four days after the pretended charter, was witnessed by James, Marquess of Hamilton. The circumstance was significant, that in the catalogue of the Scottish chancellors, appended to Spottiswood's History and other works, no mention is made of the interval between the resignation of the Archbishop of St. Andrew's and the appointment of the Earl of Loudon. In the margin of the excerpt was a reference to the register of the Great Seal Book 57, in the following form, "Reg. Mag. Sig. lib. 57;" but it was proved that this mode of marking and reference did not commence until 1806, when the registers were rebound, in order that they should have one title; and that previously to that time the title of those documents was, "Charters, book i., book ii.," and so on. In the supposed excerpt the son of the first earl was styled "*nostro consanguineo*," a mode of address never adopted in old charters in regard to a commoner; and there were other internal incongruities. This document consisted of several leaves stitched together, of a brown colour, as well under the stitching as where open; whereas if the stitching had been old, the part of the paper not exposed to the atmosphere would have been whiter than the rest. Around the margin of this excerpt were drawn red lines; but it was proved by official persons familiar with the extracts of the period, that such lines were not introduced into the Chancery Office till about 1780. A series of anachronisms conclusively disproved the authenticity of several other documents adduced by the prisoner in support of his claim. One of those documents was a copper-plate map

of Canada by Guillaume de l'Isle, " Premier Géographe
du Roi, avec privilége pour vingt ans," bearing the date
of 1703 ; on the back of which, amongst other supposed
attestations, were a note purporting to be in the handwriting of Flechier, Bishop of Nismes, dated the 3rd of
June, 1707, and another note purporting to be in the
handwriting of Fénelon, Archbishop of Cambray, of the
date of the 16th of October, 1707. It was proved that
Flechier died in 1711, and the letters-patent for the in-
stallation of his successor in the bishopric of Nismes were
produced, bearing date the 26th of February in that year;
that Fénelon died on the 7th of January, 1715 ; and that
De l'Isle was not appointed geographer to the king until
the 24th of August, 1718. In all of De l'Isle's editions
of his map the original date of 1703 was preserved as
the commencement of his copyright, but on any change
of residence or of designation, he made a corresponding
change in the original copper-plate from which all successive issues of the map were engraved, and it was proved
by a scientific witness that the title of De l'Isle had been
actually altered on the copper-plate of the map since 1718.
Of course a map issued prior to 1718 could not refer to
his appointment of geographer to the king, and any attestation of the date of 1707 to a map containing a recognition of that appointment must of necessity be spurious. The forger of the map must have been misled by
the date of 1703 upon it, and ignorant of the fact that
De l'Isle was not appointed geographer to the king until
1718; so difficult is it to preserve consistency in an
attempt to impose by means of forgery. The very ink
with which some of the pretended attestations were
made was not the usual ink of the period, but a modern
composition made to imitate ink turned old. There were

other strong grounds for impugning the genuineness of these various documents, which the jury unanimously found to be forged.*

It was observed by Lord C. B. Macdonald, that there is nothing we are so little in the habit of, as measuring with any degree of correctness small portions of time; and that if any one were to examine with a watch which marks the seconds, how much longer a space of time a few seconds or a few minutes really are than people in general conceive them to be, they would be surprised; but that in general, when we speak of a minute, or an instant, we can hardly be understood to mean more than that it was a very short space of time.† Nevertheless it is sometimes of the highest importance accurately to fix the exact time of the occurrence of an event, and a difference of a few minutes even may be of vital moment. This frequently happens in cases where the defence is that of an *alibi*. On a charge of murder, where the defence was of that nature, and it was essential to fix the precise times at which the prisoner had been seen by the several witnesses soon after the fatal event which was the subject of investigation, the object was satisfactorily effected by a comparison made by an intelligent witness on the same day, of the various time-pieces referred to by the several witnesses, with a public clock; thus affording the means of reducing the times as spoken to by them to a common standard.‡ Post-office marks are often of great importance in fixing disputed dates; but it is remarkable that in two late cases involving charges of murder, the defective manner in which they were impressed rendered them useless, and

* See the Reports of the Trial by Archibald Swinton, Esq., and William Turnbull, Esq.; Remarks on the Trial, by an English Lawyer; 1 Townsend's St. Tr. 403; and Dickson's L. of Ev., *ut supra*, 173.

† Rex *v*. Patch, Gurney's Report. 171.   ‡ Rex *v*. Thornton. *infra*.

L

became the subject of judicial animadversion,* which has led to improvements calculated to render the recurrence of any such matter of complaint most unlikely.

Scientific testimony grounded on the state of wounds and injuries to the human body, or on its condition of decay, is frequently employed indirectly in the solution of questions of time; but cases of this nature belong to the department of medical jurisprudence.

* By L. C. J. Campbell in Reg. *v.* Palmer, *infra;* and by the L. Justice Clerk in Reg. *v.* Madeleine Smith, *infra.*

CHAPTER V.

EXCULPATORY PRESUMPTIONS AND CIRCUMSTANTIAL EVIDENCE.

THE law of England recognizes several presumptions, *juris et de jure*, which create entire or partial exemption from criminal responsibility; as, that infants under the age of seven years cannot be guilty of crime, that infants above that age and under fourteen years shall be *primâ facie* adjudged *doli incapax*, and that, as to certain offences connected with physical development, minors under the age of fourteen years shall be conclusively presumed to be incapable of committing them, and that no evidence shall be admitted to the contrary.[*] Such also is the presumption that, offences committed by the wife in the presence of her husband shall, with certain exceptions, be considered to have been committed by his coercion.[†] But the presumptions which concern the subject of this essay are of a different kind, consisting mainly of maxims drawn from well-digested experience, and grounded upon considerations of natural equity, for the candid construction of the actions and motives of our fellow-men, and which are in truth but particular forms of strict justice. An enumeration of some of the principal of these presumptions will form the subject of this Chapter.

1. In the investigation and estimate of criminatory evidence there is an antecedent *primâ facie* presumption in favour of the innocence of the party accused,

---

[*] 1 Hale's P. C. ch. 3 ; 4 Bl. Comm. 2.   [†] *Ibid.*

grounded in reason and justice, and recognized in the judicial practice of all civilized nations; which presumption must prevail until it be destroyed by such an overpowering amount of legal evidence of guilt as is calculated to produce the opposite belief.* It must be admitted that in the aggregate, the number of convictions vastly exceeds that of acquittals, and that the probability is that, in a given number of cases, far the greater number of the parties accused are guilty; but according to all judicial statistics, and under every system, a considerable proportion of the persons put upon trial are legally innocent. In any particular case, therefore, the party *may* not be guilty, and it is impossible, without a violation of every principle of justice, to act upon the contrary presumption of a superior probability of guilt. It is therefore a settled and inviolable principle, that anterior to contrary proof, the accused shall be considered as legally innocent, and that his case shall receive the same dispassionate and impartial consideration as if he were really so.

2. It would be foreign to the subject of this essay to discuss the considerations which affect the credibility of evidence in general, such as the integrity, disinterestedness, and ability of the witnesses, the consistency of their testimony, its conformity with experience, and its agreement with collateral circumstances,—since these considerations apply to circumstantial only in common with all other testimonial evidence. It has been profoundly observed, that of all the various sources of error, one of the most copious and fatal is an unreflecting faith in human testimony;† and it is obvious that all reasoning

* See the language of Lord Gillies in Rex *v.* M'Kinley, 33 St. Tr. 506.
† 1 Stewart's Collected Works, 247.

upon the relevancy and effect of circumstantial evidence presupposes its absolute verity, and that such evidence necessarily partakes of the infirmities incidental to all human testimony; and facts apparently indicative of the most forcible presumption have been fabricated and supported by false testimony. Every consideration therefore, which detracts from the credibility of evidence in the abstract, applies *à fortiori* to evidence which is essentially indirect and inferential. In such cases, falsehood in the minutest particular throws discredit upon every part of a complainant's statement, according to the well-known maxim, *qui mendax in uno mendax in omnibus.* Hence, since facts can never be mutually inconsistent,* circumstantial evidence frequently affords the means of evincing the falsehood of direct and positive affirmative testimony, and even of disproving the existence of the *corpus delicti* itself, by manifesting the incompatibility of that testimony with surrounding and concomitant circumstances, of the reality of which there is no doubt.† Sir Matthew Hale mentions a very remarkable case, where an elderly man was charged with violating a young girl of fourteen years of age, but it was proved beyond all doubt, that a physical infirmity rendered the perpetration of such a crime utterly impossible.‡ The prosecutrix of an indictment against a man for administering arsenic to her, to procure abortion, deposed that he had sent her a present of tarts of which she partook, and that shortly afterwards she was seized with symptoms of poisoning. Amongst other inconsistencies, she stated that she had felt a coppery taste in the act of eating, which it was proved that arsenic does not possess; and from the quantity of arse-

* Locke on the Hum. Underst. b. iv. ch. 20, s. 8.
† Best on Pres. p. 54.   ‡ 1 P. C. c. 58.

nic in the tarts which remained untouched, she could not
have taken above two grains, while after repeated vomitings, the alleged matter subsequently preserved contained
nearly fifteen grains, though the matter first vomited
contained only one grain. The prisoner was acquitted,
and the prosecutrix afterwards confessed that she had
preferred the charge from motives of jealousy.*

3. Irrespectively of and distinct from any positive discrepancy in the account given by a complainant party,
there is a consistency of deportment and conduct grounded upon the invariable laws of our moral nature, which
is essentially characteristic of truth and honesty, and the
absence of which necessarily detracts from the credit of
such evidence, and therefore tends to create a counter-
presumption. We reasonably expect to discover in the
demeanour of a party who has just reason to complain of
personal injury or violated honour or right, prompt and
unequivocal indications of that sense of wrong and insecurity which, as the invariable consequence, is naturally
and involuntarily generated in every human mind. Sir
Matthew Hale, in reference to one of the greatest of human outrages, says, " If the party concealed the injury
for any considerable time after she had opportunity to
complain; if the place where the fact was supposed to be
committed were near to inhabitants, or common recourse
or passage of passengers, and she made no outcry when
the fact was supposed to be done, when and where it is
probable that she might be heard by others; these and
the like circumstances carry a strong presumption that
her testimony is false or feigned."† These cautionary
considerations are applicable with more or less of force

* Reg. *v.* Whalley, York Spring Assizes, 1829; Christison on Poisons, 95.   † 1 Hale's P. C. c. 58.

to accusations of every description; but they are more especially weighty and pertinent in reference to the particular crime referred to, of which the learned author has said, that "it is an accusation easily to be made, and hardly to be proved, and harder to be defended by the party accused, though never so innocent."* Such cases, he further observes, are not uncommon, and he has related the particulars of two cases, where, though the charges were groundless, the parties with difficulty escaped. "I only mention these instances," said that upright judge, "that we may be the more cautious upon trials of offences of this nature, wherein the court and jury may with so much ease be imposed upon, without great care and vigilance, the heinousness of the offence many times transporting the judge and jury with so much indignation, that they are over-hastily carried to the conviction of the persons accused thereof by the confident testimony sometimes of malicious and false witnesses."† False charges of this kind have unhappily been too common and too successful in all ages. The social consequences of female dishonour are so deadly, and the inducements to falsehood and revenge so peculiar and so powerful, that there is no class of cases in which it is more important to obtain an exact knowledge of the motives and character of the complainant. For these reasons great latitude of cross-examination is permitted in cases of this kind, and it is competent to the prisoner not only to give evidence of the prosecutrix's *general* bad character, but also to examine her with respect to particular facts, and to contradict her by evidence if she should deny them.‡

* 1 Hale's P. C. c. 58.   † *Ib.*
‡ Rex *v.* Clarke, 2 Stark Rep. 241; Rex *v.* Barker, 3 C. & P. 589;

4. Nor is the danger of false accusation confined to the particular class of offences which has been specially adverted to. Inducements to prefer false charges may operate with greater or lesser force with regard to accusations of every kind. Two women were capitally convicted of robbing a young girl named Canning, and afterwards confining her under circumstances of great cruelty for twenty-nine days without sustenance, except a quartern loaf and a pitcher of water. Public odium was intensely excited against the prisoners, and they very narrowly escaped execution, and yet it was clearly ascertained that the charge was a fabrication in order to conceal the prosecutrix's misconduct during the period of her absence from her master's house.* Canning was afterwards convicted of perjury, and sentenced to be transported ; and upon her trial thirty-eight witnesses, most of them unconnected with each other, spoke to the identity of one of her unfortunate victims, and proved a circumstantial *alibi*.† Nine persons were convicted on a charge of conspiracy to carry off from the house of her guardian, a young lady of seventeen years of age, in order to procure her clandestine marriage with a young man of low condition for whom she had formed an attachment, and with whom she had indulged in vulgar familiarities. She gave her testimony in a manner apparently so artless and ingenuous that she greatly prepossessed the judge, and so favourably impressed the jury that they stopped the

Rex v. Robins, 2 M. & R. 512; Rex v. Martin, 6 C. & P. 562; Reg. v. Clay, 5 Cox's C. C. 146; Reg. v. Dean, 6 *ib.* 23; Reg. v. Rocke, 6 *ib.* 196; and see Taylor's L. of Ev., and Roscoe's Digest, where the cases are collected.

* Rex v. Squires and Wells, 19 St. Tr. 275.

† Rex v. Canning, 19 St. Tr. 667 ; and see Lawrence's Life of Fielding, 320.

prosecutor's counsel when about to reply, and returned a verdict of guilty.* Her story was nevertheless discovered to be a fabrication, for the purpose of extricating herself from the shame of her levity and misconduct, and she as well as a witness who had corroborated her story were afterwards convicted of perjury.† Miscreants, and among them even the inferior ministers of the law, have concocted and procured the commission of robbery and other crimes for the purpose of obtaining the pecuniary rewards formerly given by Act of Parliament for the apprehension and conviction of offenders.‡

It is frequently therefore of the highest importance, to investigate the motives of the complainant party, and to ascertain whether they are such as may have led to the institution of a false charge. The just course of inquiry in such circumstances was thus laid down by Mr. Justice Coltman. "The jury," he said, "had nothing to do with the prosecutor's motives except so far as, if it should appear that there was any motive for the prosecution of an unworthy character made out, it would then be their duty to watch such a case much more narrowly than one in which no such motive appeared. Even in that case, however, if the evidence satisfied them of the truth of the charge, they had no right to look at the motives that had induced the prosecutor to prefer it, but were bound to say that the accused person was guilty."§

5. A presumption of innocence may be created by the

* Rex v. Bowditch and others, Dorchester Summ. Ass. 1818, *coram* Mr. Justice Park, Short-hand Rep.

† Rex v. Whitby, and Rex v. Glenn, K. B. Guildhall, Oct. 1820.

‡ Rex v. M'Daniel and others, Foster's Rep. 121 ; Rex v. Vaughan and others, Sessions Papers, 1816 ; Reg. v. Delahunt, Dublin, 1842 ; cited in Best's Prin., *ut supra*, 533.

§ Reg. v. Coyle, C. C. C. Oct. Session, 1851.

language, conduct, and demeanour of the party charged
with crime: and it is upon this principle that the ingenuous and satisfactory explanation of circumstances
of suspicion always operates in favour of the accused.
Mr. Justice Erle said, he thought it was extremely important, as much for the protection of innocence as
for the discovery of guilt, that the accused should have
an opportunity of making a statement,* and the Lord
Justice Clerk, in a Scotch case, said, that the declaration of a prisoner, if fairly given, and founded in truth,
often had a very favourable effect.† It is evident however, that this kind of presumption must be attended
with much uncertainty, and in its application require
the exercise of great circumspection. The deportment
of innocence may be simulated, and from the anomalies
of human nature, it may be difficult if not impracticable in some cases to determine what is the natural
and suitable conduct to be expected from a party influenced by the pressure of an accumulation of circumstances, at once threatening and fallacious. It is certain
that innocent persons have drawn upon themselves the
punishment of crime by conduct apparently consistent
only with guilt, but which has erroneously been resorted to as likely to divert or repel unjust suspicion;
of which an instructive case is mentioned by Sir Edward
Coke.‡ "In the county of Warwick," says he, "there were
two brethren; the one having issue a daughter, and
being seized of lands in fee, devised the government of
his daughter and his lands until she came to her age
of sixteen years, to his brother, and died. The uncle

* Reg. *v.* Baldwin, 21 L. J. M. C. 130.
† Rex *v.* Wishart, 1 Syme's Jud. Rep. App. 22.
‡ Third Instit. c. 104, 232.

brought up his niece very well both at her book and needle, etc., and she was about eight or nine years of age; her uncle for some offence correcting her, she was heard to say, ' Oh! good Uncle, kill me not!' After which time the child, after much inquiry, could not be heard of, whereupon the uncle, being suspected of the murder of her, the rather that he was her next heir, was upon examination, anno 8 Jac. Regis, committed to the jail for suspicion of murder; and was admonished by the justices of assize to find out the child, and thereupon bailed until the next assizes. Against which time, for that he could not find her, and fearing what would fall out against him, he took another child as like unto her both in person and years as he could find, and apparelled her like unto the true child, and brought her to the next assizes; but upon view and examination she was found not to be the true child; and upon these presumptions he was indicted, found guilty, had judgment, and was hanged. But the truth of the case was, that the child, being beaten over-night, the next morning, when she should go to school, ran away into the next county; and being well educated she was reared and entertained of a stranger; and when she was sixteen years old, at which time she should come to her land, she came to demand it, and was directly proved to be the true child." The learned author adds, " We have reported this case for a double caveat; first to judges, that they in cases of life judge not too hastily upon bare presumption, and secondly to the innocent and true man, that he never seek to excuse himself by false or undue means, lest thereby he, offending God (the author of truth), overthrow himself as the uncle did. From the foregoing considerations it follows that our judgments in regard to the conduct of parties under accusation for crime must occasionally be modified by allowances for human weakness and inconsistency, which can in no degree be admitted as qualifying the obligation of entire truthfulness and consistency justly exacted from those who voluntarily become the accusers of others.

6. Since an action without a motive would be an effect without a cause, a presumption is consequently created in favour of innocence from the absence of all apparent inducement to the commission of the imputed offence. But the investigation of human motives is often a matter of great difficulty, from their latency or remoteness ; and experience shows that aggravated crimes are sometimes committed from very slight causes, and occasionally even without any apparent or discoverable motive. This particular presumption would therefore seem to be applicable only to cases where the guilt of the individual is involved in doubt; and the consideration for the jury in general is rather whether upon the other parts of the evidence the party accused has committed the crime, than whether he had any adequate motive.*

7. A defendant party's motives, even where they are unquestionably of a criminal character, may nevertheless be susceptible of different interpretations, and indicative of very different degrees of moral and legal turpitude. Concealment of the death of an illegitimate child and the clandestine disposal of its body, for instance, may be accounted for either by a purpose to suppress evidence of a murder, or merely by the desire of preserving the reputation of female chastity. Where a woman was indicted jointly with her husband for receiving stolen pro-

* See Mr. Justice Abbott's charge in Rex *v.* Donnall, Rep. *ut supra,* 130.

perty knowing it to have been stolen, and it appeared that she had dealt with it and ultimately destroyed it, it was held to be a question for the jury whether she had so received and dealt with it to aid him in turning it to profit, or merely to conceal his guilt or screen him from the consequences.* So where a wife attempted to break up coining implements at the time of her husband's apprehension, it was held that if done with the object of screening him, it was no evidence of a guilty possession by her.† And where a man and his wife were found guilty of wounding a person with intent to disfigure him and to do him grievous bodily harm; but the jury found that the wife acted under the coercion of the husband and did not personally inflict any violence on the prosecutor; it was held by the Criminal Court of Appeal that the conviction against the wife could not be supported.‡ In all such cases, every sound principle of interpretation and judgment requires, that in the absence of contrary proof, the act shall be referred to the operation of the least guilty motive; conformably to the maxim, *præsumptio judicatur potentior quæ est benignior.*§ Of this evident principle of justice the statute 21 Jac. I. c. 27 (now happily expunged from our code), which made the concealment of the death of an illegitimate child by its mother, a conclusive presumption of murder, unless she could make proof by one witness at least that the child was born dead, was a flagrant violation. It is on this principle that, when a special intent is made by statute an essential ingredient of any offence, as in the cases of assault with intent to murder or to rob, or to commit a felony,

---

* Reg. *v.* M'Clarens, 3 Cox's C. C. 425 ; S. P. Reg. *v.* Brookes, 6 *ib.* 147.   † Reg. *v.* Boober, 5 Cox's C. C. 272.

‡ Reg. *v.* Smith and wife, 27 L. J. M. C. 201.

§ Menoch. *ut supra*, lib. v. pr. 29.

or to prevent lawful apprehension or detainer, such special intent must be proved by direct evidence or by circumstances which necessarily or reasonably lead to the inference of such intention. Thus a charge of the statutable offence of throwing upon or otherwise applying to any person any corrosive fluid or other destructive matter, with intent to burn, maim, or do some bodily harm, is not sustained by proof of throwing a corrosive fluid for the purpose of burning the clothes.* And on the trial of a man for throwing a stone at a railway carriage with intent to endanger the safety of the passengers, where it appeared that the prisoner threw a stone just as the train was setting off, at a passenger against whom he had been much excited, Mr. Justice Erle told the jury that they must be satisfied that the intent to endanger the safety of any person travelling by the railway, must have been an intent to inflict some grievous bodily harm, and such as would sustain an indictment for assaulting or wounding a person with intent to do some bodily harm ; but that as that is a question of degree, which it is impossible to define further than in those terms, it must be a question for the jury upon the facts, whether there had been such an intent.†

8. The *primâ facie* presumption in favour of innocence from the absence of all apparent motive, is greatly strengthened, where all inducement to the commission of the imputed crime is opposed by strong counteracting motives; as where a party indicted for arson with intent to defraud an insurance office had furniture on the premises worth more than the amount of his insurance,‡

---

* Reg. *v.* Coppard, Kingst. Wint. Ass. 1855, *coram* Mr. Justice Crompton ; and see Rex *v.* Coke and Woodburne, *ut supra*.

† Reg. *v.* Rooke, 1 F. & F. 107.

‡ Rex *v.* Bingham, Horsham Spr. Ass. 1811.

or where a party accused of murder had a direct interest in the continuance of the life of the party supposed to have been murdered.* *A fortiori* would this presumption seem to apply where the life of the suspected party has been endangered, as the consequence of the supposed criminal act; as where a party charged with murder by poisoning had herself partaken of the poisoned food :† but this circumstance, of apparently favourable presumption, may have been resorted to as an artifice to avert suspicion, especially if the quantity taken has not been sufficient seriously to endanger life.‡

9. Since falsehood, concealment, flight, and other like acts, are generally regarded as indications of conscious guilt, it naturally follows, that the absence of these marks of mental emotion, and still more a voluntary surrender to justice, when the party had the opportunity of concealment or flight,§ must be considered as leading to the opposite presumption; and these considerations are frequently urged with just effect, as indicative of innocence; but the force of the latter circumstance may be weakened by the consideration that the party has been the object of diligent pursuit,‖ or, as said by Lord Campbell, though the party may have abstained from flight from a sense of innocence, he may have done so from thinking that, from the course he had taken, nothing would be discovered against him.** It must be also remembered, that flight and other similar indications of fear may be refer-

---

* Rex *v.* Downing, *infra.*

† Reg. *v.* Hawkins, Stafford Summer Ass. 1839.

‡ Rex *v.* Wescombe, and Rex *v.* Nairn, *ut supra,* 90; and see Rex *v.* Fenning, *coram* the Recorder of London, Sess. Papers, 1815, *infra.*

§ Menochius, *ut supra,* lib. v. pr. 50.

‖ Rex *v.* Buish, 1 Syme's Justiciary Rep. 277.

** Reg. *v.* Palmer, Short-hand Report. *ut supra,* 310.

able, not to the precise offence charged but to other circumstances, as to disordered affairs,* or to guilt of another and less penal character than that involved in the particular charge.†

10. As is the case with other presumptions, so the inference of guilt from the recent possession of stolen property may be rebutted by circumstances which create a counter-presumption : as where the property is found in the prisoner's possession under circumstances which render it more probable that some other person was the thief.   Therefore, where, on the trial of a mother and her two sons for sheepstealing, it was proved that the carcass of a sheep was found in the house of the mother, it was considered that the presumption arising from the possession of the stolen property immediately after the theft was rebutted so far as respected her, by the circumstance that *male* footsteps only were found near the spot from which the sheep had been stolen.‡ A woman was tried for the larceny of five saws which had been stolen from the workshop of a hat-block turner during the night.   There was a hole in the building large enough for a person to have crept through it.   On the following day he pledged two of the saws with a pawnbroker in the neighbourhood.   On the following night, the house of the prosecutor was broken open and a number of articles stolen, and no communication existed between the house and the workshop.   Two days afterwards the prisoner was taken into custody for this theft, in the house of a man who

* Rex v. Crosfield, 26 S. T. 217.

† Rex v. Schofield, 31 St. Tr. 1061 ; and see the language of Tindal C. J. in Rex v. Frost, Gurney's Rep. 766, 749 ; and of the Lord Justice Clerk Boyle, in Rex v. Hunter, and others, Court of Justiciary, Jan. 1838, Short-hand Report, 368.

‡ Rex v. Arundel and others, 1 Lewin's C. C. 115.

was himself charged with having committed the burglary. Mr. Baron Gurney said it was improbable that the female should have taken these saws, but that it was extremely probable that she should have been employed by another person to pawn them, that it was hardly a case in which the general rule could apply, and that it would be safer to acquit the prisoner.* Circumstances of conduct also may repel this *primâ facie* presumption; as where the prisoner a few days after the robbery of a large quantity of plate in London, sold, to a dealer in gold and silver, some silver articles marked with the prosecutor's crest partially obliterated, which had formed part of the stolen property. Mr. Baron Bramwell said it was a circumstance in the prisoner's favour that he had disposed of the silver at a place where he had been known for several years and had been in the habit of bringing gold and silver for sale, and did not appear to have made any attempt at secrecy. The prisoner was acquitted.†

11. Circumstances of apparently the most unfavourable presumption may be susceptible of an explanation consistent with the prisoner's innocence, and really be irrelevant to the particular inference sought to be derived from them;‡ or they may be opposed by circumstances which weaken or neutralize, or even repel the imputed presumption, and induce a stronger counter-presumption,‡ to every allegation of the existence of which justice demands that dispassionate and candid consideration be given. On the trial of a shoemaker for the murder of an aged female, it appeared that his leathern apron had several circular marks made by paring away superficial

* Rex v. Collier, 4 Jurist. 703.
† Reg. v. Benjamin, C. C. C., June 1858.
‡ Rex v. Thornton, Rex v. Looker, *infra.*

pieces, which it was supposed had been removed as containing spots of blood, but it was satisfactorily proved that the prisoner had cut them off for plasters for a neighbour.*   A policeman on his examination before the Coroner, where the question was, whether a young woman had been murdered or had committed suicide, swore that a piece of rope found in the prisoner's box appeared to have been cut from the same piece that was round the neck of the deceased; but on the trial he acknowledged that he had been mistaken; the two pieces of rope had in the interim been examined by a rope-maker, and were found not to correspond, one piece being twisted to the right and the other to the left.†   The prisoner was convicted upon the general evidence, and executed.   Two men were tried for killing a sheep with intent to steal the carcass.   The prosecutor had three sheep on a common, on the 14th of December, on which evening the prisoners, one of whom had a gun, were seen near the common driving several sheep before them.   One of the witnesses, when near the prosecutor's house, heard the report of a gun in the direction of the common, and, having a suspicion of the object of the prisoners, went to the prosecutor's house and communicated his suspicion, in consequence of which the prosecutor and the witness went to the common on which the sheep had been left feeding, and discovered that one of them was not there.   The prisoners were apprehended the same night at their respective homes.   In the lodgings of one of the prisoners a gun was found which had been recently fired, and some shot and powder wrapped in a piece of newspaper, from which two small pieces had been torn; and upon the person

* Rex v. Fitter, before Mr. Justice Taunton, Warwick Summer Ass. 1834.

† Reg. v. Drory, *coram* Campbell L. C. J., Chelmsford Spr. Ass. 1851.

of the other prisoner, a knife was found discoloured with blood. No traces were found of the lost sheep at that time, but the next day the carcass was found, concealed by fern, on the common; the sheep had been shot and also stuck in the neck. Two days afterwards, on searching near the spot where the carcass was found, two small pieces of newspaper were discovered, singed and bearing marks of having been fired from a gun, which on comparison were found to be the identical pieces so torn from the paper in question. Notwithstanding these apparently conclusive circumstances, the jury acquitted the prisoners, as it appeared from the cross-examination of one of the witnesses that he had seen them shooting on the common on the previous Sunday.* A man was tried for murder on Horwich Moor, under circumstances which were extremely suspicious; but the presumption against him was greatly weakened, if not entirely destroyed, by the circumstance that six shots extracted from the deceased's brain all corresponded in weight with the shot known as No. 3, while the shot in the prisoner's bag contained a mixture of Nos. 2 and 3, and the charge in his gun was found to contain the same mixture.† A druggist's apprentice was tried for the murder by prussic acid of a female servant who was pregnant by him, and the case was one of much suspicion; but there was a strong counter-presumption from the fact that the deceased had made preparations for a miscarriage on the very night in question.‡

* Reg. *v.* Courtnage and Mossingham, *coram* Mr. Serjeant Atcherley, Winchester Spr. Ass. 1843.

† Reg. *v.* Whittall, Liverpool Spr. Ass. 1839, *coram* Mr. Baron Alderson.

‡ Reg. *v.* Freeman, Leicester Spr. Ass. 1839, *coram* Best, L. C. J.; and see Rex *v.* Barnard, 19 St. Tr. 815.

12. Nor must it be overlooked, as one of the sources of error and fallacy in these cases, that circumstances of adverse presumption, apparently the most conclusive, have been fabricated by the real offender, in order to preclude suspicion from attaching to himself, and to cause it to rest upon another; as where a party was convicted upon an indictment for privily conveying three ducats into the prosecutor's pockets, with intent to charge him with having robbed him of the same ;* or where an offender surreptitiously put on the shoes of another person while engaged in the commission of crime, in order that the impressions might lead to the inference that the crime was committed by him.†

13. In forming a judgment of criminal intention, evidence that the party has previously borne a good character is often highly important, and if the case hangs in even balance, should make it preponderate in his favour.‡ But if the evidence of guilt be complete and convincing, testimony of previous good character cannot and ought not to avail.§ The reasonable operation of such evidence is to create a presumption that the party was not likely to have committed the act imputed to him ; which presumption, however weighty in a doubtful case, cannot but be irrelevant and unavailing against evidence which irrefragably establishes the fact.

---

* Rex v. Simon, 19 St. Tr. 680; but upon a new trial the defendant was acquitted.

† See the case of Mayenc, Gabriel, *ut supra*, 403 ; and see other such cases in Wharton's C. L. of the U.S. ; and in the Theory of Presumptive Proof App. ; but Mr. Justice Park, in Rex v. Thurtell, Hertford Winter Ass., 1824, said that the latter were of no authority, and possibly mere romance.

‡ *Per* Lord Ellenborough, in Rex v. Davison, 31 St. Tr. 217 ; and see the language of L. C. J. Tindal in Reg. v. Frost, Gurney's Rep. 749.

§ *Ibid.*, and Rex v. Haigh, 31 St. Tr. 1122.

Evidence of character must of course be applicable to the particular nature of the charge ; to prove, for instance, that a party has borne a good character for humanity and kindness, can have no bearing in reference to a charge of dishonesty. The correct mode of inquiry is, as to the *general* character of the accused, and whether the witness thinks him likely to be guilty of the offence which is charged against him.[*] It is not permitted to adduce evidence that the prisoner has not borne a good character, an inquiry which is really irrelevant, and calculated to divert attention from the true point to a collateral one, since even if his general character were clearly shown to be bad, he may not have committed the act in question. This principle has been carried so far, that, on an indictment for a particular offence, evidence of an admission by the accused that he was addicted to the commission of that offence was rejected as irrelevant.[†] In the text-books of the Civil Law, much stress is laid upon the *mala fama*, and in Scotland habit and repute is an admitted aggravation in charges of theft,[‡] but there are not wanting exemplifications of the danger of permitting the influence of such evidence.

If, however, the presumption arising from the evidence of previous good character be set up by the prisoner, it is then competent to neutralize its effect by the cross-examination of his witnesses, either as to particular facts,[§] or as to the grounds of their belief[||] for the purpose of discrediting their testimony ; but it is not competent to repel such evidence by calling witnesses to give evidence

* *Per* Lord Ellenborough in Rex *v.* Davison, 31 St. Tr. 187.
† Rex *v.* Cole, Best on Pres. p. 212.
‡ 1 Dickson's L. of E., *ut supra*, 22.
§ Reg. *v.* Hodgkins, 7 C. & P. 298.
|| 2 Stark, 301 ; and Taylor's L. of Ev. 310.

of the prisoner's general bad character.* Thus where a prisoner was indicted for a highway robbery, and called a witness who deposed to having known him for years, during which time he had borne a good character, it was permitted to ask the witness on cross-examination whether he had not heard that the prisoner was *suspected* of having committed a robbery which had taken place in the neighbourhood some years before ; Mr. Baron Parke said, that " the question is not whether the prisoner was *guilty* of that robbery, but whether he was *suspected* of having been implicated in it. A man's character," added the learned judge, " is made up of a number of small circumstances, of which his being suspected of misconduct is one;"† but Mr. Justice Erle refused to permit the cross-examination of a witness to character as to circumstances of suspicion against the prisoner which occurred upon the same day as the alleged offence was committed.‡

As a general rule, neither the prosecutor nor the prisoner can enter into evidence as to *particular facts* of good or bad conduct; but an exception to the rule has been created by statute 6 and 7 William IV. c. 111, which enacts that, if upon the trial of any person for any subsequent felony, such person shall give evidence of his good character, it shall be lawful for the prosecutor in answer thereto, to give evidence of the conviction of such prisoner for the previous felony ; and that the jury shall inquire of the previous conviction and subsequent offence at the same time; and this provision has been extended by St. 14 & 15 Vict. c. 19, s. 9, to many misdemeanours. The statutes equally apply where the evidence of good

<hr>

* Reg. *v.* Burt and others, 5 Cox's C. C. 281.
† Rex *v.* Wood, 5 Jurist, 225; and Best on Pres. 215.
‡ Reg. *v.* Rogan and Elliott, 1 Cox's C. C. 201.

character is obtained by the prisoner's counsel on the cross-examination of the witnesses for the prosecution.*

14. Of all kinds of exculpatory defence, that of an *alibi*, if clearly established by unsuspected testimony, is the most satisfactory and conclusive. While the foregoing considerations are more or less of an argumentative and inconclusive character, this defence, if the element of time be definitely and conclusively fixed, and the accused be shown to have been at some other place at the time, is absolutely incompatible with, and exclusive of, the possibility of the truth of the charge. "It must be admitted," says Sir Michael Foster, "that mere *alibi* evidence lieth under a great and general prejudice, and ought to be heard with uncommon caution ; but if it appeareth to be founded in truth, it is the best negative evidence that can be offered : it is really positive evidence, which in the nature of things necessarily implieth a negative ; and in many cases it is the only evidence which an innocent man can offer."†

It is obviously essential to the proof of an *alibi* that it should cover and account for the whole of the time of the transaction in question, or at least for so much of it as to render it impossible that the prisoner could have committed the imputed act ; it is not enough that it renders his guilt improbable merely, and if the time is not exactly fixed, and the place at which the accused is alleged by the defence to have been is not far off, the question then becomes one of probabilities. A defence of an *alibi* was therefore disregarded, because all that the prisoners offered to prove was that they were in bed on the night in

---

* Reg. *v.* Shrimpton, 3 C. & K. 373.

† Foster's C. L., *ut supra*, 368 ; and see the observations of Mr. Baron George, in Rex *v.* Brennan, 30 St. Tr. 79.

question at twelve o'clock, and were found in bed next
morning, after the arson with which they were charged
had taken place, the distance being two miles, so that
they might have risen, committed the deed, and returned
to bed.* On the trial of a man for the murder of a young
woman under circumstances of the strongest adverse presumption, the proof was that the deceased had been murdered at her father's cottage in the forenoon of the day
in question, and the prisoner alleged that he was at work
the whole of that day with his fellow-labourers at a distance from the cottage : but it turned out that he had
been absent from his work about half-an-hour, an interval
sufficiently long to have enabled him to reach the cottage, commit the murder, and rejoin his fellow-workmen.
He was convicted, and before his execution confessed his
guilt.†

The credibility of an *alibi* is greatly strengthened if it
be set up at the moment when the accusation is first
made, and be consistently maintained, throughout the
subsequent proceedings.   These conditions were remarkably fulfilled in the memorable case of Abraham Thornton, of which a full account will be given hereafter.   To
all appearance the guilt of the prisoner was the necessary
conclusion from the supposed inculpatory facts, and yet
he had been seen by a number of independent and unimpeachable witnesses at such a distance from the scene of
the alleged murder, at the very time when it must have
been committed, if at all, as to render it physically impossible that the deceased could have been murdered by
him ; and all the facts supposed to have been the conclusive indications of guilt were satisfactorily explained

* Rex *v.* Fraser, Alison's Princ. 625.
† Rex. *v.* Richardson, *infra.*

by collateral circumstances, and by a different hypo-thesis.*

On the other hand, it is a material circumstance to lessen the weight of this defence, if it be not resorted to until some time after the charge has been made; or if nothing happened immediately after the transaction to lead the witnesses to watch so as to be accurate in the hour or time to which they speak, even supposing them to depose under no improper bias or influence;† or if having been once resorted to, a different and inconsis-tent defence is afterwards set up. There are many other sources of fallacy connected with this particular defence; such as mistake as to the person from want of oppor-tunity of accurate observation,—or other causes of mis-conception,—the possible difference of clocks,‡ or the fraudulent alteration of them to tally with other facts; as where one of the perpetrators of a murder hastened home, put back the clock two hours, and went to bed; and shortly afterwards awoke his servant, and told her to go down-stairs and see what was the time, which she did, not knowing that the clock had been tampered with; so that her testimony led to his acquittal.§

A group of irrelevant facts is sometimes artfully ar-ranged so as to give an appearance of reality and co-herence to the defence, the facts being true in themselves,

* Rex v. Thornton, *infra;* and see Rex v. Canning, 19 St. Tr. 283, where the prosecutrix of a capital charge was convicted of perjury on the evidence of thirty-eight witnesses who proved an *alibi.*

† *Per* Mr. Justice Le Blanc in Rex v. Mellor and others, 31 St. Tr. 1032; and see Rex v. Haigh, *ib.* 1118; and the observations of Shaw C. J., in Webster's case, Bemis's Rep., *ut supra,* 478.

‡ Rex v. Schofield, 31 St. Tr. 1063; Rex v. Mellor, *ib.* 1027.

§ Rex v. Hardy; see the ' Times' newspaper of the 28th November, 1857, where it is stated that one of the murderers made a circum-stantial confession on his death-bed.

but fraudulently referred to the critical day or time, instead of to the real time of their occurrence;* or such a misstatement may take place by unintentional mistake.† In an American case, where several persons were tried for an atrocious murder, it appears to have been a part of the plot for each of the prisoners to sleep on the night of the murder with some one who could testify to an *alibi*. One of the murderers had requested a man to sleep in his house; but the witness stated that he might have been absent while he was asleep. Another of them went several miles from the place of the murder to sleep, and the person in whose house he staid had no doubt that he was within-doors the whole night. Two others of them went to a tavern several miles from the scene of the murder, and went to bed together; but in the night one of them was discovered leaving the house, although he evidently wished to be unnoticed; and he was absent so long, not returning until the morning, as to alarm the tavern-keeper, who with his wife made diligent search for him in the neighbourhood, but his bedfellow manifested no anxiety or alarm, and got up and assisted in the search.‡

This defence is especially easy of fabrication or mistake in regard to the essential element of time, where a few minutes may be of vital moment; and the unblushing effrontery with which witnesses sometimes present themselves to speak to time, without regard to plausibility or consistency, is truly surprising. On a trial for murder, two witnesses who were called to support a defence of an *alibi*, swore that they were able to speak

---

* See a case of this kind in 8 Lond. Med. Gaz. 36.

† Rex *v.* Baines, 31 St. Tr. 1091; Rex. *v.* Haigh, *ut supra*.

‡ Case of Bauer and others, 2 Chandl. Amer. Cr. Tr. 356.

positively to the time, from having looked at a clock; but upon being required by the counsel for the prosecution to tell the time by the clock in Court, after some hesitation they admitted that they were unable to do so.* In another case it was elicited in cross-examination of a woman with whom the prisoner lived, that on his return home after an absence of an hour, during which he committed two murders, he told her to say that he had not been out more than ten minutes.†

Wherever pertinent and material evidence by which an *alibi* might, if true, have been supported, is withheld,‡ or the defence fails of being supported by credible and sufficient evidence, or is detected to be the result of afterthought or contrivance, or is contradicted, or otherwise rebutted, the attempt to set it up recoils with fatal effect upon the party who asserts it; and, in the language of a learned judge on the Irish bench, "amounts to a conviction."§

"The truth of this sort of defence," said Mr. Baron George, "is not always to be ascertained by the direct testimony of the witnesses called to prove it. Several witnesses are seldom produced in such cases without its being known that they agree with each other in the substantial and principal fact they are to relate; and as in general it is not to be expected that a prosecutor should come with evidence prepared to meet this sort of defence, the usual test of its truth or of its falsehood, where they are unknown to the jury, is a cross-examination of the witnesses, kept asunder, and fairly conducted under

* Reg. *v.* Cane and others, C. C. C. 20th of June, 1851.
† Reg. *v.* Rush, Norfolk Spr. Ass. 1849.
‡ Rex *v.* Haigh and others, *ut supra;* Rex *v.* Hunter and others, Rep., *ut supra,* 365.
§ By Mr. Baron Daly in Rex *v.* Killan, 28 St. Tr. 1085.

the eye and observation of the jury ; and here differences or contradictions, otherwise trivial, become important in showing the truth or falsehood of such narrative."[*] In such circumstances, if the story be a fabrication, it is obviously far more easy for the witnesses to agree on the mere general fact of the prisoner's presence at the time and place referred to, than on the minute surrounding particulars.[†]

The foregoing examples suffice to illustrate the subject of exculpatory presumptions; but it is obvious that as inculpatory facts are infinitely diversified, exculpatory facts must admit of the same extent of variety, and that they may be of every degree of force. In all such cases of conflicting presumptions it is the duty of the jury, with the assistance of the Court, to weigh and estimate the force of each several circumstance of presumption, and to act upon what appear to be the superior probabilities of the case ; and if there be not a decided preponderance of evidence to establish the guilt of the party, to take the safe and just course, by abstaining from pronouncing a verdict of guilt, where the necessary light and knowledge to justify them in so doing with the full assurance of moral certainty, is unattainable.[‡]

* Rex v. Brennan, 30 St. Tr. 70.
† Reg. v. Hunter, Rep., *ut supra*, 365.
‡ Mittermaier, *ut supra*, ch. 56.

CHAPTER VI.

RULES OF INDUCTION SPECIALLY APPLICABLE TO CIRCUMSTANTIAL EVIDENCE.

ALL reasoning concerning human conduct is essentially a process of induction, of which it is the object, by means of generalizations founded upon a knowledge of the faculties, emotions, and laws of the mind, to discover the moral qualities and causal origin of the voluntary actions of our fellow-men; whence it follows that the rules for the conduct of inductive inquiry belong formally to the province of LOGIC, or the science of the laws of thought. The rules of evidence are therefore a selection of maxims tacitly assumed and acted upon by all men in the ordinary affairs of life, and recognized by philosophical wisdom and judicial experience as the best means of discovering truth. The purpose of this essay requires the enumeration only of such few leading rules of evidence as are of special, though not of exclusive application, to the particular subject-matter of this treatise.*

RULE 1.—*The facts alleged as the basis of any legal inference must be clearly proved, and indubitably connected with the* factum probandum. This rule is an indispensable condition of all sound induction; and its object is, by proper rejections and exclusions, and after as many negations as are necessary,† to verify facts and clear them

---

* Mittermaier, *ut supra*, ch. 57.

† Nov. Org. lib. i.; Aphor. cv. 2; Mill's Log. b. v. ch. 2 and 3.

from all ambiguity, so that they may become the premises of logical argument and reasoning. In moral investigations the facts are generally more obscurely developed than when physical phenomena form the subjects of inquiry; and they are frequently blended with foreign and irrelevant circumstances, so that the establishment of their connection with the *factum probandum*, becomes matter of considerable difficulty. No weight therefore must be attached to circumstances which, however they may excite conjecture, do not warrant belief. Occurrences may be mysterious and justify even vehement suspicion, and yet the supposed connection between them may be but imaginary, and their co-existence indicative of accidental concurrence merely, and not of mutual correlation. " Where there is nothing but the evidence of circumstances to guide you," said Mr. Justice Bailey, " those circumstances ought to be *closely and necessarily* connected, and to be made as clear as if there were absolute and positive proof."*   Every circumstance therefore which is not clearly shown to be really connected as its correlative with the hypothesis it is supposed to support, must be rejected from the judicial balance; in other words, it must be distinctly established that there exists between the *factum probandum* and the facts which are adduced in proof of it, a real connection, either evident and necessary, or so highly probable as to admit of no other reasonable explanation.†

The following cases will serve to manifest the dangerous consequences which may ensue from the disregard of this most salutary cautionary rule.

Two brothers-in-law, Joseph Downing and Samuel

* Rex *v.* Downing, Salop Summer Ass. 1822, *infra.*
† Mittermaier, *ut supra*, ch. 55, 57.

Whitehouse, met by appointment to shoot, and afterwards to look at an estate, which on the death of Whitehouse's wife without issue would devolve on Downing. They arrived at the place of meeting on horseback, Downing carrying a gun-barrel and leading a colt. After the business of the day, and drinking together some hours, they set out to return home, Downing leading his colt as in the morning. Their way led through a gate opening from the turnpike-road, and thence by a narrow track through a wood. On arriving at the gate, Downing discovered that he had forgotten his gun-barrel; and a man who accompanied them to open the gate went back for it, returning in about three minutes. In the meantime Whitehouse had gone on in advance; and the prisoner, having received his gun-barrel, followed in the same direction. Shortly afterwards Whitehouse was found lying on the ground in the wood, at a part where the track widened, about 600 yards from the gate, with his hat off, and insensible from several wounds in the head, one of which had fractured his skull. While the person by whom he was discovered went for assistance, the deceased had been turned over and robbed of his watch and money. About the same time Downing was seen in advance of the spot where the deceased lay, proceeding homeward and leading his colt; and a few minutes afterwards two men were seen following in the same direction. Suspicion attached to Downing, partly from his interest in the estate enjoyed by the deceased, and he was put upon his trial for this supposed murder; but it was clear that he had no motive on that account to kill the deceased, as the estate was not to come to him until after failure of issue of the deceased's wife, to whom he had been married several years, without having had children;

so that it was his interest that the way should not be
opened to a second marriage. That the deceased had
been murdered at all, was a highly improbable conjecture, and it was far more probable that he had fallen
from his horse and received a kick, especially as his hat
bore no marks of injury, so that it had probably fallen
off before the infliction of the wounds. That the deceased,
if murdered at all, had been murdered by the prisoner
was in the highest degree improbable, considering how
both his hands must have been employed, nor was there
any evidence that the deceased had been robbed by the
prisoner. It thus appeared, that these accumulated circumstances, of supposed inculpatory presumption, were
really irrelevant and unconnected with any *corpus delicti.** The prisoner was acquitted; and it is instructive that about twelve months afterwards, the mystery of
the robbery, the only real circumstance of suspicion, was
cleared up. A man was apprehended upon offering the
deceased's watch for sale, and brought to trial for the
theft of it, and acquitted, the judge thinking that he
ought not to be called upon, at so distant a period, to
account for the possession of the deceased's property,
which he might have purchased, or otherwise fairly acquired, without being able to prove it by evidence. The
accused, when no longer in danger, acknowledged that
he had robbed the deceased, whom he found lying drunk
on the road, as he believed; but that he had concealed
the watch, on learning that it was supposed that he had
been murdered, in order to prevent suspicion from attaching to himself.

A farmer was tried under the special commission for
Wiltshire, in January 1831, upon an indictment which

* Rex *v.* Downing, Salop Sum. Ass. 1822, *coram* Mr. Justice Bayley.

charged him with having feloniously sent a threatening letter, which was alleged to have been written by him. That the letter was in the prisoner's handwriting was positively deposed by witnesses who had had ample means of becoming acquainted with it, while the contrary was as positively deposed on the part of the prisoner by numerous witnesses equally competent to speak to the fact. But the scale appears to have been turned by the circumstance that the letter in question, and two others of the same kind sent to other persons, together with a scrap of paper found in the prisoner's bureau, had formed one sheet of paper; the ragged edges of the different portions exactly fitting each other, and the water-mark name of the maker, which was divided into three parts, being perfect when the portions of paper were united. The jury found the prisoner guilty, and he was sentenced to be transported for fourteen years. The judge and jury having retired for a few minutes, during their absence the prisoner's son, a youth about eighteen years of age, was brought to the table by the prisoner's attorney, and confessed that he had been the writer of the letter in question, and not his father. He then wrote on a piece of paper from memory a copy of the contents of the anonymous letter, which on comparison left no doubt of the truth of his statement. The writing was not a verbatim copy, although it differed but little; and the bad spelling of the original was repeated in the copy. The original was then handed to him, and on being desired to do so, he copied it, and the writing was exactly alike. Upon the return of the learned judge the circumstances were mentioned to him, and two days afterwards the son was put upon his trial and convicted of the identical offence which had been imputed to the father.

It appeared that he had had access to the bureau, which was commonly left open. The writing of the letter constituted in fact the *corpus delicti;* there having been no other evidence to inculpate the prisoner as the *sender* of the letter, which would however have been the natural and irresistible inference if he had been the *writer*. The correspondence of the fragment of paper found in the prisoner's bureau with the letter in question, and with the two others of the same nature sent to other persons, was simply a circumstance of suspicion, but foreign, as it turned out, to the *factum* in question; and considering that other persons had access to the bureau, its weight as a circumstance of suspicion seems to have been overrated.[*]

But, perhaps, the most extraordinary and instructive case of this kind that has ever occurred, was that of Abraham Thornton, who was tried at the Warwick Autumn Assizes, 1817, before Mr. Justice Holroyd, for the alleged murder of a young woman, who was found dead in a pit of water, about seven o'clock in the morning, with marks of violence about her person and dress, from which it was supposed that she had been violated, and afterwards drowned. The deceased's bonnet and shoes and a bundle were found on the bank of the pit. Upon the grass, at the distance of forty yards, there was the impression of an extended human figure, and a large quantity of blood was upon the ground near the lower extremity of the figure, where there were also the marks of large shoe-toes. Spots of blood were traced for ten yards in a direction leading from the impression to the pit upon a footpath, and about a foot and a half from the path upon

* Rex *v.* Isaac Looker, Rex *v.* Edward Looker, A. R. 1831, 9; and see Selections from the charges of Mr. Baron Alderson.

the grass on one side of it.   When the body was found, there was no trace of any footstep on the grass, which was covered with dew not otherwise disturbed than by the blood ; from which circumstances it was insisted that the spots of blood must have fallen from the body while being carried in some person's arms. Upon the examination of the body, about half a pint of water and some duckweed were found in the stomach, so that the deceased must have been alive when immersed in the water. There were lacerations about the parts of generation, but nothing which might not have been caused by sexual intercourse with consent.   Soon after the discovery of the body, there were found in a newly harrowed field adjoining that in which the pit was situate, the recent footmarks of the right and left footsteps of the prisoner and also of the footsteps of the deceased, which, from the length and depth of the steps, indicated that there had been running and pursuit, and that the deceased had been overtaken.   From that part of the harrowed field where the deceased had been overtaken, her footsteps and those of the prisoner proceeded together, walking in a direction towards the pit and the spot where the impression was found, until the footsteps came within the distance of forty yards from the pit, when from the hardness of the ground they could be no longer traced. The marks of the prisoner's running footsteps were also discovered in a direction leading from the pit across the harrowed field ; from which it was contended that he had run alone in that direction after the commission of the supposed murder.   The mark of a man's left shoe (but not proved to have been the prisoner's) was discovered near the edge of the pit, and it was proved that the prisoner had worn right and left shoes. On the prisoner's shirt

and breeches were found stains of blood, and he acknowledged that he had had sexual intercourse with the deceased, but alleged that it had taken place with her own
consent. The defence set up was an *alibi*, which, notwithstanding these apparently decisive facts, was most
satisfactorily established. The prisoner and the deceased
had met at a dance on the preceding evening at a public-
house, which they left together about midnight. About
three in the morning they were seen talking together at
a stile near the spot, and about four o'clock the deceased
called at the house of Mrs. Butler, at Erdington, where
she had left a bundle of clothes the day before. Here
she appeared in good health and spirits, changed a part
of her dress for some of the garments which she had
left there, and quitted the house in about a quarter of
an hour. Her way home lay across certain fields, one of
which had been newly harrowed, and adjoined that in
which the pit was situate. The deceased was successively
seen after leaving Mrs. Butler's house by several persons,
proceeding alone in a direction towards her own home,
along a public road where the prisoner, if he had rejoined
her, could have been seen for a considerable distance ; the
last of such persons saw her within a quarter of an hour
afterwards, that is to say, before or about half-past four.
At about half-past four, and not later than twenty-five minutes before five, the accused was seen by four persons,
wholly unacquainted with him, walking slowly and leisurely along a lane leading in an opposite direction from
the young woman's course towards her home. About a
mile from the spot where the prisoner was seen, he was
seen by another witness about ten minutes before five,
still walking slowly in the same direction, with whom he
stopped and conversed for a quarter of an hour, after

which, at twenty-five minutes past five, he was again seen
walking towards his father's house, which was distant
about half a mile. From Mrs. Butler's house to the pit
was a distance of upwards of a mile and a quarter; and
allowing twenty minutes to enable the deceased to walk
this distance, would bring the time of her arrival at the
pit to twenty-five minutes before five; whereas the prisoner was first seen by four persons above all suspicion
at half-past four or twenty-five minutes before five, and
the distance of the pit from the place where he was
seen, was two miles and a half. Upon the hypothesis
of his guilt, the prisoner must have rejoined the deceased after she left Mrs. Butler's house, and a distance
of upwards of three miles and a quarter must have been
traversed by him, accompanied for a portion of it by
the deceased, and the pursuit, the criminal intercourse,
the drowning, and the deliberate placing of the deceased's bonnet, shoes, and bundle, must have taken
place within twenty or twenty-five minutes. The defence
was set up at the instant of the prisoner's apprehension,
which took place within a few hours after the discovery
of the body, and was maintained without contradiction
or variation before the coroner's inquest and the committing magistrates, and also upon the trial, and no inroad
was made on the credibility of the testimony by which
it was supported. The various timepieces to which the
witnesses referred, and which differed much from each
other, were carefully compared on the day after the occurrence and reduced to a common standard, so that
there could be no doubt of the real times as spoken to
by them. Thus, it was not within the bounds of possibility that the prisoner could have committed the crime
imputed to him; nevertheless public indignation was so

strongly excited that his acquittal, though it afforded a fine example of the calm and unimpassioned administration of justice, occasioned great public dissatisfaction. There was nevertheless a total absence of all conclusive evidence of a *corpus delicti*, which the jury were required to infer from circumstances of apparent suspicion. The deceased might have drowned herself, in a moment of bitter remorse, after parting from her seducer, and excited to agonizing reflection by the sight of so many appalling marks of her ruin. It was possible that she might have sat down to change her dancing-shoes for the boots which she had worn the preceding day and carried in her bundle, and fallen into the water from exhaustion; for she had walked to and from market in the morning, had exerted herself in dancing in the evening, and had been wandering all night in the fields without food. The allegation that the prisoner had violated the deceased, and therefore had a motive to destroy her, was mere conjecture; and from the circumstance of her having been out all night with the prisoner, with whom she was previously unacquainted, and from the state of the garments which she took off at Mrs. Butler's, as compared with those for which she exchanged them, it was clear that the sexual intercourse had taken place before she called there, at which time she made no complaint, but appeared composed and cheerful. Again, the inference contended for, from the state of the grass, with drops of blood upon it where the dew had not been disturbed, was equally groundless; for there was no proof that the dew had not been deposited after the drops of blood; and it clearly appeared that the footsteps of the prisoner and the deceased could not be traced on other parts of the grass where, beyond all doubt, they had been together in the course of the night. Now, suppose that the *alibi* had been incapable of satisfactory proof, that the prisoner had not been seen after parting from the deceased, and that the inconclusiveness of the inference suggested from the discovery of drops of blood on the grass, where there were no footmarks, had not been manifested by the absence of those marks in other places where they had unquestionably been together in the night,—the guilt of the prisoner would have been considered indubitable, and his execution certain ; and yet these exculpatory circumstances were entirely collateral, and independent of the facts which were supposed to be clearly indicative of guilt.*

Rule 2.—*The burden of proof is always on the party who asserts the existence of any fact which infers legal accountability.*† This is a universal rule of jurisprudence, founded upon evident principles of justice ; and it is a necessary consequence, that the affirmant party is not absolved from its obligation because of the difficulty which may attend its application. No man can be justly deprived of his social rights but upon proof that he has committed some act which legally involves the forfeiture of them. The law respects the *status in quo*, and regards every man as legally innocent until the contrary be proved. To prove a negative is in most cases difficult, in many impossible. Criminality therefore is never to be presumed. But nevertheless the operation of this rule

* The friends of the deceased brought an appeal of death, in which the defendant tendered wager of battle, and the proceedings led to the abolition, by St. 59 G. III. c. 46, of that barbarous relic of feudal times. See Ashford *v.* Thornton, 4 B. & Ald. 405 ; Short-hand Rep., and Observations upon the case of Abraham Thornton, by Edward Holroyd, Esq., where the judge's notes of the evidence are given.

† 1 Starkie's L. of Ev. 162 ; 1 Greenleaf's L. of Ev. c. 3.

may, to a certain extent, be modified by circumstances which create a counter-obligation, and shift the *onus probandi.* Lord Brougham said that the burden of proof often shifts about from one party to the other in the progress of a cause, according as the evidence raises a presumption one way or the other.* It follows, from the very nature of circumstantial evidence, that, in drawing an inference or conclusion as to the existence of a particular fact from other facts that are proved, regard must always be had to the nature of the particular case, and the facility that appears to be afforded either of explanation or contradiction.† Lord Ellenborough said that no person accused of crime is bound to offer any explanation of his conduct, or of circumstances of suspicion which attach to him; but nevertheless, if he refuse to do so, where a strong *primâ facie* case has been made out, and when it is in his own power to offer evidence, if such exist, in explanation of such suspicious appearances, which would show them to be fallacious and explicable in consistency with his innocence, it is a reasonable and justifiable conclusion that he refrains from doing so only from the conviction that the evidence so suppressed or not adduced would operate adversely to his interest.‡ It is therefore a qualification of the rule in question, that in every case the *onus probandi* lies on the person who is interested to support his case by a particular fact, which lies more particularly within his own knowledge, or of which he is supposed to be cognizant. This indeed is not allowed to supply the want of necessary proof, whether direct or presumptive, against a defendant, of the crime

* Wareing *v.* Wareing, 6 Moore's P. C. Rep. 355.
† *Per* Lord Chief Justice Abbott in Rex *v.* Burdett, 4 B. & Ald. 161.
‡ Rex *v.* Cochrane, Gurney's Rep.

with which he is charged; but when such proof has been given, it is a rule to be applied in considering the weight of the evidence against him, whether direct or presumptive, when it is unopposed, unrebutted, or not weakened by contrary evidence, which it would be in the defendant's power to produce, if the fact directly or presumptively proved were not true.* It has been well observed, that in such case we have something like an admission that the presumption is just.† "In drawing an inference or conclusion, regard must always be had," said the Lord Chief Justice Abbott,‡ "to the nature of the particular case, and the facility that appears to be afforded either of explanation or of contradiction. No person is to be required to explain or contradict, until enough has been proved to warrant a reasonable and just conclusion against him, in the absence of explanation or contradiction; but when such proof has been given, and the nature of the case is such as to admit of explanation or contradiction, if the conclusion to which the proof tends be untrue, and the accused offers no explanation or contradiction, can human reason do otherwise than adopt the conclusion to which the proof tends? The premises may lead more or less strongly to the conclusion, and care must be taken not to draw the conclusion hastily; but in matters that concern the conduct of men, the certainty of mathematical evidence cannot be required or expected; and it is one of the peculiar advantages of our jurisprudence, that the conclusion is to be drawn by the unanimous judgment and conscience of twelve men conversant with the affairs and business of life, and who know that when reasonable

* *Per* Mr. Justice Holroyd in Rex *v.* Burdett, 4 B. & Ald. 140.
† *Per* Mr. Justice Best, *ib.* 122.
‡ *Ibid.* 161; and see the language of Mr. Justice Bayley, *ib.* 150.

doubt is entertained, it is their duty to acquit; and not of one or more lawyers, whose habits might be suspected of leading them to the indulgence of too much subtlety and refinement." To the same effect Lord Chief Justice Tindal, on a trial for high-treason, said, that " the offence charged against the prisoner must be proved by those who make the charge. The proof of the case against the prisoner must depend for its support not upon the absence or want of any explanation on the part of the prisoner himself, but upon the positive affirmative evidence of the guilt that is given by the crown. It is not however an unreasonable thing," said the learned judge, " and it daily occurs in investigations, both civil and criminal, that if there is a certain appearance made out against a party, if he is involved by the evidence in a state of considerable suspicion, he is called upon for his own sake and his own safety to state and bring forward the circumstances, whatever they may be, which might reconcile such suspicious appearances with perfect innocence.* But this doctrine, it has been well observed, is to be cautiously applied, and only in cases where it is manifest that proofs are in the power of the accused, not accessible to the prosecution."†

It is a necessary consequence of this rule, rather than a substantive rule, that the *corpus delicti* must be clearly proved before any effect is attached to circumstances supposed to be inculpatory of a particular individual; but this is a branch of the subject of so much importance

---

* Reg. *v.* Frost, Monmouth Sp. Comm. Jan. 1840, Gurney's Report, 689; and see the language of Lord Ellenborough in Rex *v.* Despard. 28 St. Tr. 521; and in Rex *v.* Watson, 32 *ib.* 583; and that of Le Blanc J. in Rex *v.* Mellor and others, 31 St. Tr. 1032.

† *Per* Shaw C. J. in Webster's case, *ut supra.* 467.

and of such comprehensive extent, as to require consideration in a separate chapter.

RULE 3.—*In all cases, whether of direct or circumstantial evidence, the best evidence must be adduced which the nature of the case admits.* The suppression or non-production of pertinent and cogent evidence necessarily raises a strong presumption against the party who withholds such evidence when he has it in his power to produce it; of which some interesting exemplifications appear in other parts of this Essay.* This rule applies *à fortiori* to circumstantial evidence, a kind of proof which, for reasons which have been already urged, is inherently inferior to direct and positive testimony; and therefore whenever such evidence is capable of being adduced, the very attempt to substitute a description of evidence not of the same degree of force, necessarily creates a suspicion that it is withheld from corrupt and sinister motives.† Nor is the application of the rule confined to the proof of the principal fact; it is "the master rule which governs all the subordinate rules,"‡ and applies alike to the proof of every individual constituent fact, whether principal or subordinate. Thus, in a trial for murder, Mr. Baron Maule refused to receive evidence of the contents of a coffin-plate in order to establish the identity of the deceased, on the ground that, being removable, it might have been produced, and there being no other case of identity, stopped the case.§ The rule is however necessarily relaxed, where its application becomes impracticable by the wrongful act of the party who would otherwise be entitled to claim its protection;

* See *ante*, Ch. III., ss. 5. 7.   † See *ante*, 31.
‡ 2 Burke's works, *ut supra*, 618; Mittermaier, *ut supra*, ch. 57.
§ Reg. *v.* Edge, Chester Spr. Ass. 1842.

as where a witness is kept out of the way by or on his behalf,* or a deed or other instrument in his possession, which he refuses, after notice, to produce.†

Considering moreover the inherent infirmity of human memory, in the fair construction and application of this rule, evidence ought in all criminal cases, and *à fortiori* in cases of circumstantial evidence, to be received with distrust, wherever any considerable time has elapsed since the commission of the alleged offence. The justice and efficacy of punishment, and more especially of capital punishment, inflicted after the lapse of any considerable interval, at least where the offender has not withdrawn himself from the reach of justice, are more than questionable.‡ An unavoidable consequence of great delay is, that the party is deprived of the means of vindicating his innocence, or of proving the attendant circumstances of extenuation ; the crime itself becomes forgotten, or is remembered but as matter of tradition, and the offender may have become a different moral being : in such circumstances punishment can seldom, perhaps never, be efficacious for the purpose of example. On these accounts judges and juries are now always reluctant to convict parties charged with offences committed long previously.

RULE 4.—*In order to justify the inference of guilt,*

* Hawk. P. C. Bk. 2. c. 46. s. 15 ; R. *v.* Guttridge, 9 C. & P. 471; Reg. *v.* Scaife, 20 L. J., M. C. 220.

† Rex *v.* Hunter, 3 C. & P. 491 ; 4 *ib.*, 128 ; Rex *v.* Haworth, 4 C. & P. 254 ; and see *ante*, Ch. III. s. 7.

‡ See Rex *v.* Horne, executed at Nottingham in 1759, for the murder of his natural child forty years before, 4 Cel. Trials, 396 ; and Rex *v.* Wall, 28 St. Tr. 51, whose execution took place after the lapse of twenty years from the commission of the offence; and see the strictures of Lord Campbell on the case, 3 Lives of the C. Justices, 147 ; and Rex *v.* Roper, Leicester Sum. Ass. 1836, for a murder committed thirty-four years before, A. R. 1836.

*the inculpatory facts must be incompatible with the inno-
cence of the accused, and incapable of explanation upon
any other reasonable hypothesis than that of his guilt.*
This is the fundamental rule, the *experimentum crucis* by
which the relevancy and effect of circumstantial evidence
must be estimated. The awards of penal law can be
justified only when the strength of our convictions is
equivalent to moral certainty; which, as we have seen,
is that state of the judgment, grounded upon an adequate
amount of appropriate evidence, which induces a man of
sound mind to act without hesitation in the most important concerns of human life. In cases of direct credible evidence, that degree of assurance immediately and
necessarily ensues; but in estimating the effect of circumstantial evidence, there is of necessity an ulterior intellectual process of inference which constitutes an essential element of moral certainty. The most important
part of the inductive process, especially in moral inquiries,
is the correct exercise of the judgment in drawing the
proper inference from the known to the unknown, from
the facts proved to the *factum probandum.* A number
of secondary facts of an inculpatory moral aspect being
given, the problem is, to discover their causal moral
source, not by arbitrary assumption, but by the application of the principles of experience in relation to the immutable laws of human nature and conduct. It is not
enough, however, that a particular hypothesis will explain all the phenomena; nothing must be inferred, because, if true, it would account for the facts; and if the
circumstances are equally capable of solution upon any
other reasonable hypothesis, it is manifest that their true
moral cause is not exclusively ascertained, but remains in
uncertainty; and they must therefore be discarded as

conclusive presumptions of guilt. Every other reasonable supposition by which the facts may be explained consistently with the hypothesis of innocence must therefore be rigorously examined and successively eliminated ; and only when no other supposition will reasonably account for all the conditions of the case, can the conclusion of guilt be legitimately adopted.* In a late case before the Court of Justiciary at Edinburgh, the Lord Justice Clerk Cockburn said that the matter might remain most mysterious, wholly unexplained ; they might not be able to account for it on any other supposition than that of the prisoner's guilt ; but that still that supposition or inference might not be a ground on which they could safely and satisfactorily rest their verdict against her.† But nevertheless it seems hardly possible to conceive of such a state of facts. If however the hypothesis fulfils the required conditions, the conclusion is no longer a gratuitous assumption, but becomes as it were part of the induction ; and an additional test is obtained, by which, as by the application of a theorem of verification, the conclusion may be tested, and, if true, corroborated and confirmed ; since, if it be true, it must harmonize with, and satisfactorily account for, all the facts, to the exclusion of every other reasonable hypothesis.* In accordance with these sound principles of reasoning and inference, Lord Chief Baron Macdonald said that he had ever understood the rule as to circumstantial evidence to be that where the circumstances are true, where they are well connected, where they support each other in a clear and lucid manner, and where they cannot reasonably be accounted for unless the charge be true that is imputed

* See Mittermaier, *ut supra*, ch. 59.
† Reg. *v*. Madeleine Smith, Rep., *ut supra*, 303.

to the prisoner, then the jury were justified in convicting upon that evidence.* On another occasion the same learned Judge said, that the nature of circumstantial evidence was this, that the jury must be satisfied that there is no rational mode of accounting for the circumstances, but upon the supposition that the prisoner is guilty.† Mr. Baron Alderson, with more complete exactness, said, that to enable the jury to bring in a verdict of guilty, it was necessary, not only that it should be a rational conviction, but that it should be the only rational conviction which the circumstances would enable them to draw.‡ In Humphreys' case, Lord Meadowbank said to the jury, " Your duty is to consider what is the reasonable inference to be drawn from the whole circumstances; in short, whether it is possible to explain the circumstances upon grounds consistent with the innocence to the panel, or whether, on the contrary, they do not necessarily lead to a result directly the reverse."§

It follows, as a consequence of this rule, that wherever several persons are jointly charged with any offence, joint complicity must be proved. In the case of the two Mannings their counsel severally endeavoured to throw the guilt exclusively on the other; and Lord C. B. Pollock told the jury that if they thought one of the prisoners was guilty, but could not possibly decide which was the guilty party, they might be reduced to the alternative of returning a verdict of not guilty as to both ; but, that if, looking at the whole transaction, they came to the conclusion that both must, according to the ordinary course

* Rex v. Smith, for arson, *ut supra*, p. 30.
† Rex v. Patch, Surrey Spr. Ass. 1805.
‡ Rex v. Hodges, 2 Lewin's C. C. 227.
§ Swinton's Rep., *ut supra*, 353.

of human affairs, have been concerned in the murder, it would be their duty to find both the prisoners guilty.*

A learned writer thinks that almost all writers have attempted to estimate the force of evidence upon a wrong principle; that the true principle is to estimate its value entirely by the effect which it does in fact produce upon the minds of those who hear it, and that the value of evidence is measured as exactly by the state of mind which it produces, as a force is measured by the weight which it will lift.† But, not to dwell upon the fallacy of every attempt to compare the conclusions of moral reasoning with the constrained and inevitable consequence of mechanical force, this would be to give up a safe, practical, and philosophic test, the validity and sufficiency of which are recognized in every other branch of philosophical and scientific research, for an indeterminate and empirical result incapable of independent verification, and would virtually justify the most erroneous determinations of the tribunals.

RULE 5.—*If there be any reasonable doubt of the guilt of the accused, he is entitled as of right to be acquitted.* In other words, there must be no uncertainty as to the reality of the connection of the circumstances of evidence with the *factum probandum*, or as to the sufficiency of the proof of the *corpus delicti*, or, supposing those points to be satisfactorily established, as to the personal complicity of the accused. This is in strictness hardly so much a distinct rule of evidence as a consequence naturally flowing from, and virtually comprehended in, the preceding rules. Indeed, it is more properly a test of the right ap-

* Reg. *v.* Manning and wife, C. C. C. Oct., 1849.

† See an able and interesting essay on the characteristics of English Law, Camb. Ess. 1857, p. 27.

plication of those rules to the facts of the particular case. The necessity and value of such test is manifest from the consideration of the numerous fallacies incidental to the formation of the judgment on indirect evidence and contingent probabilities, and from the impossibility in all cases of drawing the line between moral certainty and doubt. In questions of civil right the magistrate is obliged to decide according to the greatest amount of probability in favour of one or the other of the litigant parties; but where life or liberty are in the balance, it is neither just nor necessary that the accused should be convicted but upon conclusive evidence. While it is certain that circumstantial evidence is frequently most convincing and satisfactory, it must never be forgotten, as was remarked by that wise and upright magistrate, Sir Matthew Hale, that " persons really innocent may be entangled under such presumptions, that many times carry great probabilities of guilt;"* wherefore, as he justly concludes, " this kind of evidence must be very warily pressed." Many adverse appearances may be outweighed by a single favourable one, and all the probabilities of the case may not be before the court. The Lord Justice Clerk Cockburn, in his charge in the case of Madeleine Smith before mentioned, said, " I wish you to keep in mind that although you may not be satisfied with any of the theories that have been propounded on behalf of the prisoner, still nevertheless the case for the prosecution may be radically defective in evidence."† It is safer, therefore, as wisely said by Sir Matthew Hale, to err in acquitting than in convicting, and better that many guilty persons should escape, than that one inno-

---

* 2 P. C. ch. 39; see Rex v. Thornton, *ante.* p. 178.
† Report, *ut supra*, 281.

cent man should suffer.* Paley controverts the maxim, and urges that " he who falls by a mistaken sentence may be considered as falling for his country, while he suffers under the operation of those rules, by the general effect and tendency of which the welfare of the community is maintained and upheld."† There is no judicial enormity which may not be palliated or justified under colour of this execrable doctrine, which is calculated to confound all moral and legal distinctions ; its sophistry, absurdity, and injustice have been unanswerably exposed by one of the ablest of lawyers and most upright of men.‡ Justice never requires the sacrifice of a victim ; an erroneous sentence is calculated to produce incalculable and irreparable mischief to individuals, to destroy all confidence in the justice and integrity of the tribunals, and to introduce an alarming train of social evils as the inevitable result. Every consideration of truth, justice, and prudence requires, therefore, that where the guilt of the accused is not incontrovertibly established, however suspicious his conduct may have been, he shall be acquitted of legal accountability. No rule of procedure is more firmly established, as one of the great safeguards of truth and innocence, than the rule in question ; and it is the invariable practice of judges to advise juries to acquit whenever they entertain any fair and reasonable doubt. The doubt however must be not a trivial one, such as speculative ingenuity may raise, but a conscientious one which may operate upon the mind of a rational man acquainted with the affairs of life.§ " If," said Lord Chief Baron

* 2 P. C. c. 39.
† Mor. and Pol. Phil. b. vi. ch. 9.
‡ Romilly's Obs. on the C. L. of England, 72 ; Best on Pres. 292.
§ Per Mr. Baron Parke in Reg. *v.* Tawell, *ut supra.*

Pollock to the jury, in a late case, "the conclusion to which you are conducted be that there is that degree of certainty in the case that you would act upon it in your own grave and important concerns, that is the degree of certainty which the law requires, and which will justify you in returning a verdict of guilty."*

The rules of evidence, as founded on reason and consecrated in the judgments of the courts, constitute the best means for discovering truth, and are an integral part of our legal system, essential alike for private and social security. Nevertheless, language of most dangerous tendency in regard to them, has occasionally fallen from learned judges, which implies that they may be modified, according to the enormity of the crime, or the weightiness of the consequences which attach to conviction. Lord Finch, afterwards Lord Chancellor Nottingham, on the trial of Lord Cornwallis, said, " The fouler the crime is, the clearer and the plainer ought the proof to be."† "The more flagrant the crime is," said Mr. Baron Legge, " the more clearly and satisfactorily you will expect that it shall be made out to you."‡   Mr. Justice Holroyd is represented to have said, that " the greater the crime, the stronger is the proof required for conviction."§

Upon a trial for high treason, Lord Chief Justice Dallas, after adverting to the extreme guilt of the crime, as seeking the subversion of the established government, and

* Reg. v. Manning and Wife, C. C. C.. Oct. 1849 ; and see the language of Mr. Justice Parke in Doe d. Pattershall v. Turford, 3 B. & Ad. 897 ; of Lord Meadowbank in Reg. v. Humphreys, Swinton's Rep. 353 ; and of C. J. Shaw in Prof. Webster's Case, Bemis's Rep. 470.

† 7 St. Tr. 149, and see Rex v. Crossley, 26 St. Tr. 218.

‡ Rex v. Blandy, 18 St. Tr. 1186.

§ Rex v. Hobson, 1 Lewin's C. C. 261.

aiming at the property, the liberty, and the lives of all, said, " Still, however, nothing will depend upon the comparative magnitude of the offence ; for be it great or small, every man standing in the situation in which the prisoner is placed, is entitled to have the charge against him clearly and satisfactorily proved ; with only this difference (and I make the observation at the outset, as being in favour of the prisoner), that in proportion to the magnitude of the offence, and the consequences which result from his conviction, ought the proof to be clear and satisfactory."* In the case of the Glasgow cotton-spinners for conspiracy and murder, the learned Lord Justice Clerk Boyle said, that the magnitude of the charge ought to have no other effect than rendering it more necessary that the jury should be fully satisfied that the evidence is clear upon the subject.† The distinction was more broadly laid down by the late Lord Justice Clerk Cockburn, in Madeleine Smith's case. " In drawing an inference," said the learned judge, " you must always look to the import and character of the inference which you are asked to draw ;" and the same distinction pervades the whole of the charge in that celebrated case.

These dicta are opposed to the principles of reason, and inconsistent with all established rules of law. No legal doctrine is more firmly settled than that there is no difference between the rules of evidence in civil and criminal cases ; but if under any circumstances they may be relaxed according to notions of supposed expediency, they cease to be, in any correct and intelligible sense, rules for the discovery of truth, and the most valued rights of civilized men become the sport of chance. The

* Rex v. Ings, 33 St. Tr. 1135.
† Reg. v. Hanson and others, Court of Justiciary, 1838 ; Short-hand Rep. 366.

logical consequences of any such power of relaxation would be, that the rules of evidence are radically different in civil and criminal cases, and different even in criminal cases, as they are applied to particular classes of crime, according to some arbitrary and imaginary measure for estimating their relative enormity and penalty. Is the dictum, it may be asked, to be restricted to cases where the consequence of conviction may be loss of life? Is it to be repudiated when it may be followed by the inferior penalties of transportation or imprisonment? Is it to be applied or rejected in application to the numerous cases, civil as well as criminal, where physical and social consequences may follow, which, though of a different kind, may be scarcely less fatal to the individual than loss of liberty, or even of life itself? And if the maxims of evidence may be made more stringent in one direction, there is no reason why they may not be relaxed in another, according to the greater difficulties incidental to the proof of the more atrocious and dangerous forms of crime, as some writers on the civil law have actually maintained. A late noble and distinguished historical writer, whose opinions on every question of legal science or of constitutional principle, are eminently entitled to respect, with the strictest philosophical truth, and with great felicity of illustration, has thus denounced the doctrine under review:—"The rules of evidence no more depend on the magnitude of the interests at stake than the rules of arithmetic. We might as well say that we have a greater chance of throwing a size when we are playing for a penny, than when we are playing for a thousand pounds, as that a form of trial which is sufficient for the purposes of justice, in a matter of liberty and property, is insufficient in a matter affecting life.

Nay, if a mode of proceeding be too lax for capital cases, it is, *à priori*, too lax for all others; for in capital cases the principles of human nature will always afford considerable security. No judge is so cruel as he who indemnifies himself for scrupulosity in cases of blood, by license in affairs of smaller importance. The difference in tale on the one side far more than makes up for the difference in weight on the other."*

* 1 Macaulay's Ess. 143, 1st ed.

CHAPTER VII.

PROOF OF THE CORPUS DELICTI.

SECTION 1.

GENERAL DOCTRINE AS TO THE PROOF OF THE CORPUS DELICTI.

EVERY allegation of the commission of legal crime involves the establishment of two distinct propositions; namely, that an act has been committed from which legal responsibility arises, and that the guilt of such act attaches to a particular individual, though the evidence is not always separable into distinct parts, or applicable to each of those propositions.

Such a complication of difficulties occasionally attends the proof of crime, and so many cases have occurred of convictions for alleged offences which have never existed, that it is a fundamental and inflexible rule of legal procedure, of universal obligation, that no person shall be required to answer, or be involved in the consequences of guilt without satisfactory proof of the *corpus delicti*, either by direct evidence or by cogent and irresistible grounds of presumption.* If it be objected that rigorous proof of the *corpus delicti* is sometimes unattainable, and that the effect of exacting it must be, that crimes will occasionally pass unpunished, it must be admitted that

* Rex *v.* Burdett, 4 B. & Ald. 123.

such may possibly be the result; but, it is answered that, where there is no proof, or, which is the same thing, no sufficient legal proof of crime, there can be no legal criminality. In penal jurisdiction there can be no middle term; the party must be absolutely and unconditionally guilty or not guilty. Nor under any circumstances can considerations of supposed expediency ever supersede the immutable obligations of justice; and occasional impunity of crime is an evil of far less magnitude than the punishment of the innocent. Such considerations of mistaken policy led some of the writers on the civil and canon laws to modify their rules of evidence, according to the difficulties of proof incidental to particular crimes, and to adopt the execrable maxim, that the more atrocious was the offence, the slighter was the proof necessary; *in atrocissimis leviores conjecturæ sufficiunt, et licet judici jura transgredi.* Such indeed is the logical and inevitable consequence, when, from whatever motive, the plea of expediency is permitted to influence judicial integrity. The clearest principles of justice require, that whatever the nature of the crime, the amount and intensity of the proof shall in all cases be such as to produce the full assurance of moral certainty.*

SECTION 2.

PROOF OF THE CORPUS DELICTI BY CIRCUMSTANTIAL EVIDENCE.

But it is clearly established, that it is not necessary that the *corpus delicti* should be proved by direct and positive evidence, and it would be most unreasonable to require such evidence. Crimes, and especially those of the worst

---

* See *ante*, Ch. I. s. 3.

kinds, are naturally committed at chosen times, and in darkness and secrecy; and human tribunals must act upon such indications as the circumstances of the case present or admit, or society must be broken up. Nor is it very often that adequate evidence is not afforded by the attendant and surrounding facts, to remove all mystery, and to afford such a reasonable degree of certainty as men are daily accustomed to regard as sufficient in the most important concerns of life: to expect more would be equally needless and absurd. In Burdett's case* this subject underwent much discussion, and was elaborately treated by the Bench. Mr. Justice Best said, " When one or more things are proved from which experience enables us to ascertain that another, not proved, must have happened, we presume that it did happen, as well in criminal as in civil cases. Nor is it necessary that the fact not proved should be established by irrefragable inference. It is enough if its existence be highly probable, particularly if the opposite party has it in his power to rebut it by evidence, and yet offers none ; for then we have something like an admission that the presumption is just. It has been solemnly decided, that there is no difference between the rules of evidence in civil and criminal cases. If the rules of evidence prescribe the best course to get at truth, they must be and are the same in all cases and in all civilized countries. There is scarcely a criminal case, from the highest down to the lowest, in which courts of justice do not act upon this principle." His Lordship added, " It therefore appears to me quite absurd to state that we are not to act upon presumption. Until it pleases Providence to give us means beyond those our present faculties afford of knowing things done

* 4 B. & Ald. 95.

in secret, we must act on presumptive proof, or leave the worst crimes unpunished. I admit, where presumption is intended to be raised as to the *corpus delicti*, that it ought to be strong and cogent." Mr. Justice Holroyd said, "No man is to be convicted of any crime upon mere naked presumption. A light or rash presumption, not arising either necessarily, probably, or reasonably, from the facts proved, cannot avail in law. But crimes of the highest nature, more especially cases of murder, are established, and convictions and executions thereupon frequently take place for guilt most convincingly and conclusively proved, upon presumptive evidence only of the guilt of the party accused; and the well-being and security of society much depend upon the receiving and giving due effect to such proof. The presumptions arising from those proofs should, no doubt, and most especially in cases of great magnitude, be duly and correctly weighed. They stand only as proofs of the facts presumed till the contrary be proved, and those presumptions are either weaker or stronger according as the party has, or is reasonably to be supposed to have it in his power to produce other evidence to rebut or to weaken them, in case the fact so presumed be not true, and according as he does or does not produce such contrary evidence." Mr. Justice Bayley said, "No one can doubt that presumptions may be made in criminal as well as in civil cases. It is constantly the practice to act upon them, and I apprehend that more than one-half of the persons convicted of crimes, are convicted on presumptive evidence. If a theft has been committed, and shortly afterwards the property is found in the possession of a person who can give no account of it, it is presumed that he is the thief, and so in other criminal cases; but the question always is, whether there are sufficient premises to warrant the conclusion." Lord Chief Justice Abbott said, " A fact must not be inferred without premises which will warrant the inference; but if no fact could be thus ascertained by inference in a court of law, very few offences would be brought to punishment. In a great proportion of trials, as they occur in practice, no direct proof that the party accused actually committed the crime, is or can be given; the man who is charged with theft, is rarely seen to break the house or take the goods; and in cases of murder, it rarely happens that the eye of any witness sees the fatal blow struck, or the poisonous ingredient poured into the cup." The law on this point was also very emphatically declared by Mr Baron Parke in Tawell's case. His Lordship said, " The jury had been properly told by the counsel for the prosecution, that circumstantial evidence is the only evidence which can in cases of this kind lead to discovery. There is no way of investigating them except by the use of circumstantial evidence; but Providence has so ordered the affairs of men that it most frequently happens that great crimes committed in secret leave behind them some traces, or are accompanied by some circumstances which lead to the discovery and punishment of the offender;* therefore the law has wisely provided that you need not have, in cases of this kind, direct proof, that is, the proof of eye-witnesses, who see the fact and can depose to it upon their oaths. It is impossible, however, not to say

* " Ces circonstances sont autant de témoins muets, que la Providence semble avoir placés autour du crime, pour fair jaillir la lumière de l'ombre dans laquelle l'agent s'est efforcé d'ensevelir le fait principal ; elles sont comme un fanal qui éclaire l'esprit du juge, et le dirige vers des traces certains, qu'il suffit de suivre pour atteindre à la vérité."— Mittermaier, *ut supra*, ch. 53.

that is the best proof, if that proof is offered to you upon
the testimony of men whose veracity you have no reason
to doubt ; but on the other hand it is equally true with
regard to circumstantial evidence, that the circumstances
may often be so clearly proved, so closely connected with
it, or leading to one result in conclusion, that the mind
may be as well convinced as if it were proved by eye-
witnesses.   This being a case of circumstantial evidence,
I advise you," said the learned judge, " as I invariably
advise juries, to act upon a rule, that you are first to
consider what facts are clearly, distinctly, indisputably
proved to your satisfaction ; and you are to consider
whether those facts are consistent with any other rational
supposition than that the prisoner is guilty of that offence.
If you think that the facts in this case are all consistent
with the supposition that the prisoner is guilty, and can
offer no resistance to that, except the character the prisoner has borne, and except the supposition that no man
would be guilty of so atrocious a crime as that laid to the
charge of the prisoner, that cannot much influence your
minds ; for we all know that crimes are committed, and
therefore the existence of the crime is no inconsistency
with the other circumstances, if those circumstances lead
to that result. The point for you to consider is, whether,
attending to the evidence, you can reconcile the circumstances adduced in evidence with any other supposition
than that he has been guilty of the offence? If you cannot, it is your bounden duty to find him guilty; if you
can, then you will give him the benefit of such a supposition.   All that can be required is,—not absolute, positive proof,—but such proof as convinces you that the
crime has been made out."*

* Reg. v. Tawell, ut supra.

The same general principle prevails with regard to the proof of crimes of every description, and of every element of the *corpus delicti*. Thus, on the trial of a man for stealing pepper, it appeared that on the first floor of a warehouse a large quantity of pepper was kept in bulk, and that the prisoner was met coming out of the lower room of the warehouse where he had no business to be, having on him a quantity of pepper of the same description with that in the room above. On being stopped he threw down the pepper, and said, "I hope you will not be hard with me." From the large quantity in the warehouse it could not be proved that any pepper had been taken from the bulk. It was urged on behalf of the prisoner that there must be direct and positive evidence of a *corpus delicti*, and that presumptive evidence was insufficient for that purpose; but the Court of Criminal Appeal held that the prisoner had been rightly convicted.* Mr. Justice Maule said that the offence with which the prisoner is charged must be proved, and that involves the necessity of proving that the prosecutor's goods have been taken. But why, continued the learned Judge, is that to be differently proved from the rest of the case? If the circumstances satisfy the jury, what rule is there which renders some more positive and direct proof necessary? And he mentioned the case of a father and two sons, who were convicted of stealing from their employers a quantity of shoes and materials for making shoes, though the prosecutors said their stock was so large that they could not say they had missed any one of the articles alleged to have been stolen.†

But it is not necessary that every individual fact should

---

* Reg. *v.* Burton, 23 L. J. N. S. M. C. 52; and see Reg. *v.* Dredge, 1 Cox, 235; and *ante*, 108.   † *Ibid.*

be indisputably proved. On a trial for forgery, in Scotland, Lord Meadowbank said :—"I must tell you that the learned counsel for the panel stated the law incorrectly; when he said that you must have decisive, irrefragable, and conclusive proof of every point in a case like the present, before finding the instrument to be forged. The law is quite the reverse. You are to take all the evidence together, and you are bound to consider whether it amounts and comes up to affording a moral conviction in your minds equivalent to the positive and direct proof of a fact."[*]

SECTION 3.

APPLICATION OF THE GENERAL PRINCIPLE TO PROOF OF THE CORPUS DELICTI IN CASES OF HOMICIDE.

THE general principles of evidence under discussion are so supremely important in reference to cases of homicide, that it will be expedient to illustrate the application of them at some length.

(1) The discovery of the body necessarily affords the best evidence of the fact of death, and of the identity of the individual, and most frequently also of the cause of death.[†] A conviction for murder is therefore never allowed to take place, unless the body has been found, or there is equivalent proof of death by circumstantial evidence leading directly to that result,[‡] and many cases have shown the danger of a contrary practice. Three persons were executed in the year 1660, for the murder of a person who had suddenly disappeared,[§] but about two

---

[*] Reg. v. Humphreys, *ut supra.*

[†] Mittermaier, *ut supra,* ch. 24.

[‡] Per Mr. Baron Parke, in Reg. v. Tawell, *ut supra.*

[§] Rex v. Perrys, 14 St. Tr. 1312; and see 11 St. Tr. 463; see also the Scotch case of Green and others, 14 St. Tr. 1197, where, in 1705, the

years afterwards he reappeared. It appeared that he had been out to collect his mistress's rents, and had been robbed by highwaymen, who put him on board a ship which was captured by Turkish pirates, by whom he was sold into slavery. Sir Matthew Hale mentioned a case where A. was long missing, and upon strong presumptions B. was supposed to have murdered him, and to have consumed the body to ashes in an oven, whereupon B. was indicted of murder, and convicted, and executed; and within one year afterwards A. returned, having been sent beyond sea by B. against his will; "and so," that learned writer adds, "though B. justly deserved death, yet he was really not guilty of that offence for which he suffered."* Sir Edward Coke also gives the case of a man who was executed for the murder of his niece, who was afterwards found to be living, of which the particulars have been given in a former part of this Essay.† Sir Matthew Hale, on account of these cases, says, " I will never convict any person of murder or manslaughter, unless the fact were proved to be done, or at least the body found.‡ The judicial history of all nations, in all times, abounds with similar warnings and exemplifications of the danger of neglecting these salutary cautions.§

But, nevertheless, to require the discovery of the body in all cases would be unreasonable and lead to absurdity

captain of a vessel and several of his crew were executed on a charge of piracy and murder ; but the party supposed to have been murdered reappeared many years afterwards, having been taken at sea and carried into captivity.

* 2 Hale's P. C. c. 39.

† See *ante*, p. 155; and for other cases of the same kind, see Green's case, 14 St. Tr. 1311.

‡ 2 P. C. ch. 39.

§ See the case of the two Boorns, 1 Greenleaf's L. of Ev. § 214, and *ante*, p. 71.

and injustice, and it is indeed frequently rendered impossible by the act of the offender himself. It is said that on the trial for murder of the mother and reputed father of a bastard child, whom they had stripped and thrown into the dock of a seaport town, after which it was never seen again, Mr. Justice Gould advised an acquittal on the ground that as the tide of the sea flowed and reflowed into and out of the dock it might possibly have carried out the living infant.* Mr. Justice Story said of the proposition in question that "it certainly cannot be admitted as correct in point of common reason or of law, unless courts of justice are to establish a positive rule to screen persons from punishment who may be guilty of the most flagitious offences. In the cases of murder committed on the high seas the body is rarely if ever found, and a more complete encouragement and protection to the worst offences of this sort, could not be invented than a rule of this strictness. It would amount to a universal condonation of all murders committed on the high seas."† It is now clearly established that the fact of death may be legally inferred from such strong and unequivocal circumstances of presumption as render it morally certain, and leave no ground for reasonable doubt; as where, on the trial of a mariner for the murder of his captain at sea, a witness stated that the prisoner had proposed to kill him, and that, being alarmed in the night by a violent noise, he went upon deck and saw the prisoner throw the captain overboard, and that he was not seen or heard of afterwards, and that near the place on the deck where the captain was, a billet of wood was

* Per Garrow *arguendo* in Hindmarsh's case, 2 Leach's C. C. 371.

† United States *v.* Gilbert, 2 Sumner, 19, quoted in Berrill on Cir. Ev. 679.

found, and that the deck and part of the prisoner's dress were stained with blood. It was urged that, as there were many vessels near the place where the transaction was alleged to have occurred, the probability was that the party had been taken up by some of them and was then alive ; but the Court, though it admitted the general rule of law, left it to the jury to say upon the evidence, whether the deceased was not killed before the body was cast into the sea, and the jury being of that opinion, the prisoner was convicted and executed ;* but it is not easy to perceive why the natural presumption from these facts should have been thus restricted to a presumption that the party had been killed before he was thrown overboard.

The rule and its qualifications are well exemplified by the case of Elizabeth Ross, who was tried for the murder of Caroline Walsh. The deceased had been repeatedly solicited by the prisoner to live with her and her husband, but had refused. However she at last consented, and went for that purpose to the prisoner's lodgings, in Goodman's Fields, in the evening of the 19th of August 1831, taking with her her bed and an old basket, in which she was accustomed to carry tape and other articles for sale. Notwithstanding all inquiry, from that evening all traces of the deceased were lost, and when the prisoner was required by her relatives to account for her disappearance she prevaricated, but finally asserted that she had gone out early in the morning of the next day, and had not returned. Many circumstances confirmed their suspicions that she had been murdered, and in the month of October the prisoner was apprehended, and charged with the murder of the old woman. From

* Rex v. Hindmarsh, 2 Leach's C. C. 648.

the testimony of the prisoner's son, a boy of twelve years of age, it appeared that she had suffocated the deceased on the evening of her arrival, by placing her hands over her mouth, and pressing on her chest; and he deposed that the following morning he saw the dead body in the cellar of the house, and that in the evening he saw his mother leave the house with something large and heavy in a sack. A medical man deposed that the means described would be sufficient to cause death. It happened most singularly that on the evening of the day following that of the alleged murder, an old woman was found lying in the street in the immediate neighbourhood, in a completely exhausted condition, and in a most filthy and squalid state. On being questioned she stated that her name was Caroline Welsh, and that she was a native of Ireland. Her hip was found to be fractured, in consequence of which she was conveyed to the London Hospital, where she subsequently died. The prisoner when apprehended insisted that this was the female whom she was accused of having murdered. The resemblance of names and the coincidence of time were very remarkable, but by the examination of numerous witnesses the following points of difference were established. They were both Irishwomen; but Caroline Walsh came from Kilkenny; Caroline Welsh from Waterford. Walsh was eighty-four years of age, tall, of a sallow complexion, grey hair, and had very perfect incisor teeth in both jaws, having lost only a side tooth in the upper and lower jaws from the effect of continual smoking with a tobacco-pipe. Welsh (the woman who died in the hospital) was about sixty years of age, tall, dark like a mulatto, but had no front teeth, and the alveolar cavities corresponding to them had been obliterated for a considerable time. Walsh was healthy, cleanly, and neat in her person, and her feet were perfectly sound; Welsh was considerably emaciated; in a dirty and filthy condition; her hip broken, her feet covered with bunions and excrescences, and the toes overlapped one another. The two women were differently dressed : Walsh was dressed in a black stuff gown, a broken old willow bonnet, and a faded blue shawl with a broad border; Welsh wore a striped blue cotton gown, a dark or black silk bonnet, and a snuff-coloured shawl with little or no border. Walsh's clothing was proved to have been sold by the prisoner to different persons, and almost every article was produced in court and identified. The clothes of Welsh, on account of their disgusting condition, had been burnt by order of the parish authorities. Both of these women had similar baskets : that of Walsh had no lid or cover, while that found on Welsh had. Lastly, the body of the latter was taken up from the burial-ground of the London Hospital for the purpose of identification, and it was sworn by two of the granddaughters of Walsh not to be the body of their grandmother. The prisoner was convicted and executed.* The corpse of the murdered woman was most probably sold by the prisoner for the purpose of dissection; and other murders were committed about the same time both in England and Scotland from the same motive.†

(2) It is another necessary step in the establishment of the *corpus delicti* in cases of homicide, that the body, when discovered, be satisfactorily identified as that of the person whose death is the subject of inquiry. Mr.

* R. *v.* Ross, O. B. Sess. Pap. 1831.

† See Rex *v.* Burke, Alison, *ut supra*, p. 74, Syme's Jud. Rep. 345. Rex *v.* Bishop and others. O. B. Sess. Pap. 1832.

Justice Park stopped the trial of a woman, charged with the murder of her illegitimate child, because the supposed body was nothing but a mass of corruption, so that there were no lineaments of the human face, and it was impossible even to distinguish its sex.*   On the trial of a woman for the murder of her brother, a child eight years of age, by poison, the sexton proved the interment on the 29th of June, and the exhumation on the 12th of August following, of a body which he believed to be that of the deceased, from the coffin plate, and the place from which he had exhumed it, but he had not seen the body in the coffin at the time of interment, and could not recognize it independently of those circumstancces, on account of its state of decay.   Mr. Baron Maule refused to receive evidence of the contents of the coffin plate, on the ground that, being removable, it ought to have been produced, and there being no other evidence of identity stopped the case.†   On the trial of a girl for the murder of her illegitimate child, it appeared that she was proceeding from Bristol to Llandago, and was seen near Tintern at six o'clock in the evening, with the child in her arms, and that she arrived at Llandago between eight and nine without it, and that the body of a child was afterwards found in the river Wye near Tintern, but which appeared from circumstances not to be the prisoner's child; Lord Abinger held that the prisoner could not be called upon to account for her child, or to say where it was, unless there was evidence to show that her child was actually dead; the jury were not sitting, he said, to inquire what the prisoner had done with her child, which might be

* See Mr. Justice Park's charge to the grand jury in Rex v. Thurtell, Hertford winter assizes, 1824; Reg. v. Edge, *ante*, p. 187.

† Reg. v. Edge, *ante*, p. 187; and see Reg. v. Henley, 1 Cox, C. C. 112.

then alive and well.* In a similar case Mr. Baron Bramwell observed that the evidence of identity was not complete; that still, if the jury thought there was reasonable evidence upon the point, they might think that if the child was still alive the prisoner would probably produce it in a case where her life was at stake, but that she was at liberty to act upon the defect of proof, and to say that the prosecutor had failed to prove the identity.†

But, nevertheless, it is not necessary that the remains should be identified by direct and positive evidence, where such proof is impracticable, and especially if it has been rendered so by the act of the party accused. A man was convicted of the murder of a creditor who had called to obtain payment of a debt, and whose body he had cut into pieces and attempted to dispose of by burning; the effluvium and other circumstances alarmed the neighbours, and a portion of the body remained unconsumed, sufficient to prove that it was that of a male adult; and various articles which had belonged to the deceased were found on the person of the prisoner, who was apprehended putting off from the Black Rock at Liverpool, after having ineffectually endeavoured to elude justice by drowning himself.‡ The remains of a man which had lain undiscovered upwards of twenty-three years, were identified by his surviving widow from peculiarities in the teeth and skull, and from a carpenter's rule found with them.§ The identification of human remains has been facilitated by the preservation of the head and other parts

* Reg. v. Hopkins, 8 C. and P. 591.

† Reg. v. Rudge, Hereford Summer Assizes, 1857.

‡ Rex v. Cook, Leicester Summer Assizes, 1834; and see Reg. v. Good, Sess. Pap., May, 1842.

§ Rex v. Clewes, Worcester Spring Assizes. 1830, *coram* Mr. Justice Littledale.

in spirits;* by the antiputrescent action of the substances
used to destroy life; by the similarity of the undigested
remains of food found in the stomach, with the food
which it has been known that the party has eaten,† by
means of clothing or other articles of the deceased traced
to the possession of the prisoner, and unexplained by any
evidence that he became innocently possessed of them;‡
by means of artificial teeth,§ and by numerous other mechanical coincidences.

(3) In the proof of criminal homicide the true cause
of death must be clearly established; and the possibility
of accounting for the event by self-inflicted violence, accident or natural cause, excluded; and only when it has
been irrefragably proved that no other hypothesis will explain all the conditions of the case, can it be safely and
justly concluded, that it has been caused by intentional
injury.   But in accordance with the principles which
govern the proof of every other element of the *corpus
delicti*, it is not necessary that the cause of death should
be verified by direct and positive evidence; it is sufficient
if it be proved by circumstantial evidence, which produces
a moral conviction in the minds of the jury, equivalent
to that which is the result of positive and direct evidence.‖

Suicide, accident, and natural causes are frequently
suggested and plausibly urged, as the causes of death,
where the pretence cannot receive direct contradiction,
and where the truth can be ascertained only by a compa-

* Rex *v*. Hayes and others, 3 Par. and F. 73.
† Rex *v*. MacDougal, Burnett's C. L. of Scotl. p. 540.
‡ Rex *v*. Ross, *ante*, p. 209; Reg. *v*. Good. Sess. Pap., May, 1842.
§ Reg. *v*. Manning and wife, and Webster's case, *ut supra*.
‖ See the language of Lord Meadowbank in Reg. *v*. Humphreys,
Swinton's Rep. 315.

rison of all the attendant circumstances; some of which, if the defence be false, are commonly found to be irreconcilable with the cause alleged. A young woman who had borne a child to him, was taken by her seducer from her father's house under the pretence of conveying her to Ipswich to be married. The prisoner having represented that the parish officers meant to apprehend the deceased, she left her house on the 18th of May in disguise, a bag containing her own clothes having been taken by the prisoner to a barn belonging to his mother, where it was agreed that she should change her dress. The deceased was never heard of afterwards; and the various and contradictory accounts given of her by the prisoner having excited suspicious, which were confirmed by other circumstances, it was ultimately determined to search the barn; where, on the 19th of April, after an interval of nearly twelve months, the body of a female was found, which was clearly identified as that of the deceased. A handkerchief was drawn tight round the neck, and a wound from a pistol-ball was traced through the left cheek, passing out at the right orbit; and three other wounds were found, all of which had been made by a sharp instrument, and one of which had entered the heart. The prisoner, who in the interval had removed from the neighbourhood, upon his apprehension denied all knowledge of the deceased; but in his defence he admitted the identity of the remains, and alleged that an altercation took place between them at the barn, in consequence of which, and of the violence of temper exhibited by the deceased, he expressed his determination not to marry her, and left the barn; but that immediately afterwards he heard the report of a pistol, and going back found the deceased on the ground apparently dead;

and that, alarmed by the situation in which he found himself, he formed the determination of burying the corpse and accounting for her absence as well as he could. But the variety of the means and instruments employed to produce death, some of them unusual with females, in connection with the contradictory statements made by the prisoner to account for the absence of the deceased, entirely discredited the account set up by him. He afterwards made a full confession, and was executed pursuant to his sentence.[*] But these heads of evidence belong rather to the department of medical jurisprudence. Such auxiliary evidence is frequently of the highest value in demonstrating the falsehood and impossibility of the alleged defence; but, when uncorroborated by conclusive moral circumstances, it must be received with a certain amount of circumspection and reserve, of the necessity for which some striking illustrations have occurred in other parts of this essay.[†] These preliminary considerations naturally lead to the application of them to the proof of the *corpus delicti* in some special cases of great importance and interest.

SECTION 4.

APPLICATION OF THE GENERAL PRINCIPLE TO THE PROOF OF THE CORPUS DELICTI IN CASES OF POISONING.

THERE are two classes of cases of criminal homicide, in which the cause of death can rarely be proved by direct evidence, and in which the proof of it by circumstantial

* Rex *v.* Corder, Bury St. Edmund's Summ. Ass.
† See particularly, Rex *v.* Booth and Reg. *v.* Newton, *ante*, c. s.

evidence is attended with peculiar difficulties; those, namely, of poisoning and infanticide. An examination of the principles on which courts of law proceed in the investigation of such cases, will afford an instructive commentary upon the foregoing principles of evidence and procedure.

1. Among the most important grounds upon which the proof of criminal poisoning commonly rests are, the symptoms during life, and *post-mortem* appearances; but these subjects belong to another department of science, and have only an incidental connection with the subject of this treatise. As is the case with regard to all other questions of science, courts of justice must derive their knowledge from the testimony of persons who have made them the objects of their special duty, applying to the *data* thus obtained those principles of interpretation and judgment which constitute the tests of truth in all other cases.

It is obviously essential that the particular symptoms and *post-mortem* appearances should be shown to be not incompatible with the hypothesis of death from poison. In general such appearances are inconclusive, since though they are commonly characteristic of death from poison, they not unfrequently resemble the appearance of disease, and may have been produced by some natural cause. Nevertheless, as to some particular poisons, the symptoms may be so characteristic as to afford unmistakeable evidence of poisoning, and preclude all possibility of referring the event of death to any other cause. Thus in Palmer's case, it was conclusively shown by numerous witnesses of the greatest professional experience, that the symptoms in the course of their progress were clearly distinguishable from those of tetanus or any other known form of disease, and were not only consistent with, but specially characteristic of, poisoning by strychnine.*

It is a very important circumstance in corroboration of the reality of alleged poisoning, if several persons are simultaneously affected with symptoms indicative of poisoning, after partaking of the same food, as when four members of a family were taken ill after having eaten of yeast dumplings made by the prisoner, who was the cook, while those members of it who had not partaken of them were not affected.†

The probability in such cases is greatly strengthened if the violence of the symptoms has been in proportion to the quantities of the suspected food taken by the parties;‡ and on the other hand, a favourable presumption is created, if only one member of a family is taken ill after partaking of food of which other members of it have eaten with impunity.§

From the nature of the case, these elements of proof never occur alone; but are necessarily blended with facts of a more conclusive character.

* In a late case involving much conflicting evidence as to morbid appearances supposed to have been indicative of death by slow poisoning, a pardon was granted after conviction, on the ground of the imperfection of medical science, and of the fallibility of judgment, with respect to an obscure malady, even of skilful and experienced medical practitioners. Reg. v. Smethurst, C. C. C. Sess. Pap. Aug. 1859.

† Rex v. Fenning, *ut supra.* The evidence against this young girl was most unsatisfactory, and she was long thought to have been unjustly convicted (3 Mem. of Romilly, 235; Suggestions for the Repression of Crime, by M. D. Hill, 31), but it has been recently stated on good authority that she made a confession to a minister of religion, who had her confidence (see the 'Times' Newspaper of Aug. 5, 1857). It is unaccountable that the statement should have been withheld, and the public suffered to remain for nearly half a century under the belief that she was wrongfully executed.

‡ Rex v. Alcorn, 1 Syme's Just. Rep. 221.

§ Rex v. Bickle, Exeter Summ. Ass. 1834, *coram* Mr. Justice Patteson.

2. The possession of poisonous matter by the party charged with the administration of it, is always an important fact, and when death has been caused by poison of the same kind, and no satisfactory explanation of that fact is given by the accused or suggested by the surrounding circumstances, a strong inference of guilt may be created against the accused; especially if he has attempted to account for such possession by false statements. In Palmer's case, Lord Chief Justice Campbell said that if the jury should come to the conclusion that the symptoms which the deceased had exhibited were consistent with strychnia, a fearful case was made out against the prisoner. "I have listened," said the learned Judge, "with the most anxious attention to know what explanation would be given respecting the strychnia that has been purchased by the prisoner. There is no evidence of the intention with which it was purchased, there is no evidence how it was applied, what became of it, or what was done with it."*

3. Not only must it appear that the accused possessed the deadly agent, but it is indispensable to show that he had the *opportunity* of administering it. Upon the effect of these heads of evidence, and upon the caution with which they ought to be received, some valuable observations were made by Mr. Baron Rolfe in a case before him. The prisoner was indicted for the murder of his wife, who was taken ill on the morning of the 25th of November, and died two days afterwards with symptoms resembling those of an irritant poison. Poisoning not having been suspected, the body was interred without examination; but suspicions having afterwards arisen, it was exhumed in the month of June following, and a large quantity of

* Report, *ut supra*, 313.

arsenic was discovered in the stomach. Several weeks
after the apprehension of the prisoner, the police took
possession of some of his garments, which were found
hanging up in his lodgings, in the pockets of which arsenic was found. In his address to the jury, Mr. Baron
Rolfe said, " Had the prisoner the opportunity of administering poison?—that was one thing. Had he any
motive to do so?—that was another. There was also
another question, which was most important ; it was
whether the party who had the opportunity of administering poison had poison to administer? If he had not the
poison, the having the opportunity became unimportant.
If he had the poison, then another question arose,—did
he get it under circumstances to show that it was for a
guilty or improper object? The evidence by which it
was attempted to trace poison to the possession of the
prisoner was, that on a certain occasion, after the death
of the wife, and after he himself was apprehended, the
contents of the pockets of a coat, waistcoat, and trousers,
on being tested by the medical witnesses, were found to
contain arsenic ; and that, a week afterwards, another
waistcoat which came into the possession of the policeman, on being examined, was also found to contain arsenic.
Did that bring home to the prisoner the fact that he had
arsenic in his possession in November? It was not conclusive that, because he had it in June, he had it in
November. He (the learned Judge) inferred from what
had been stated by the medical men, that the quantity
of arsenic found in the pockets of the clothes was very
small. Now, if he had it in a larger quantity in November, and it had been used for some purpose, being a
mineral substance, such particles were likely to remain
in the pockets, and finding it there in June was certainly

evidence that it might have been there in larger quantity in November; but obviously, by no means conclusive, as it might have been put in afterwards. But connected with the arsenic being found in the clothes, there were other considerations which he thought were worthy to be attended to. The prisoner was apprehended on the 9th of June, and he knew long before that time that an inquiry was going on. He was taken up, not in the clothes in which the arsenic was found; and a fortnight afterwards a batch of clothes was given up in which arsenic was detected. Now, if arsenic had been found in the clothes he was wearing, it would be perfectly certain, in the ordinary sense, that he had arsenic in his possession. But it was going a step further to say that because arsenic was discovered in clothes of his, accessible to so many people between the time of his apprehension and their being given up, it was there when he was apprehended; in all probability, he thought, it was, but that was by no means the necessary consequence. That observation was entitled to still more weight, with regard to the waistcoat last given up to the police, because it was not given up till three weeks after the prisoner was apprehended, and had been hanging in the kitchen, accessible to a variety of persons. . . . It was urged also that arsenic was used for cattle. It might be so, and it might be that the prisoner might innocently have had arsenic. The circumstance of there being arsenic in so many pockets ought not to be lost sight of, for it could scarcely be conceived that a guilty person should be so utterly reckless as to put the poison he used into every pocket he had. One would have thought that he would have kept it concealed, or put it only in some safe place for the immediate purpose of being used; and it was worthy of observation that it did not appear to have been put into the clothes in such a way as it would have been put had the prisoner been desirous to conceal it."   The prisoner was acquitted.*

In a late case of the deepest interest, before the High Court of Justiciary at Edinburgh, a question whether or not the prisoner had the opportunity of administering arsenic to the deceased was the turning-point of the case. The prisoner, a young girl of nineteen, was tried upon an indictment charging her, in accordance with the law of Scotland, with the administration to the same person of arsenic, with intent to murder, on two several occasions in the month of February, and with his murder by the same means on the 22nd of March following. She had returned home from a boarding-school in 1853, and in the following year formed a clandestine connection with a foreigner of inferior position, named L'Angelier, whose addresses had been forbidden by her parents, which early in 1856 became of a criminal character, as was shown by her letters.   In the month of December following, another suitor appeared, whose addresses were accepted by her with the consent of her parents, and arrangements were made for their marriage in June. During the earlier part of this engagement, the prisoner kept up her interviews and correspondence with L'Angelier; but the correspondence gradually became cooler, and she expressed to him her determination to break off the connection, and implored him to return her letters; but this he refused to do, and declared that she should marry no other person while he lived.   After the failure of her efforts to obtain the return of her letters, she resumed in her correspondence her former tone of passionate affection, assuring him that she would marry him

* Reg. v. Graham, Carlisle Summer Assizes, 1845.

and no one else, and denying that there was any truth in the rumours of her connection with another. She appointed a meeting on the night of the 19th of February, at her father's house, where she was in the habit of receiving his visits, after the family had retired to rest, telling him that she wished to have back her "cool letters," apparently with the intention of inducing him to believe that she remained constant in her attachment to him. In the middle of the night after that interview, at which he had taken coffee prepared by the prisoner, L'Angelier was seized with alarming illness, the symptoms of which were similar to those of poisoning by arsenic. There was no evidence that the prisoner possessed arsenic at that time, but on the 21st she purchased a large quantity, professedly for the purpose of poisoning rats, an excuse for which there was no pretence. On the night of the 22nd, L'Angelier again visited the prisoner, and about eleven o'clock on the following day was seized with the same alarming symptoms as before; and on this occasion also he had taken cocoa from the hands of the prisoner. After this attack L'Angelier continued extremely ill, and was advised to go from home for the recovery of his health.

On the 6th of March the prisoner a second time bought arsenic; and on the same day she went with her family to the Bridge of Allan, (where she was visited by her accepted lover,) and remained till the 17th, when they returned to Glasgow. On the day before her departure for the Bridge of Allan, L'Angelier wrote a letter to her, in which he reproached her for the manner in which she had evaded answering the questions which he had put to her in a former letter respecting her rumoured engagement with another person, expressed his conviction that there was foundation for the report, and after repeating his inquiries threatened, if she again evaded them, to try some other means of coming at the truth. To this letter, the prisoner, although she had been engaged nearly two months, and was receiving the visits of her affianced at the Bridge of Allan, from which place she wrote, replied that there was no foundation for the report, and that she would answer all his questions when they met, and informed him of her expected return to Glasgow on the 17th of March. L'Angelier, pursuant to medical advice, on the 10th of March went to Edinburgh, leaving directions for the transmission of his letters, and having become much better, left that place on the 19th for the Bridge of Allan. During this interval, namely, on the 17th, he returned to his lodgings at Glasgow, and inquired anxiously of his landlady if there was no letter waiting for him, as the prisoner's family were to be at home on that day, and she was to write to fix another interview. He left Glasgow again on Thursday the 19th for the Bridge of Allan, leaving directions as before for the transmission to him of any letter which might come for him during his absence. On the 18th of March, the prisoner a third time purchased a large quantity of arsenic, alleging, as before, that it was for the purpose of killing rats. A letter from the prisoner to L'Angelier came to his lodgings on Saturday the 21st, from the date and contents of which it appeared that she had written a letter appointing to see him on the 19th; he had not, however, received it in time to enable him to keep her appointment. In that letter she urged him to come to see her, and added, "I waited and waited for you, but you came not. I shall wait again to-morrow night, same time and arrangement." This letter was immediately transmitted to L'Angelier, and in consequence he returned to his lodgings at Glasgow about eight o'clock on the evening of Sunday the 22nd, in high spirits and improved health, having travelled a considerable distance by railway, and walked fifteen miles. He left his lodgings about nine o'clock, and was seen going leisurely in the direction of the prisoner's house, and about twenty minutes past nine he called at the house of an acquaintance who lived about four or five minutes' walk from the prisoner's residence. After leaving his friend's house, all trace of him was lost, until two o'clock in the morning, when he was found at the door of his lodgings, unable to open the latch, doubled up and speechless from pain and exhaustion, and about eleven o'clock the same morning he died, from the effects of arsenic, of which an enormous quantity was found in his body. The prisoner stated in her declaration that she had been in the habit of using arsenic as a cosmetic, and denied that she had seen the deceased on that eventful night; whether she had done so or not was the all-momentous question. As there was no evidence that the prisoner possessed poison at the time of the first illness, nor any analysis made of the matter ejected on either the first or second illness, the learned Lord Justice Clerk Cockburn said, that there was no proof of the administration of poison on either of those occasions; that the first charge therefore had entirely failed, and that it was safer not to hold that the second illness was caused by poison. As to the principal charge of murder, his Lordship said, " Supposing the jury were quite satisfied that the prisoner's letter brought L'Angelier again into Glasgow, were they in a situation to say, with satisfaction to their consciences, that as an inevitable and just result from this, they could find it proved that the pri-

soner and deceased had met that night?—that was the
point in the case. But it is for you to say here, whether
it has been proved that L'Angelier was in the house that
night. If you can hold that that link in the chain is
supplied by just and satisfactory inference,—remember
that I say, just and satisfactory,—and it is for you to say
whether the inference is satisfactory and just, in order to
complete the proof ;—if you really feel that you may have
the strongest suspicion that he saw her,—for really no one
need hesitate to say that, as a matter of moral opinion,
the whole probabilities of the case are in favour of it—
but if that is all the amount that you can derive from
the evidence, the link still remains wanting in the chain,
the catastrophe and the alleged cause of it are not found
linked together. And therefore you must be satisfied
that you can here stand and rely upon the firm foundation, I say, of a just and sound, and perhaps I may add,
inevitable inference. That a jury is entitled often to draw
such an inference there is no doubt. . . If you find this
to be a satisfactory and just inference, I cannot tell you
that you are not at liberty to act upon it, because most
of the matters occurring in life must depend upon circumstantial evidence, and upon the inferences which a
jury may feel bound to draw. But it is an inference of
a very serious character,—it is an inference upon which
the death of this party by the hand of the prisoner really
must depend. And then, you will take all the other circumstances of the case into your consideration, and see
whether you can infer from them that they met. If you
think they met together that night, and he was seized
and taken ill, and died of arsenic, the symptoms beginning shortly after the time he left her, it will be for you
to say, whether in that case there is any doubt as to

whose hand administered the poison." In another part of his charge the learned Judge said :—" In the ordinary matters of life, when you find the man came to town for the purpose of getting a meeting, you may come to the conclusion that they did meet; but, observe that becomes a very serious inference indeed to draw in a case where you are led to suppose that there was an administration of poison and death resulting therefrom. It may be a very natural inference, looking at the thing morally. None of you can doubt that she waited for him again; and if she waited the second night, after her first letter, it was not surprising that she should look out for an interview on the second night, after the second letter. . . . She says, ' I shall wait again to-morrow night, same hour and arrangement.' And I say there is no doubt—but it is a matter for the jury to consider—that after writing this letter he might expect she would wait another night —that is the observation I made, and therefore it was very natural that he should go to see her that Sunday night.

"But, as I said to you, this is an inference only. If you think it such a just and satisfactory inference that you can rest your verdict upon it, it is quite competent for you to draw such an inference from such letters as these, and from the conduct of the man coming to Glasgow for the purpose of seeing her—for it is plain that that was his object in coming to Glasgow. It is sufficiently proved that he went out immediately after he got some tea and toast, and had changed his coat. But then, gentlemen, in drawing an inference, you must always look to the important character of the inference which you are asked to draw. If this had been an appointment about business, and you found that a man came to

Glasgow for the purpose of seeing another upon business, and that he went out for that purpose, having no other object in coming to Glasgow, you would probably scout the notion of the person whom he had gone to meet saying, I never saw or heard of him that day; but the inference which you are asked to draw is this, namely, that they met upon that night, where the fact of their meeting is the foundation of a charge of murder. You must feel, therefore, that the drawing of an inference in the ordinary matters of civil business, or in the actual intercourse of mutual friends, is one thing, and the inference from the fact that he came to Glasgow, that they did meet, and that, therefore, the poison was administered to him by her at that time, is another, and a most enormous jump in the category of inferences. Now, the question for you to put to yourselves is this—Can you now, with satisfaction to your own minds, come to the conclusion that they did meet on that occasion, the result being, and the object of coming to that conclusion being, to fix down upon her the administration of the arsenic by which he died?

" She has arsenic before the 22nd; and that is a dreadful fact, if you are quite satisfied that she did not get it and use it for the purpose of washing her hands and face. It may create the greatest reluctance in your mind, to take any other view of the matter, than that she was guilty of administering it somehow, though the place where may not be made out, or the precise time of the interview. But, on the other hand, you must keep in view that arsenic could only be administered by her if an interview took place with L'Angelier; and that interview, though it may be the result of an inference that may satisfy you *morally* that it did take place, still rests upon an inference alone; and that inference is to be the ground, and must be the ground, on which a verdict of guilty is to rest. Gentlemen, you will see, therefore, the necessity of great caution and jealousy in dealing with any inference which you may draw from this. You may be perfectly satisfied that L'Angelier did not commit suicide; and of course it is necessary for you to be satisfied of that, before you could find that anybody administered arsenic to him. Probably none of you will think for a moment that he went out that night, and that, without seeing her, and without knowing what she wanted to see him about, if they had met, he swallowed above 200 grains of arsenic in the street, and that he was carrying it about with him. Probably you will discard that altogether, . . . yet, on the other hand, gentlemen, keep in view that that will not of itself establish that the prisoner administered it. The matter may remain most mysterious—wholly unexplained; you may not be able to account for it on any other supposition; but still that supposition or inference may not be a ground on which you can safely and satisfactorily rest your verdict against the panel. Now then, gentlemen, I leave you to consider the case with reference to the views that are raised upon this correspondence. I don't think you will consider it so unlikely as was supposed, that this girl, after writing such letters, may have been capable of cherishing such a purpose. But still, although you may take such a view of her character, it is but a supposition that she cherished this murderous purpose—the last conclusion of course that you ought to come to merely on supposition and inference and observation, upon this varying and wavering correspondence, of a girl in the circumstances in which she was placed. It receives more importance, no doubt, when you find the purchase of arsenic just before she expected, or just at the time she expected, L'Angelier. But still these are but suppositions; they are but suspicions. . . .

" I don't say that inferences may not competently be drawn; but I have already warned you as to inferences which may be drawn in the ordinary matters of civil life, and those which may be drawn in such a case as this; and therefore if you cannot say, We find here satisfactory evidence of this meeting, and that the poison must have been administered by her at a meeting,—whatever may be your suspicion, however heavy the weight and load of suspicion is against her, and however you may have to struggle to get rid of it, you perform the best and bounden duty as a jury to separate suspicion from truth, and to proceed upon nothing that you do not find established in evidence against her." The jury returned, in conformity with the law of Scotland, a verdict of not guilty on the first, and of not proven on the second and third charges.* On the supposition that the parties met on the fatal evening in question, there could be but one conclusion as to the guilt of the prisoner, the hypothesis of suicide being considered by the learned Judge as out of the question, as it obviously was ; and in the language of the learned Judge, " that this man, ardent to see this girl again, hoping to get the satisfactory answer which she had promised to give him respecting her rumoured engagement with another, should hurry home on the Sunday night, and go out from his lodgings in the hope that he could find her waiting, and that there was the greatest probability of his seeing her, was, he thought, the only conclusion the jury could come to in the matter." With-

---

* Reg. v. Madeleine Smith, June, 1857 ; Reports of A. F. Irvine, Advocate, and John Morrison, Advocate.

out presumption, it may be observed that the distinction
thus drawn between " a very natural inference, looking at
the thing morally," " an inference that may satisfy a jury
morally," so that " no one need hesitate to say as a matter of moral opinion, the whole probabilities of the case
are in favour of it," and " as the only conclusion the jury
could come to," and that moral certainty which is the
only foundation of our confidence in the sufficiency and
safety of conclusions based upon circumstantial evidence,
and which in every case can be but inferential, is fine
and shadowy in the extreme. Nor is it easy to reconcile
with sound principle, as recognized in other cases, English and Scotch, any distinction in the application of the
rules of evidence and inference according as the subject-
matter relates to the ordinary or the uncommon events
of life.* And even upon that supposition, surely no
matter or occasion of ordinary business could have been
more important to her, or have more deeply interested
the parties, or be more likely to bring two young persons
so mutually implicated together, than the object of the
anxiously looked-for meeting appointed for the night in
question.

4. The science of chemistry generally affords most important auxiliary evidence as to the *corpus delicti* in the investigation of cases of imputed poisoning. As with regard
to scientific evidence of every other kind, the processes
and results of chemical analysis in application to the discovery or reproduction of poison are subordinated to the
control of those general principles of law which, in all
other cases, govern the admissibility of evidence and the
estimation of its weight and effect : indeed, those rules

---

* See Rex *v.* Ings, and Reg. *v.* Hanson and others, *ante*, p. 196.

have received some of their most instructive illustrations from cases of this nature.

Of the various chemical tests, unquestionably those which, applied to the human body or its contents or *excreta*, reproduce the particular poison which has been employed, are the most satisfactory, since, if the re-agents employed are free from impurities, they give an infallible result.

A remarkable exemplification of the necessity of this qualification occurred in a late trial, in which Reinsch's test, which had previously been regarded as infallible in the separation of arsenic, turned out to be fallacious when applied to chlorate of potass; and, in fact, the arsenic which was found in the mixture had been liberated from the copper gauze employed in the experiment.*

In general, therefore, it may be considered as a sound rule of procedure, founded in justice and prudence, that such evidence, whenever it is capable of being obtained, ought to be adduced, and in such circumstances the failure to adduce such evidence, unexplained by satisfactory reasons, gives serious ground for doubt as to the reality of the alleged poisoning.

But some of the vegetable poisons, in the present state of science, are beyond the reach of chemical processes. The offender himself, by his chemical knowledge and choice of means, by the administration of minimum doses, or by the destruction of the portions of the body containing the suspected matter, or by the destruction, dilution, or other tampering with its *excreta* or contents, may have rendered detection by the reproduction of the deadly agent impracticable; or the absorption of the poison, or

---

* Reg. *v.* Smethurst, C. C. C. Sess. Pap., Aug. 1859, *ut supra.* But arsenic was also found in an evacuation not complicated with the same source of fallacy.

a want of skill in the experimenter, or failure to employ
the proper means, or other cause, may have rendered the
necessary chemical researches impracticable, unsatisfactory, or inconclusive.*   The concurrence, moreover, of a
plurality of characteristic tests, separately fallacious, but
fallacious from different causes, may, in connection with
strong moral facts, yield a result of so high a degree of
probability as to be perfectly convincing, though the poison has not been reproduced.†

It would be most unreasonable, therefore, and lead to
the grossest injustice, and in some circumstances to impunity of the worst of crimes, to require, as an imperative
rule of law, that the fact of poisoning shall be proved
by any special and exclusive medium of proof, when that
kind of proof is unattainable, and especially if it has been
rendered so by the act of the offender himself.   No universal and invariable rule, therefore, can be laid down;
and every case must depend upon its own particular circumstances; and as, in all other cases, the *corpus delicti*
must be proved by the best evidence which is capable of
being adduced, and by such an amount and combination
of relevant facts, whether direct or circumstantial, as
establish the imputed guilt to a moral certainty, and to
the exclusion of every other reasonable hypothesis.

In Tawell's case it was strenuously urged by the counsel for the prisoner that it was a rule of law, that there
ought to be positive proof of the *mode* of death, and that
such a quantity of poison was found in the body of the
deceased, as would necessarily occasion death.   But this
doctrine was peremptorily repudiated by Mr. Baron
Parke, who told the jury, that "if the evidence satisfied

* Rex *v.* Donellan; Reg. *v.* Smethurst, *ut supra*; Reg. *v.* Palmer,
post.

† Rex *v.* Elder, 1 Syme's Jud. Rep. 71; and see Rex *v.* Donnall, *post.*

them that the death was occasioned by poison, and that that poison was administered by the prisoner,—if that," said his Lordship, " is proved by circumstantial evidence, it is not necessary to give direct and positive proof what is the quantity which would destroy life, nor is it necessary to prove that such a quantity was found in the body of the deceased, if the other facts lead you to the conclusion that the death was occasioned by poison, and that it was knowingly administered by the prisoner. You must take this fact, just the same as all the other parts of the case, and see if you are satisfied, as reasonable men, whether the prisoner is guilty or not. The only fact which the law requires to be proved by direct and positive evidence is the death of the party, by finding the body ; or when such proof is absolutely impossible, by circumstantial evidence leading closely to that result, —as where a body was thrown overboard far from land,— when it is quite enough to prove that fact without producing the body." His Lordship, in a subsequent part of his charge, said, " There is very reasonable evidence, supposing that to be required which I tell you is not, that the quantity of prussic acid in the stomach amounted to one grain ; and although that is not necessary to be proved, the scientific evidence shows that one grain may be enough to destroy life." In reference to the argument urged by the prisoner's counsel, that the deceased might have died from some sudden emotion, the learned Judge said, that it was within the range of possibility that a person might so die without leaving any trace on the brain ; *they* were to judge whether they could attribute death to that cause, if they found strong evidence of the presence of poison ; because they were not to have recourse to mere conjecture ; that, where the result of the evidence gave them the existence of a cause to which it might be rationally attributed, they were not to suppose it was to be attributed to any other cause.*

Lord Campbell, in Palmer's case, said that it was not to be expected that witnesses should be called to state that they saw the deadly poison administered by the prisoner, or mixed up by the prisoner openly before them. Circumstantial evidence, as to that, continued the learned Judge, is all that can be reasonably expected; and if there were a series of circumstances leading to the conclusion of guilt, a verdict of guilty might satisfactorily be pronounced.† With respect to the consideration that no strychnia was found in the body, it was for them to consider, but there was no rule of law according to which the poison must be found in the body of the deceased, and all that they knew respecting the poison not being in the body was, that in that part of the body that was analyzed by the witnesses no strychnia had been found.‡

5. Of the various heads of evidence in charges of poisoning, that of moral conduct is of most general interest. The *data* of physiological and pathological and chemical science must always be matter of opinion testified to by skilled witnesses ; whereas in the forensic discussion of moral facts, appeal is necessarily made to those psychological principles of our nature which give them pertinence and significance, and upon which every intelligent person is capable of forming a trustworthy judgment. It would be absurd to suppose that such facts, when clearly connected by adequate independent evidence with a *corpus delicti*, are simply fortuitous and phenomenal;

* Short-hand Rep., *ut supra*.   † Report. *ut supra*, p. 308.
‡ Ib. pp. 319–396.

on the contrary, they are the natural and unmistakeable manifestations of the secret workings of the mind, not only throwing light upon and bringing into relief the character of the act itself, but tending also to discriminate the individual guilty actor. His necessities, his antipathies, or other motives, his reluctance to permit examination of the body, or its contents or *excreta*, or of other suspected matter—his contrivances to prevent it, his attempts to tamper with the witnesses or the officers of justice, or with such suspected matter, or with any other article of real evidence—his falsehoods, subterfuges, and evasions,—these and many other circumstances constitute most material explanatory parts of the *res gestæ*, and afford relevant and frequently conclusive evidence, from which his guilt may be reasonably inferred.

In most criminal charges, the evidence of the *corpus delicti* is separable from that which applies to the indication of the offender; but in cases of poisoning, it is scarcely ever possible to obtain conclusive evidence of the *corpus delicti*, irrespectively of the explanatory evidence of moral conduct: and Mr. Justice Buller, in Donellan's case, told the jury that "if there was a doubt upon the evidence of the physical witnesses, they must take into their consideration all the other circumstances, either to show that there was poison administered, or that there was not, and that every part of the prisoner's conduct was material to be considered."* So in Donnall's case, Mr. Justice Abbott in summing up said to the jury that there were two important questions: first, did the deceased die of poison? and if they should be of opinion that she did, then, whether they were satisfied from the evidence that the poison was administered by

* Gurney's Short-hand Report, *ut supra*, p. 53.

the prisoner or by his means ?   There were some parts
of the evidence which appeared to him equally applicable
to both questions, and those parts were what related to
the conduct of the prisoner during the time of the opening and inspection of the body ; his recommendation of
a shell and the early burial ; to which might be added
the circumstances, not much to be relied upon, relative
to his endeavours to evade his apprehension.   His Lordship also said, as to the question whether the deceased
died by poison, " in considering what the medical men
said upon the one side and the other, you must take into
account the conduct of the prisoner in urging a hasty
funeral, and his conduct in throwing away the contents
of the jug into the chamber utensil."*   Lord Chief Justice Campbell, in his charge to the jury in Palmer's case,
said that " in cases of this sort the evidence had often
been divided into medical and moral evidence ; the medical
being that of the scientific men, and the moral the circumstantial facts which are calculated to prove the truth
of the charge against the party accused.   They cannot,"
he continued, " be finally separated in the minds of the
jury, because it is by the combination of the two species
of evidence that their verdict ought to be found.   In this
case you will look at the medical evidence to see whether
the deceased, in your opinion, did die by strychnia or by
natural disease ; and you will look at what is called the
moral evidence, and consider whether that shows that the
prisoner not only had the opportunity, but that he actually availed himself of that opportunity, to administer to
the deceased the deadly poison of which he died."†   His
Lordship also said that " it was impossible they should
not pay attention to the conduct of the prisoner, and

* Frazer's Short-hand Rep., *ut supra,* pp. 127, 177.

† Reg. *v.* Palmer, Report, *at supra,* p. 308.

that there were some instances of his conduct as to which
they would say whether they belonged to what might be
expected from an innocent or a guilty man.   He was
eager to have the body fastened down in the coffin.
Then with regard to the betting-book, there is certainly
evidence from which you may infer that he did get possession of the deceased's betting-book, and that he abstracted it and concealed it.   Then, gentlemen, you must
not omit his conduct in trying to bribe the post-boy to
overturn the carriage in which the jar was being conveyed to be analyzed in London, and from which evidence might be obtained of his guilt.   Again, you find
him tampering with the post-master, and procuring from
him the opening of a letter from the person who had
been examining the contents of the jar, to the attorney
employed in the case.   And then, gentlemen, you have
tampering with the coroner, and trying to induce him to
procure a verdict from the coroner's jury, which would
amount to an acquittal.   These are serious matters for
your consideration, but you, and you alone, will say what
inference is to be drawn from them.   If not answered,
they certainly present a serious case for your consideration."*

Among the most important circumstances of moral
conduct, and in analogy with the rules which prevail in
the proof of the *corpus delicti* in other cases, may be mentioned former acts of poisoning, or attempts to poison,
whether the same individual, or other members of the
same family, where such successive administrations throw
light upon the particular act which forms the subject of
inquiry.   On a trial for murder by the administration
of prussic acid in porter, evidence was admitted that
the deceased had been taken ill several months before,

* Report, *at supra*, p. 320.

after partaking of porter with the prisoner.* And upon the trial of a woman for the murder of her husband by arsenic in September, evidence was admitted of arsenic having been taken by two of her sons, one of whom died in December, and the other in March following, and also by a third son, who took arsenic in April following, but did not die. Evidence was also admitted of a similarity of symptoms in the four cases, that the prisoner lived in in the same house with her husband and sons, and prepared their tea, cooked their victuals, and distributed them to the four parties. Lord Chief Baron Pollock said his opinion was that evidence was receivable that the deaths of two sons, and the illness of the third, proceeded from the same cause, namely, arsenic. The tendency of such evidence, he said, was to prove, and to confirm the proof already given, that the death of the husband, whether felonious or not, was occasioned by arsenic. In that case he thought it wholly immaterial whether the deaths of the sons took place before or after the death of the husband. The domestic history of the family during the period that the four deaths occurred, was also receivable in evidence to show that during that time arsenic had been taken by four members of it, with a view to enable the jury to determine whether such taking was accidental or not. The evidence, he said, was not inadmissible, by reason of its tendency to prove, or to create a suspicion of a subsequent felony. His Lordship, after taking time to consider, refused to reserve the point for the opinion of the Judges, under the 11 & 12 Vict. c. 78, and stated that Mr. Baron Alderson and Mr. Justice Talfourd concurred in opinion with him.†

* Reg. *v.* Tawell, *ut supra.*
† Reg. *v.* Geering, 27 L. J. M. C. 215 ; and see Reg. *v.* May, 1 Cox's

But nevertheless, moral facts apparently calculated to create the greatest suspicion, may not be of a suspicious nature, or may be too fallacious and uncertain to justify conviction, especially where the *corpus delicti* is matter of inference only, and not established on a basis of independent evidence. Justice requires that such facts should be interpreted in a spirit of candour, and with proper allowance for the weaknesses of men who may be suddenly placed in circumstances of suspicion and difficulty. It is well known, for example, that many persons, more especially in the humbler classes, feel great repugnance to permit the bodies of their friends to be subjected to anatomical examination. The manifestation of such repugnance is a fact to be taken into account like all other facts. But although in the case of violent or sudden death, and particularly when caused by poison, it must be known that the *post-mortem* examination is of the highest importance, it by no means follows that objection to permit such examination proceeds from the consciousness of guilt. In a case of this kind, Mr. Baron Rolfe said that the question was, from what motive the reluctance arose? On the one hand, it was suggested that it was because the prisoner did not wish the cause of his wife's death to be investigated, being afraid it would be discovered that she had died from arsenic;—on the other, that his reluctance arose from his horror of the notion of his wife's dead body being taken up, and exposed to the investigation of the surgeons, at which the feelings were apt to revolt. Many persons, no doubt, feel very great horror at the notion of such things being done to themselves, or those connected with them, whilst others, again,

C. C. 236. Reg. *v.* Calder, *ib.* 348, and the language of Mr. Baron Maule, in Reg. *v.* Dossett, 2 C. & K. 306.

were indifferent on the subject, leaving their own bodies to be dissected. But few persons liked to have their wives or their daughters so exposed; the prisoner, said the learned Judge, might not be one of them, and his feelings on that subject might have prompted the remark alleged against him; and surely he must have known that any reluctance expressed by him to an inquiry, or wish to stop it, would only tend to make those who were about to make it, persevere.*

· It happens of necessity that in every case of the kind under discussion, there is a concurrence of evidence derived, if not from all, at least from several of the sources which have been mentioned; so that the strength of the conviction finally produced depends not merely upon the sum of the separate forces, but upon that superior force analogous to a geometrical progression, which is the consequence of their combination.

An analysis of some of the most remarkable recorded cases of criminal poisoning which have occurred in our judicial annals, will form an interesting commentary upon the general rules of evidence, and more especially in their application to the interpretation of moral inculpatory facts.

John Donellan, Esq., was tried at Warwick spring assizes, 1781, before Mr. Justice Buller, for the murder of Sir Theodosius Boughton, his brother-in-law, a young man of fortune, twenty years of age, who up to the moment of his death had been in good health and spirits, with the exception of a trifling venereal ailment, for which he occasionally took a laxative draught. Mrs. Donellan was the sister of the deceased, and together with Lady Boughton his mother lived with him at Lawford

* Reg. *v.* Graham, *ut supra.*

Hall, the family mansion. On attaining twenty-one, Sir Theodosius would have been entitled absolutely to an estate of £2000 per annum, the greater part of which, in the event of his dying under that age, would have descended to the prisoner's wife. For some time before the death of Sir Theodosius, the prisoner had on several occasions falsely represented his health to be very bad, and his life to be precarious, and not worth a year's purchase, though to all appearance he was well and in good health. On the 29th of August the apothecary in attendance sent him a mild and harmless draught, to be taken the next morning. In the evening the deceased was out fishing, and the prisoner told his mother that he had been out with him, and that he had imprudently got his feet wet, both of which representations were false. When he was called on the following morning, he was in good health; and about seven o'clock his mother went to his chamber for the purpose of giving him his draught, of the smell and nauseousness of which he immediately complained, and she remarked that it smelt like bitter almonds. In about two minutes he struggled very much, as if to keep the medicine down, and Lady Boughton observed a gurgling in his stomach; in ten minutes he seemed inclined to doze, but in five minutes afterwards she found him with his eyes fixed, his teeth clenched, and froth running out of his mouth, and within half an hour after taking the draught he died. Lady Boughton ran downstairs to give orders to a servant to go for the apothecary, who lived about three miles distant; and in less than five minutes the prisoner came into the bedroom, and after she had given him an account of the manner in which Sir Theodosius had been taken, he asked where the physic-bottle was, and she

showed him the two bottles. The prisoner then took up
one of them and said, " Is this it?" and being answered
" Yes," he poured some water out of the water-bottle,
which was near, into the phial, shook it, and then emptied
it into some dirty water, which was in a washhand basin.
Lady Boughton said, " You should not meddle with the
bottle;" upon which the prisoner snatched up the other
bottle and poured water into that also, and shook it, and
then put his finger to it and tasted it. Lady Boughton
again asked what he was about, and said he ought not
to meddle with the bottles; on which he replied, he did
it to taste it, though he had not tasted the first bottle.
The prisoner ordered a servant to take away the basin,
the dirty things, and the bottles, and put the bottles into
her hands for that purpose; she put them down again,
on being directed by Lady Boughton to do so, but subsequently, while Lady Boughton's back was turned, removed them on the peremptory order of the prisoner.
On the arrival of the apothecary, the prisoner said the
deceased had been out the preceding evening fishing,
and had taken cold, but he said nothing of the draught
which he had taken. The prisoner had a still in his
own room, which he had used for distilling roses; and a
few days after the death of Sir Theodosius he brought
it full of wet lime to one of the servants to be cleaned.
The prisoner made several false and inconsistent statements to the servants and others as to the cause of the
young man's death, attributing it at one time to his
having been out late fishing, and getting his feet wet,
and at another to the bursting of a blood-vessel, and
again to the malady for which he was under treatment,
and the medicine given to him. On the day of his
death he wrote to Sir William Wheeler, his guardian,

to inform him of the event, but made no reference to
its suddenness. The coffin was soldered up on the fourth
day after the death. Two days afterwards, Sir William,
in consequence of the rumours which had reached him
of the manner of his friend's death, and that suspicions
were entertained that he had died from the effects of
poison, wrote a letter to the prisoner, requesting that
an examination might take place, and mentioning the
gentlemen by whom he wished it to be conducted. He
accordingly sent for them, but did not exhibit Sir William Wheeler's letter, alluding to the suspicion that the
deceased had been poisoned, nor did he mention to
them that they were sent for at his request. Having
been induced by the prisoner to suppose the case to be
one of ordinary sudden death, and finding the body in
an advanced state of putrefaction, the medical gentlemen declined to make the examination, on the ground
that it might be attended with personal danger. On
the following day, a medical man, who had heard of their
refusal to examine the body, offered to do so; but the
prisoner declined his offer, on the ground that he had
not been directed to send for him. On the same day
the prisoner wrote to Sir William a letter, in which he
stated that the medical men had fully satisfied the family,
and endeavoured to account for the event by the ailment
under which the deceased had been suffering; but he
did not state that they had not made the examination.
Three or four days afterwards, Sir William, having been
informed that the body had not been examined, wrote to
the prisoner insisting that it should be done, which however he prevented, by various disingenuous contrivances,
and the body was interred without examination. In the
meantime, the circumstances having become known to

the coroner, he caused the body to be disinterred, and examined on the eleventh day after death. Putrefaction was found to be far advanced; and the head was not opened, nor the bowels examined, and in other respects the examination was incomplete. When Lady Boughton, in giving evidence before the coroner's inquest, related the circumstance of the prisoner having rinsed the bottles, he was observed to take hold of her sleeve, and endeavour to check her; and he afterwards told her that she had no occasion to have mentioned that circumstance, but only to answer such questions as were put to her; and in a letter to the coroner and jury, he endeavoured to impress them with the belief, that the deceased had inadvertently poisoned himself with arsenic, which he had purchased to kill fish. Experiments made by the administration of laurel-water on various animals produced convulsions and sudden death, and on opening one of them a strong smell of laurel-water was perceived. Upon the trial, four medical men, three physicians and an apothecary, were examined on the part of the prosecution, and expressed a very decided opinion, —mainly grounded upon the symptoms, the suddenness of the death, the *post-mortem* appearances, the smell of the draught as observed by Lady Boughton, and the similar effects produced by experiments upon animals,— that the deceased had been poisoned with laurel water; and one of them stated that, on opening the body, he had been affected with a peculiar biting acrimonious taste in the hands and mouth, like that which affected him in all the subsequent experiments with laurel-water. An eminent surgeon and anatomist examined on the part of the prisoner, stated a positive opinion, that the symptoms did not necessarily lead to the conclusion that the deceased had been poisoned, and that the appearances presented upon dissection explained nothing but putrefaction.

Mr. Justice Buller, in his charge to the jury, called their attention to the suddenness of the death immediately after the administration of a draught by the prisoner,—to the opinions of the medical witnesses that there was nothing to lead them to attribute death to any other cause than that draught,—to the prisoner's misrepresentations as to the deceased's state of health at a time when he appeared to others to be in good health and spirits,—to his contrivances to prevent the examination of the body, and emphatically to the fact of his having rinsed out the bottle from which the draught had been taken, "which," said the learned Judge, " does carry with it strong marks of knowledge by him that there was something in that bottle which he wished should never be discovered;" and finally, to his attempts to check the witness who spoke to that circumstance while giving her evidence before the coroner. The prisoner was convicted and executed.

This trial has given rise to much difference of opinion, and assuredly the scientific evidence was very imperfect and unsatisfactory. But the manner in which death occurred, at the very instant of taking the draught from the hand of the prisoner, was all but conclusive that it contained some poisonous ingredient which was the cause of death; and though the mere coincidence of the two events would not alone have been exclusive of the hypothesis of a sudden death from accident or natural cause, the conjunction of those events with so many circumstances of moral conduct of deep inculpatory import, could admit of explanation only on the hypothesis of the prisoner's guilt. It is impossible to regard those circumstances in any other light than as the necessary indications, on the ordinary principles of human nature, of the moral causal origin of the fatal catastrophe.*

Robert Sawle Donnall, a surgeon and apothecary, was tried at Launceston spring assizes, 1817, before Mr. Justice Abbott, for the murder of Mrs. Elizabeth Downing, his mother-in-law.

The prisoner and the deceased were next-door neighbours, and lived upon friendly terms; and there was no suggestion of malice, nor could any motive be assigned which could have induced the prisoner to commit such an act, except that he was in somewhat straitened circumstances, and in the event of his mother-in-law's death would have become entitled to a share of her property. On the 19th of October the deceased drank tea at the prisoner's house, which was handed to her by him, and returned home much indisposed, retching and vomiting, with a violent cramp in her legs, from which she did not recover for several days. About a fortnight afterwards, after returning from church, and dining at home on boiled rabbits smothered with onions, upon the invitation of her daughter she drank tea in the evening at the prisoner's house with a family party. The prisoner on this occasion also handed to the deceased cocoa and bread and butter, proceeding towards her chair by a circuitous route; but it was stated to have been his habit to serve his visitors himself, and not to allow them to rise from their chairs. When Mrs. Downing had drunk

* The account of this case in 'The Theory of Presumptive Proof' suppresses many of the most important facts, and is in other respects partial, garbled, and inaccurate; the strictures upon the trial are most unfair, and the book itself is utterly unworthy of the author to whom it is commonly ascribed.

about half of her second cup, she complained of sickness and went home, where she was seized with retching and vomiting, attended with frequent cramps ; and then a violent purging took place, and at eight o'clock the next morning she died.   None of the other persons who had been present on either of these occasions were taken ill. To a physician called in by the prisoner two or three hours before her death, he stated that she had had an attack of *cholera morbus*.   The nervous coat of the stomach was found to be partially inflamed or stellated in several places, and the villous coat was softened by the action of some corrosive substance; the blood-vessels of the stomach were turgid, and the intestines, particularly near the stomach, inflamed.   The contents of the stomach were placed in a jug, in a room to which the prisoner (to whom at that time no suspicion attached) had access, for examination ; but he clandestinely threw them into another vessel containing a quantity of water.   The prisoner proposed that the body should be interred on the following Wednesday, assigning as a reason for so early an interment that from the state of the corpse there would be danger from keeping it longer. This representation was entirely untrue.   He also evinced much eagerness to accelerate the funeral, urging the person who had the charge of it, and the men who were employed in making the vault, to unusual exertions. The physician called in to the deceased concluded from the symptoms, the shortness of the illness, and the morbid appearances, that she had died from the effects of some active poison ; and in order to discover the particular poison supposed to have been used, he applied to the contents of the stomach the tests of the ammoniacal sulphate of copper, or common blue vitriol, and the ammoniacal nitrate of silver, or lunar caustic, in solution, which severally yielded the characteristic appearances of arsenic, the sulphate of copper producing a green precipitate, whereas a blue precipitate is formed if no arsenic is present, and the nitrate of silver producing a yellow precipitate, instead of a white precipitate, resulting if no arsenic is present. He stated that he considered these tests conclusive and infallible, and that he had used them because they would detect a minuter portion of arsenic; on which account he considered them to be more proper for the occasion, as, from the smallness of the quantity, from the frequent vomitings and purgings, and the appearance of the tests, he found there could not be much. Concluding that bile had been taken into the stomach, he mixed some bile with water, and applied to the mixture the same tests, but found no indication of the presence of arsenic; from which he inferred that the presence of bile would not alter the conclusion which he had previously drawn. Having been informed that the deceased had eaten onions, he boiled some in water; and after pouring off the water in which they were boiled, he poured boiling water over them and left them standing for some time, after which he applied the same tests to the solution thus procured, and ascertained that it did not produce the characteristic appearances of arsenic. The witness, upon his cross-examination, admitted that the symptoms and appearances were such as might have been occasioned by some other cause than poisoning; that the reduction test would have been infallible; and that it might have been adopted in the first instance, and might also have been tried upon the matter which had been used for the other experiments. Upon his re-examination he accounted for his omission of the reduction test by stating that the quantity of matter left after the frequent vomitings and the other experiments would have been too small, and that it would not have been so correct to use the matter which had been subjected to the preceding experiments.

Séveral medical witnesses called on the part of the prisoner, stated that the symptoms and morbid appearances, though they were such as might and did commonly denote poisoning, did not exclude the possibility that death might have been occasioned by *cholera morbus* or some other disease ; that the tests which had been resorted to were fallacious, since they had produced the same characteristic appearances upon their application to innocent matter, namely, the sulphate of copper a green, and the nitrate of silver a yellow precipitate, on being applied to an infusion of onions ; and that the experiment with the bile was also fallacious, since from the presence of phosphoric acid, which is contained in all the fluids of the human body, the same coloured precipitate would be thrown down by putting lunar caustic into a solution of phosphate of soda. The learned Judge, in his charge to the Jury, said, that none of the evidence of the witnesses for the prisoner went to show that the tests employed by the medical witnesses on the other side would not prove that arsenic was there if it were really there,—that the experiments made by the witnesses for the prisoner were made with onions in a different state from what onions boiled with rabbits are—as by that mode could be got a great portion of the juice or strength of the onions, in water, whereas in regard to onions prepared for the table, or boiled with a considerable quantity of water, a good portion of their juice is withdrawn from them—that as to the experiment with the bile, if there were no phos-

phoric acid in the stomach of the deceased, or no quantity of it sufficient to produce that appearance, whatever might have been the appearance if sufficient were put in, then the experiment was tried on something that did not contain a sufficient quantity of that matter; that although the same result might be produced by that matter, if there, yet if there is no reason to suppose that that matter was there or there in sufficient quantity, then he thought the suspicion that arsenic was there was very strong. His Lordship also said, " If the evidence as to the opinions of the learned persons who have been examined on both sides should lead you to doubt whether you should attribute the death of the deceased to arsenic having been administered to her, or to the disease called *cholera morbus*,—then, as to this question as well as to the other question, the conduct of the prisoner is most material to be taken into consideration ; for he, being a medical man, could not be ignorant of many things as to which ignorance might be shown in other persons : he could hardly be ignorant of the proper mode of treating *cholera morbus ;* he could not be ignorant that an early burial was not necessary ; and when an operation was to be performed in order to discover the cause of the death, he should not have shown a backwardness to acquiesce in it ; and when it was performing, and he attending, he could not surely be ignorant that it was material for the purposes of the investigation that the contents of the stomach should be preserved for minute examination."*
His Lordship also said, "The conduct of the prisoner, his eagerness in causing the body to be put into a shell, and afterwards to be speedily interred, was a circumstance most material for their consideration, with reference to

* Frazer's Short-hand Rep., 161.

both the questions he had stated ; for although the examination of the body in the way set forth, and the experiments that were made, might not lead to a certain
conclusion as to the charge stated, that the deceased got
her death by poison administered to her by the prisoner,
yet if the prisoner as a medical man had been so wicked
as to administer that poison, he must have known that
the examination of the body would divulge it."*   Notwithstanding this adverse charge of the learned Judge,
the prisoner was acquitted.

A medical man was tried for the murder of his wife,
by the administration of prussic acid.   They left their
place of residence at Sunderland on a journey of pleasure
to London, where they arrived on the 4th of June, and
went into lodgings.   On the morning of the 8th, being
the Saturday after their arrival in town, the prisoner rang
the bell for some hot water, a tumbler, and a spoon, and
he and his wife were heard conversing in their chamber.
About a quarter before eight he called the landlady up-
stairs, saying that his wife was very ill, and she found
her lying motionless on the bed, with her eyes shut and
her teeth closed, and foaming at the mouth.   The prisoner said she had had fits before, but none like this,
and that she would not come out of it ; and on being
urged to send for a doctor, he said he was a doctor himself, and should have let blood before, but that there was
no pulse, and that this was an affection of the heart, and
that her mother died in the same way nine months before, and he put her feet and hands in warm water, and
applied a mustard plaister to her chest.   In the meantime a medical man was sent for, but she died before
his arrival.   There was a tumbler close to the head of the

* *Ibid.*, 170.

bed, about one-third full of a clear white fluid, and an empty tumbler on the other side of the table, and a paper of Epsom salts. In reply to a question from the medical man, the prisoner stated that the deceased had taken nothing but a little salts. On the same morning he ordered a grave for interment on the Tuesday following. The contents of the stomach were found to contain prussic acid and Epsom salts; and it was deposed that the symptoms were similar to those of death by prussic acid, but they might be the effect of any powerful sedative poison, and that the means resorted to by the prisoner were not likely to promote recovery, but that artificial respiration and stimulants were the appropriate remedies, and might probably have been effectual. The prisoner had purchased prussic acid and acetate of morphine on the previous day, from a vender of medicines with whom he was intimate, and he had been in the habit of using these poisons, under advice, for a complaint in the stomach. Two days after the fatal event, he stated to the medical man who had been called in, that on the morning in question he was about to take some prussic acid; that on endeavouring to remove the stopper he had some difficulty, and used some force with the handle of a toothbrush; that the neck of the bottle was broken by the force, and some of the acid spilt; that he placed the remainder in the tumbler, and went into the front room to fetch a bottle in which to place the acid, but instead of doing so, began to write to his friends in the country, when in a few minutes he heard a scream from his wife's bed-room; that he immediately went to her; that she exclaimed that she had taken some hot drink, and called for cold water, and that the prussic acid was undoubtedly the cause of her death. Upon being asked what he had done with the bottle, he said he had destroyed it, and assigned as the reason why he had not mentioned the circumstances before, that he was distressed and ashamed at the consequences of his negligence. According to the opinions of the medical witnesses, after the scream or shriek, volition and sensibility must have ceased, and speech would have been impossible. To various persons in the north of England the prisoner wrote false accounts of his wife's state of health. In one of them, dated from the Euston Hotel, the 6th of June, he stated that she was unwell, and had two medical gentlemen attending her, and that he was apprehensive of a miscarriage. In another, dated the 8th, he stated that he had had her removed to private lodgings, where she was under the care of two medical men, dangerously ill; that symptoms of premature labour had come on, and that one of the medical men pronounced her heart to be diseased. At the date of this letter his wife was cheerful and well, and all these statements respecting her health were false; and in fact they had gone into lodgings on their arrival in London on the 4th. In a letter dated the 9th, he stated the fact of her death, but without any allusion to the cause of it; which suppression, in a subsequent letter, he stated to have been caused by the desire of concealing the shame and reproach of his negligence. His statement to his landlady that his mother-in-law had died from disease of the heart was a falsehood, he himself having certified to the registrar of burials that bilious fever was the cause of her death. The deceased was entitled to some leasehold property, to which the prisoner would become entitled absolutely if he survived her, and to a copyhold estate which was limited to the joint use of herself and her husband, so that the survivor would take the absolute interest. The motive suggested for the commission of the alleged murder was, that the prisoner might become at once the absolute owner of his wife's property.

Mr. Baron Gurney said that this case differed from almost every other case he had ever known, in this circumstance, that generally there was a difficulty in ascertaining whether the death had been caused by poison, and whether the poison came from the hands of the person charged with the crime; but that in this case there could be no doubt that the deceased had come to her death by a poison most certain, fatal, and speedy in its effects, and that it was equally certain that it came from the hands of the prisoner. It had been proved beyond all doubt that the prisoner had bought the poison, and had placed or left it unprotected in the chamber of his wife, and the question was, whether, she having died from poison, it had been administered to her by his hand, or whether he had purposely placed it in her way in order that she might herself take it. The secrets of all hearts were known to God alone, and human tribunals could only judge of those secrets from the conduct of the individual at the time. In this case, the jury had the conduct of the prisoner, his words, his writing, his demeanour, proved before them, and it would be for them to decide, upon the whole case, whether they believed he had administered the poison, or placed it within the reach of the deceased in order that she might take it. If he had done either of those things, he would be guilty of murder; if they thought he had acted incautiously and negligently by leaving the poison in the way he had done, he had not been guilty of murder. He dwelt upon the circumstances that the parties had lived for a year and a half together upon terms of mutual affection, that the marriage took place with the consent of the lady's mother, with whom they had lived till her death, that the visit to London was well known to their friends, and that the place to which she was taken was where he had lodged before, and near the residence of the only two persons with whom he was acquainted in London. When any person committed a heinous crime, it was usual and natural, said the learned Judge, to look whether there existed any adequate motive to the commission of it. The prisoner being about thirty, and his wife about twenty-two years of age, it would be a good deal to say, that the desire to possess her property should be brought forward as a great motive of interest to excite to the commission of such a crime. Nevertheless, it was sometimes found, as they could not dive into the heart and ascertain motives, that a grave crime might be committed, although no motive for it could be found. Inasmuch as the great question the jury had to decide was the intention of the prisoner, it should be remembered that a man was entitled to a candid construction of his words and actions, particularly if placed in circumstances of great and unexpected difficulty, and they would take care to give what fair allowance they could in putting a construction upon the prisoner's words and actions. He also laid stress upon the conduct of the prisoner to his wife, and his general good character for kindness. He could not conceive the motive which should have induced the prisoner, in the letter posted on the 6th, when his wife was well and cheerful, to write so complete a fabrication from beginning to end, of her being unwell and attended by two medical men, and the jury would observe that it was written on the very day on which the prisoner had made arrangements for her residence with a friend, during his absence abroad. When the letter of the 8th was written did not appear, but it was proved to have been posted on the evening of that day. If it was written before the death, it told against the prisoner. It concurred with the letter written on the 6th, and practised the same deception, as to the two medical men, upon those to whom it was addressed. The defence was, that the prisoner had been guilty of a lamentable indiscretion; that a sudden event, fatal to his wife, had happened; that he was overpowered and overwhelmed by the result of his own carelessness, and that he did not like to divulge the truth. The awkward fact, however, was, that in his last letter he had pursued exactly the same system as that adopted in the letter written two days before. They would recollect, with reference to the letter of the 8th, that on that day he had more than once exclaimed, "This is all my fault." These outbreaks were of some importance for the consideration of the jury in giving, as compared with the letters, all indulgent consideration to any language used by the prisoner, after an event had occurred which placed him in a situation of difficulty and embarrassment. In comparing the statement set up for the defence with the evidence of the medical witnesses, two things were of a good deal of importance. The prisoner's statement was, that when he entered the bedchamber, his wife told him what had occurred, and that he took the tumbler out of her hand. The medical men had told the jury that with the scream that had been spoken of, all volition and power of speech would cease; but here it must not be forgotten that the judgment of these gentlemen must be received with this caution, that none of them had ever witnessed the effect of prussic acid on the human frame. It was for the jury to decide

s

whether they were convinced, beyond any reasonable
doubt, that the prisoner either administered, or in effect
caused to be administered, poison to the deceased; if
on the other hand they should be of opinion that he had
been merely guilty of indiscretion, and that, in consequence of the sudden and awful event which had occurred, he had been driven to conceal it by falsehood,
they would acquit him. No doubt, falsehood often placed
persons having recourse to it under awkward and menacing circumstances. In this case, falsehood had been
much resorted to. It was shown before the death, in the
statement about the two medical men; that falsehood
was followed up and repeated in the second letter; another falsehood appeared in the representation that his
mother-in-law, who had died of bilious fever, as appeared
by an entry in the register under his own hand, had
died of disease of the heart. If they thought the case
conclusive, however painful it might be, it would be
their duty to pronounce the prisoner guilty; but if they
thought it left in doubt and mystery, so that they could
not safely proceed, they would remember that it was
better that many guilty men should escape than that
one innocent man should perish. The prisoner was acquitted.*

Palmer's case is perhaps the most remarkable one of
this nature on record. The prisoner had been a medical practitioner, but had given up his profession for the
pursuits of the turf, in the course of which he became
intimate with a young man named Cook, who was addicted to the same pursuits. By his extensive gambling
transactions he became involved in great pecuniary difficulties, and was ultimately driven to the desperate expe-

* Reg. v. Belaney, C. C. C., Aug. 1844.

dient of borrowing money at exorbitant rates of interest, and to the commission of forgeries on a large scale. In 1855 he was indebted in about £20,000, borrowed at sixty per cent. interest upon bills, all of which bore the forged acceptances of his mother, and secured in part by the assignment of a policy of assurance for £13,000 on the life of his brother, who died in August of that year. To this source the prisoner had looked for relief from his embarrassments, but the office having become acquainted with circumstances which induced them to dispute the validity of the policy on the ground of fraud, declined to pay the sum assured; and in consequence the holder of some of these bills issued writs against the prisoner and his mother, which were sent into the country, to be served unless he should effect some satisfactory arrangement. Exposure, ruin, and punishment thus became imminent, unless some means could be devised of averting the impending disclosures. On the 13th of November, Cook won, by one of his horses and by bets at Shrewsbury races, between £2,000 and £3,000, of which he received £700 or £800 on the course; the remainder was payable in London, on Monday, the 20th. He was greatly excited by his success, and the prisoner and several other persons spent the following evening with him, after the conclusion of the races, at his inn in Shrewsbury. In the course of the evening the prisoner was seen in the passage outside of his own room, holding up a tumbler to a gas-light; after which he went, with the tumbler in his hand, into the room where Cook and his other friends were sitting. Soon afterwards, on drinking some brandy and water, Cook became suddenly ill, with violent vomiting, and it was necessary to call in medical assistance. He said he had been dosed by the prisoner, and handed the money he had about him, between £700 and £800, to a friend to take care of, who returned it to him the next morning, after his recovery. Notwithstanding these suspicious circumstances, such was the prisoner's influence over his infatuated victim, that Cook returned from Shrewsbury to Rugeley in company with him on the evening of Thursday, the 15th, when, on their arrival, the former went to his lodgings at the Talbot Arms, and the prisoner to his own house opposite. On the Saturday and Sunday the prisoner called many times to see Cook, who was repeatedly taken sick and ill after taking coffee and broth from the hands of the prisoner. On Monday (the 18th) he got up much better; and the prisoner called upon him early in the morning, but did not see him again until eight and nine in the evening, having in the interim, as it turned out, been to London. In the course of that evening Cook's medical attendant, who had previously seen him, left at the Talbot Arms a box of morphine pills, which was taken into his bedroom and administered by the prisoner, soon after which the household was disturbed by screams proceeding from the patient's room, who was found sitting up in bed, in great agony, beating the bed-clothes, gasping for breath, convulsed with a jerking and twitching motion all over his body, and one hand clenched and stiff, but conscious, and calling to those about him to send for the prisoner. In about half an hour the paroxysm subsided, and he became composed. On the morning of Tuesday (the 19th), after taking coffee from the hand of the prisoner, Cook was again affected with violent vomiting, which continued throughout the day; but in the evening was better, and in good spirits. About seven o'clock he was visited by his medical attendant, and the prisoner urged him to repeat the morphine pills, as on the night before; and they went together to the surgery, where pills were prepared and delivered to the prisoner, who took them away, and went to Cook's room about eleven o'clock, as was intended and supposed, for the purpose of administering them to him; so that he had the opportunity in the interval of changing them, which there can be no doubt he did. Cook strongly objected to take them, because he had been made so ill the night before; but his objections were overcome by the prisoner, and at length he swallowed the pills presented to him. Soon after midnight he became ill with the same agonizing symptoms as on the preceding night, and again desired that the prisoner should be sent for. Such was the rigidity of his limbs that it was found impossible to raise him up, and he asked to be turned over on his side; after which the action of the heart gradually ceased, and in a quarter of an hour he was a corpse. When dead, the body was bent back like a bow, and if it had been placed upon a level surface, it would have rested upon the head and heels. Upon receiving information of the young man's death, his step-father, who lived in London, went to Rugeley on Friday, the 23rd, to make arrangements for his funeral, and to inquire into the state of his affairs, as well as into the circumstances of his illness. On stating to the prisoner that he understood he knew something of his affairs, he told him that there were £4,000 worth of bills of the deceased's out, to which his name was attached, and that he had got a paper drawn up by a lawyer, signed by the deceased, to show that he had never received any benefit from them. The step-father then inquired if there were no sporting debts owing to him, to which the

prisoner said there was nothing of the sort; and on asking about the betting-book, which could not be found,
the prisoner said it would be of no use if found, as when
a man dies, his bets are done with. Other facts now began to transpire throwing a sinister light upon the mysterious events of the last few days. It was discovered
that the prisoner had procured three grains of strychnia
on the evening of Monday, and a second quantity of six
grains on the following day,—that he had been seen to
search the pockets, and under the pillow and bolster of
the unfortunate man before his body was cold,—that although his betting-book was kept on the dressing-table of
the deceased's bedroom, and was seen there on the previous night, it was never seen after his death,—that the
prisoner handed to a friend of the deceased five guineas
as the whole of the money that was found belonging to
him,—that he had been to London on Monday, the day
before the death, and procured payment of upwards of
£1,000 on account of the wagers won by the deceased at
Shrewsbury, and appropriated the amount in payment of
his own losses, and in part payment of the forged acceptances on which writs had been issued,—that before
the races he was short of money, and had borrowed £25,
and lost largely at the races, but had subsequently paid
considerable sums to various other creditors,—that two
or three days after Cook's death he had endeavoured to
obtain the attestation by an attorney to a forged acknow-
ledgment in the name of the deceased that £4,000 of
bills had been negotiated by the prisoner for his benefit,
—and finally had prevailed upon the medical man who
had attended the deceased, who was of a very advanced
age, to certify that he had died of apoplexy. A *post-
mortem* examination was made, at which the prisoner was

present, and the stomach and intestines were placed in a jar to be taken to London for examination. While the operation was going on, the prisoner pushed against the medical men engaged in it, so as to shake a portion of the contents of the stomach into the body. The jar was then covered with parchment, tied down, and sealed and placed aside; and while the attention of the medical men was still engaged in examining the body, the prisoner removed the jar to a distance near a door not the usual way out of the room, and it was found that two slits had been cut with a knife through the double skin which formed the covering. The prisoner having learned that the jar was to be sent to London the same evening, offered the driver who was to carry the persons in charge of it to the railway station, £10 to upset the carriage and break the jar. The analytical chemists to whom the stomach and intestines, and subsequently other parts of the body were sent, found traces of antimony, but none of strychnia, or any other poison; and sent their report by post, directed to the attorney at Rugeley employed in the investigation. The prisoner incited the post-master to betray to him the contents of this report; and wrote a confidential letter to the coroner, to whom during the course of the inquiry he sent presents of fish and game, stating that he had seen it in black and white that no strychnia, prussic acid, or opium had been found, and expressing his hope that on the next day to which the inquest stood adjourned, the verdict would be that of death from natural causes. The coroner's jury found a verdict of wilful murder against the prisoner. Upon the trial the chemical witnesses examined on the part of the prosecution stated that the stomach and intestines were received in an unfavourable state for finding strychnia had it been there, the stomach having been cut from end to end, and the contents gone, and the mucous surface, in which any poison, if present, would be found, lying in contact with the intestines and their succulent contents, and shaken together; that the non-discovery of strychnia was not conclusive that death had not been caused by that poison, inasmuch as they had failed to discover it in animals killed for the purpose of experiment; that if a minimum dose is administered, it disappears by absorption into the blood, but that it is discoverable, and had been discovered, when administered to animals in excess of the quantity required to destroy life, and that there is no known process by which it can be discovered in the tissues, if present there only in a small quantity. On the other hand, witnesses were called on behalf of the prisoner, who disputed the theory of absorption, and stated that strychnia, if present, is always discoverable, not only in the blood and in the stomach and intestines, and their contents, but also in the tissues,—that there was nothing in the condition of the parts of the body submitted to examination, to preclude the detection of strychnia; and that if present, it might have been found, even if it had been administered in a minimum dose, though on this latter point there was some difference of opinion among them. Numerous medical witnesses of the highest professional experience and character, called on the part of the Crown, deposed that many of the symptoms, especially in the progress and termination of the attack, were not those of any of the ordinary forms of tetanus, idiopathic or traumatic, or of any known disease of the human frame, but were the peculiar characteristics of poisoning by strychnia. Nor were there in these respects any such differences between their opi-

nions and those of many respectable professional witnesses called on the part of the prisoner, as might not
be accounted for by the imperfect state of knowledge
of all the forms of tetanic affection, or by the obscuri-
ties of physiological and pathological science. Of the
numerous professional witnesses examined on behalf of
the prisoner, some ascribed the symptoms to tetanic affection; others of them to various forms of disease from
which they were shown to be clearly distinguishable;
while others again ascribed them to physical causes
absolutely absurd and incredible. The contradictions
and inconsistencies in the testimony of some of the prisoner's witnesses, and their obtrusive zeal and manifest
purpose of obtaining an acquittal, deprived it of all moral
effect, and drew down upon several of them the severe
reprehension of the Court. After a protracted trial of
twelve days, the prisoner was found guilty, and was executed pursuant to his sentence;* and there is no doubt
that this was only one of several murders perpetrated by
this great criminal, by the same nefarious means, for the
purpose of obtaining money secured by fraudulent life
assurances.†

Section 5.

Application of the general principle to proof of the corpus delicti in cases of infanticide.

Of the various forms of criminal homicide, that of Infan-

---

* Short-hand Report, *ut supra*, and Sess. Pap.

† See An. Reg. 1855, p. 190. The technical nature of the evidence
in Smethurst's case, *ut supra*, would render it inapplicable in illustration of *legal* principles, even if doubt had not been thrown upon the
verdict by the grant of a pardon.

ticide, by which is popularly understood the murder of a recently born infant for the purpose of concealing its birth, perhaps presents the greatest difficulties in the establishment of the *corpus delicti*.

1.) In addition to the sources of difficulty and fallacy which are incidental to charges of homicide in general, there are many circumstances of embarrassment peculiar to cases of this nature, amongst which must be mentioned the occasional uncertainty and inconclusiveness of the symptoms of pregnancy, the fundamental fact to be proved,[*] which may resemble and be mistaken for appearances caused by obstructions or spurious gravidity.[†] In a remarkable case of imputed murder of an adult female, the suspicion of pregnancy arose principally from the bulk of the deceased while living, coupled with circumstances of conduct which denoted the existence of an improper familiarity between the parties, and from the discovery upon *post-mortem* examination of what was believed by the witnesses for the prosecution to be the placental mark. Four medical witnesses expressed the strongest belief that the deceased had been recently delivered of a child nearly come to maturity; while on the other hand, it was proved that she had been subject to obstructions; and it was deposed that the appearances of the uterus might be accounted for by hydatids, a species of dropsy in that part of the body, and that what was thought to be the placental mark might be the *pediculi* by which they were attached to the internal surface of the womb.[‡] The learned Judge said to the jury, that it

* Hume's Comm. *ut supra*, 464.

† Rex *v.* Bate, Warwick Summer Assizes, 1809. Rex *v.* Ferguson, Burnett's C. L. *ut supra*, 574.

‡ Rex *v.* Angus, Lancaster Autumn Assizes, 1808, *coram* Mr. Justice Chambre, Shorthand Report; and see Burnett's C. L. of Scotl. 575.

was a very unfortunate thing, that upon every particular point they had to rest upon conjecture; that it was a conjecture to a certain extent that the deceased was with child, that it was conjecture to a certain degree that any means were used to procure abortion; and, if they were used, that it was conjecture that the prisoner was privy to the administration of them.

2.) It must be clearly shown that a child has been born alive, and acquired an independent circulation and existence; it is not enough that it has breathed in the course of its birth;* but if a child has been wholly born, and is alive, and has acquired an independent circulation, it is not material that it is still connected with its mother by the umbilical cord,† nor is it essential that it should have breathed at the time it was killed, as many children are born alive and yet do not breathe for some time after birth.‡

Whether a child has been born alive or not is frequently a question of considerable difficulty; and it is an admonitory consideration, that scientific tests which have been considered as infallible, with the advance of knowledge have been found to be fallacious. Such is the case with respect to the hydrostatic test, from the indications of which in former times many women have suffered the last penalty of the law. On the trial of a woman at Winchester spring assizes, 1835, it was proved that the lungs were inflated; which the medical witness said would not have been the case if the child had been still-

* Rex v. Poolton, 5 C. & P. 399; Rex v. Enoch, *ib.* 539; Rex v. Crutchley, 7 *ib.* 814; Rex v. Sellis, *ib.* 856.

† Reg. v. Reeves, 9 *ib.* 25; Reg. v. Wright, *ib.* 754; Reg. v. Trilloe, 1 C. & M. 650.

‡ Rex v. Brain, 6 C. & P. 350.

born; but he stated, in answer to a question from Mr. Baron Gurney, that if the child had died in the birth, the lungs might have been inflated, upon which he stopped the case.* A single sob, it appears, is sufficient to inflate the lungs, though the child died in the act of birth.† A young woman was tried before Mr. Baron Parke for the murder of her female child; the throat was cut, and the wound had divided the right jugular vein; the lungs floated in water, and were found on cutting them to be inflated; but it was deposed that this test only showed that the child must have breathed, and not that it had been born alive, and that there are instances of children being lacerated in the throat in the act of delivery. On the close of the case for the prosecution, the learned Judge asked the jury whether they were satisfied that the child was born alive, and that the wound was inflicted by the prisoner with the intention of destroying life; as, if they entertained any doubt on these points, it would be unnecessary to go into the evidence on behalf of the prisoner. The jury returned a verdict of acquittal.‡

3.) It is a further source of uncertainty in cases of this nature, that circumstances of presumption frequently adduced as indicative of the crime of murder, may commonly be accounted for by the agency of less malignant motives. Concealment of pregnancy and delivery may proceed even from meritorious motives; as where a married woman resorted to such concealment in order to screen her husband, who was a deserter, from discovery.§

---

* Rex v. Simpson, Cummin on the Proof of Infanticide, 40.
† Rex v. Davidson, 1 Hume's Comm. *ut supra*, 486.
‡ Rex v. Grounall, Worcester Spring Assizes, 1837.
§ Rex v. Stewart, Burnett's C. L. *ut supra*, 572.

Severe must be the struggle between the opposing motives of shame and affection, before a mother can contemplate, and still more so before she can form and execute, the dreadful and unnatural resolution of taking away the life of her own offspring. The unhappy object of these conflicting motives is commonly the victim of brutality and treachery. Deserted by a heartless seducer, and scorned by a merciless world, scarcely any condition of human weakness can be imagined more calculated to excite the compassion of the considerate and humane.* The wisdom and humanity of the legislature, in accordance with the spirit of the times, have led, though tardily, to the repeal† of the cruel rule of presumption created by Statute 21 Jac. I. c. 27, and suggested by a corresponding edict of Henry II. of France, which made the concealment of the birth of an illegitimate child by its mother conclusive evidence of murder, unless she made proof by one witness at least that the child was born dead; a rule which had too long survived the barbarous age in which it originated, and under which it is but too probable that many women have unjustly suffered:‡ and the endeavour to conceal the birth of a child by secret burying, or otherwise disposing of the body, instead of being treated as a conclusive presumption of murder, has been made a substantive misdemeanour.§

4.) The casualties which, even in favourable circumstances, are inseparable from parturition, must be incalculably aggravated by the perplexities incidental to illegitimate, clandestine and unassisted birth, from the impulses of shame and alarm, the desire of concealment, the want of assistance and sympathy, and occasionally

---

* See 1 Hume's Comm. 462. † St. 43 Geo. III. c. 58. s. 3.
‡ See 1 Hume's Comm. 486. § St. 9 Geo. IV. c. 31. s. 14.

from the mother's inability to render the attentions requisite to preserve infant life; and there have been cases in which even the very means resorted to, under the terror of the moment, to facilitate birth, have been the unintentional cause of death. For these reasons, wounds and other marks of violence are not necessarily considered as indicative of wilful injury, and are not therefore sufficient to warrant a conviction of murder, unless the concomitant circumstances clearly manifest that they were knowingly inflicted upon a body born alive. Nor are these principles of construction peculiar to our own law; it is believed that they prevail generally, if not universally, in the application of the criminal law to cases of this nature.*

It follows from these considerations, that though the facts may justify extreme suspicion that death has been the result of intentional violence, yet if they do not entirely exclude every other possible hypothesis by which it may be reasonably accounted for, the soundest principles of justice, and a proper regard to the fallibility of human judgment in cases so mysterious as these generally are, combine to forbid the adoption of a conclusion so abhorrent to nature and humanity, and the infliction of a punishment which admits of no recall.

It has been thought that in these cases the feelings of humanity have been permitted to bias the strict course of judicial truth, and that countenance has been given to subtle and strained hypotheses for the explanation of circumstances of conclusive presumption.† It is to be feared that to some extent this opinion is correct, and if so, it is a conclusive proof that the law is not in har-

---

* Alison's Princ. 159.

† Whately on Secondary Punishments, 108.

mony with public feeling : but it may be doubted whether in this reproach sufficient weight has always been given to the difficulties inseparably incidental to the proof of this crime, and whether, in fact, acquittals take place so frequently as has been supposed, where it has been so clearly and satisfactorily proved as entirely to dispel all doubt, and to produce complete and undoubting assurance. It is however well deserving of consideration, whether the ends of public justice and social protection might not be better promoted by the abolition of capital punishment in a class of cases in which society will not concur in its infliction, and by the substitution of a minor punishment, not only in the case of concealment of birth, but generally in all cases where death has been caused by the wilful omission of the mother to take the necessary means for the preservation of infant life,* so as to avoid on the one hand the scandal and ill-example of acquittals in the face of convincing evidence of guilt, and on the other, of doing violence to public feeling by the denunciation of capital punishments against a crime which, atrocious as it is, is nevertheless wanting, as an eminent prelate has remarked, " in all the attributes which distinguish the murder of adults, viz. the wickedness of the motive, the danger to the community, and the feeling of alarm and insecurity which it occasions."†

The discussion and illustration of the rules and principles of evidence, in reference to the proof of the *corpus delicti*, might be extended to an examination of their application to other offences ; but the subject has been

* See Code Pénal d'Autriche, prem. partie, ch. xvi. art. 122.

† Whately on Secondary Punishments, p. 108, App. No. 2; and see Selections from the Charges, etc., of Mr. Baron Alderson, 78.

sufficiently exemplified for the purposes of this Essay, and such an extended examination would therefore be superfluous and transgress its legitimate limits. The cases which have been cited strikingly exhibit the strict accordance between judicial practice and the dictates of enlightened reason.

CHAPTER VIII.

OF THE FORCE AND EFFECT OF CIRCUMSTANTIAL EVIDENCE.—CONCLUSION.

SECTION 1.

GENERAL GROUNDS OF THE FORCE OF CIRCUMSTANTIAL EVIDENCE.

In considering the force and effect of circumstantial evidence, the credibility of the *testimony*, as distinguished from the credibility of the *fact*, is assumed, since it is a quality essential to the value of circumstantial, in common with all moral, evidence.

Our faith in moral evidence is grounded, as we have seen, upon our confidence in the permanence of the order of nature, and in the reality and fidelity of the impressions received by means of the senses, which place us in connection with the external world and with other men; and upon the laws of our moral and intellectual being, the immutability of moral distinctions, and the authority of conscience;[*] so that if we could correctly estimate, and were able to eliminate, the various disturbing influences which tend to divert men from the path of truth and rectitude, our reasonings and conclusions would possess all the force of demonstration.

The silent workings, and still more the fearful explo-

* See *ante*, 10.

T

sions, of human passion, which bring to light the darker elements of man's nature, must ever present to the philosophical observer considerations of deep intrinsic interest; while to the jurist, the moral and mechanical coincidences which connect different facts with each other, are relevant and all-important, as they are the intermediate connecting links between criminal actions and the malignant feelings and dispositions in which they originate.

The distinct and specific proving power of circumstantial evidence, as incidentally stated in a former part of this Essay, depends upon its incompatibility with, and incapability of explanation upon, any reasonable hypothesis, consistent with the ordinary course of nature, other than that of the truth of the principal fact in proof of which it is adduced:* so that, after the exhaustion of every other possible and admissible mode of solution, we must either conclude that the accused has been guilty of the fact imputed, or renounce as illusory and deceptive all the results of consciousness and experience, and all the operations of the human mind.†

Conclusions thus formed are simple inferences of the understanding, aided and corrected by the application of those rules of evidence and those processes of reason which sound and well-ripened experience has consecrated as the best methods of arriving at truth; and they constitute that MORAL CERTAINTY upon which men securely act in all other great and important concerns, and upon which they may therefore safely rely for the truth and correctness of their conclusions in regard to those events which fall within the province of criminal jurisprudence.

Many Continental codes, following the principles of the civil law, prescribe imperative *formulæ* descriptive of the

* *Supra,* p. 28.   † Mittermaier, *ut supra,* ch. 59.

kind and amount of evidence requisite to constitute legal proof. Those principles prevail also to a certain extent in the reception of evidence in the ecclesiastical and some other courts of special jurisdiction in this country, so far as to require the testimony of a plurality of witnesses. But the diversities of individual men render it impracticable thus definitely to estimate the fleeting shades and infinite combinations of human motives and actions ; or thus to fix, with arithmetical exactness, a common standard of proof, which shall influence with unvarying intensity and effect the minds of all men alike. Such restrictive rules are not merely harmless, nor simply superfluous ; they are in some cases positively pernicious and dangerous to the cause of truth ; and while they operate as snares for the conscience of the Judge, obliging him occasionally to determine contrary to his own convictions of truth, they are unnecessary for the protection of the innocent, and effective only for the impunity of the guilty.* A learned Judge of one of our ecclesiastical courts, after commenting on the rule of those courts, that one witness is not sufficient to establish the fact of adultery, said, " To this authority I readily submit, and I am bound to do so ; but I must honestly say that I do it upon compulsion. I am bound by this rule, and so long as it remains a rule of these courts, so long as more evidence is required to prove an act of adultery than to find a man guilty of murder, it will be my duty to obey that rule."†

The very few cases in which the law of England requires a particular amount of evidence, as on trials for high-treason, where two witnesses are required, and in cases of perjury, where there must be two witnesses, or

* Mittermaier, *ut supra*, ch. 8.
† *Per* Dr. Lushington in Taylor *v.* Taylor, 6 Eccl. & Mar. Cases, 563.

the testimony of one witness confirmed by some independent corroborative evidence, are obviously grounded upon different principles ; in the former, upon motives of policy and justice, for the protection of persons charged with political crime from becoming the victims of party violence ; and in the latter, because the mere contradiction by the oath of a single witness is obviously not of itself sufficient to prove that the person accused has been guilty of wilful falsehood.*

If it be proved that a party charged with crime has been placed in circumstances which commonly operate as inducements to commit the act in question,—that he has so far yielded to the operation of those inducements as to have manifested the disposition to commit the particular crime,—that he has possessed the requisite means and opportunities of effecting the object of his wishes,—that recently after the commission of the act he has become possessed of the fruits or other consequential advantages of the crime,—if he be identified with the *corpus delicti* by any conclusive mechanical circumstances, as by the impressions of his footsteps, or the discovery of any article of his apparel or property at or near the scene of the crime,—if there be relevant appearances of suspicion, connected with his conduct, person, or dress, and such as he might reasonably be presumed to be able, if innocent, to account for, but which nevertheless he cannot or will not explain,—if, being put upon his defence *recently* after the crime, under strong circumstances of adverse presumption, he cannot show where he was at the time of its commission,—if he attempt to evade the force of those circumstances of presumption by false or incredible pre-

---

* See also 7 & 8 Vict. c. 101, s. 3, and 8 & 9 Vict. c. 10, s. 6, as to confirmatory evidence in orders of affiliation.

tences, or by endeavours to evade or pervert the course of justice,—the concurrence of all or of many of these cogent circumstances, inconsistent with the supposition of his innocence and unopposed by facts leading to a counter-presumption, naturally, reasonably, and satisfactorily establishes the moral certainty of his guilt,—if not with the same kind of assurance as if he had been seen to commit the deed, at least with all the assurance which the nature of the case and the vast majority of human actions admit. In such circumstances we are justly warranted in adopting, without qualification or reserve, the conclusions to which, " by a broad, general, and comprehensive view of the facts, and not relying upon minute circumstances with respect to which there may be some source of error,"* the mind is thus naturally and inevitably conducted, and in regarding the application of the sanctions of penal law as a mere corollary.

Nor can any practice be more absurd and unjust, than that perpetuated in some modern codes, which, while they admit of proof by circumstantial evidence, inconsistently deny to it its logical and ordinary consequences. Thus the penal code of Austria† prohibits the application of capital punishment to the crime of murder, " où l'inculpé n'est convaincu que par le concours des circonstances;" but nevertheless the party may be sentenced to an imprisonment of twenty years; and the same indefensible practice prevails in many other States, though with a considerable diversity as to the maximum penalty.‡ How wise and just the emphatic condemnatory language of the French Papinian: "Ut veritas, ita probatio, scindi non potest : quæ non est plena veritas est plena falsitas,

---

* *Per* Lord C. B. Pollock in Reg. *v.* Manning and wife, *ut supra.*

† Première partie, art. 430.

‡ See note, *ante,* p. 26, and Mittermaier, *ut supra,* c. 61.

non semiveritas; sic, quæ non est plena probatio, plane nulla probatio est."*

Section 2.

CONSIDERATIONS WHICH AUGMENT THE FORCE OF CIR-CUMSTANTIAL EVIDENCE IN PARTICULAR CASES.

Such are the considerations which constitute the force and effect of circumstantial evidence in *general;* but there are some collateral considerations which augment the force of circumstantial evidence in *particular* cases, and greatly increase the strength and security of our convictions, upon which it will be expedient to dilate.

(1) The principal of these auxiliary considerations arises from the concurrence of many or of several separate and independent circumstances pointing to the same conclusion, especially if they be deposed to by unconnected witnesses. In proportion to the number of cogent circumstances, each separately bearing a strict relation to the same inference, the stronger their united force becomes, and the more secure becomes our conviction of the moral certainty of the fact they are alleged to prove, as the intensity of light is increased by the concentration of a number of rays to a common focus. It is forcibly remarked by a learned writer, that "the more numerous are the particular analogies, the greater is the force of the general analogy resulting from the fuller induction of facts, not only from the mere accession of particulars, but from the additional strength which each particular derives by being surveyed jointly with other particulars, as one among the correlative parts of a system."†   Although neither the combined effect of the

* Cujas, Cod. t. de Leg., and see Gabriel, *ut supra*, 67.
† Hampden's Essay, *ut supra*, 63.

evidence, nor any of its constituent elements, admits of numerical computation, it is indubitable, that the proving power increases with the number of the independent circumstances and witnesses, according to a geometrical progression. The effect of a body of circumstantial evidence is sometimes compared to that of a chain, but the metaphor is obviously inaccurate, since the weakest part of a chain is, of necessity, its strongest. Such evidence is more aptly compared to a rope made up of many slender filaments twisted together. The rope has strength more than sufficient to bear the stress laid upon it, though no one of the filaments of which it is composed would be sufficient for that purpose.* These remarks are applicable with especial force to the written enumeration of a number of minute facts "multiplying beyond calculation the means of detecting imposture; serving the purpose of an accuser by hints and allusions only, such as would be found in genuine correspondence, not by those clear and positive manifestations of guilt by which an eager partisan betrays his forgeries."†

The increase of force produced by the concurrence of independent *circumstances*, is analogous to that which is the result of the concurrence of several independent *witnesses* in relating the same fact; and if these elements admitted of numerical evaluation, their combined effect would be capable of being represented by a fraction, having for its numerator the product of the chances favourable to the testimony of each witness, and for its denominator, the sum of all the chances, favourable and unfavourable, the unfavourable chances being the product of the several deficiencies of the witnesses. But if in such

* Reid's Essay on the Intell. Pow. c. iii.
† 2 Mack. Hist. *ut supra.* 331.

case the witnesses be dependent on each other, so that
the testimony of the second depends for its truth upon
the first, that of the third upon the second, and so on,
then the effect of the evidence diminishes with every increase in the number of the witnesses or the facts, just
as an increase in the denominator of a fraction reduces it
to one of inferior value.*

A learned writer has illustrated the subject by a case
which at first sight seems an extreme one, and it has occasionally been pressed in argument with much force.†
" Let it be supposed," says he, " that A. is robbed, and
that the contents of his purse were one penny, two sixpences, three shillings, four half-crowns, five crowns, six
half-sovereigns, and seven sovereigns, and that a person
apprehended in the same fair or market where the robbery takes place is found in possession of the same remarkable combination of coin and of no other, but that
no part of the coin can be identified; and that no circumstances operate against the prisoner except his possession of the same combination of coin : here, notwithstanding the very extraordinary coincidence as to the
number of each individual kind of coin, although the
circumstances raise a high probability of identity, yet it
still is one of a definite and inconclusive nature."‡   The
probability that the coins lost and those discovered are
the same is so great, that perhaps the first impulse of
every person unaccustomed to this kind of reasoning is
unhesitatingly to conclude that they certainly are so;
yet, nevertheless, the case is one of probability only, the

* 2 Kirwan's Logic, c. vii.   Hartley's Obs. c. iii. s. 2. prop. LXXX.

† Trial of the Rev. Ephraim Avery, charged with the murder of
Sarah Maria Cornell, before the Supreme Court of Rhode Island, May,
1833. (Boston.)   ‡ 2 Starkie's L. of Ev. 506.

degree of which is capable of exact calculation : but if that degree of probability, high as it is, were sufficient to warrant conviction in the particular case, it would be impossible to draw the distinction between the degree of probability which would and that which would not justify the infliction of penal retribution in other cases of inferior probability. In the case of a small number of coins, two or three for instance, the probability of their identity would be very weak ; and yet the two cases, though different in degree, are in principle the same ; and the chance of identity is in both cases equally capable of precise determination. The learned writer adds, that " although the fact taken nakedly and alone, without any collateral evidence, would in principle be inconclusive, yet, if coupled with circumstances of a conclusive tendency, such as flight, concealment of the money, false and fabricated statements as to the possession, it might afford strong and pregnant evidence of guilt for the consideration of the jury." In like manner it would be difficult to resist the inference of the identity of the coins, if in the case supposed they were scarce or foreign ones.

From the number of qualifying considerations connected with facts which are the subjects of testimonial evidence, and the impracticability of forming a numerical estimate of such facts, or of the veracity of witnesses, the cases to which this kind of reasoning is applicable, if there be any such, must be very rare. Every combination of moral incidents and contingent probabilities must give a product of the same nature, and affected by the same sources of error and uncertainty, as affect its separate elements ; and in all judgments grounded upon circumstantial evidence, this fundamental difference between moral and mathematical certainty must be borne in mind. "It were absurd," declares an eminent philosopher, "to say that the sentiment of belief produced by any probability is proportioned to the fraction which expresses that probability; but it is so related to it, or ought to be so, as to increase when it increases, and to diminish when it diminishes."[*] It is manifest, however, that the consequence of the concurrence of a plurality of witnesses, and the conjunction of separate circumstances, is to add immensely to the force of each; and if the credit of the witnesses be unimpeachable, and the hypotheses of confederacy and error be excluded, then no other conclusion can be rationally adopted, than that the facts to which they depose are true. The case suggested is that of circumstantial evidence in its most cogent form; and in such case, the conclusion to which its various elements converge must be regarded as morally irresistible.

(2) Independently of the direct effect of that probability which results from a concurrence of independent witnesses or circumstances, the security of our judgments is further increased from the considerations, that in proportion to the number of such witnesses or circumstances, confederacy is rendered more difficult, and that increased opportunities and facilities are afforded of contradicting some or all of the alleged facts if they be not true. To preserve consistency in a work even professedly of fiction, where all the writer's art and attention are perpetually exerted to avoid the smallest appearance of discrepancy, is an undertaking of no common difficulty; and it is obvious that the difficulty must be incomparably greater of preserving coherency and order in a fabricated case which must be supported by the confederacy of several persons, where, since by the hypothesis the congruity results from

* 4 Playfair's Works, 437.

artifice, the slightest variation in any of the minute circumstances of the transaction or of its concomitants may lead to detection and exposure. On the other hand, though if the main features of the case do not satisfactorily establish guilt, it is not safe to rely upon very minute circumstances,* yet, if the statements of the witnesses are based upon realities, the more rigorously they are sifted the more satisfactory will be the general result, from the development of minute, indirect, and unexpected coincidences in the attendant minor particulars of the main event. It was happily remarked by Dr. Paley, that " the *undesignedness* of the agreements (which undesignedness is gathered from their latency, their minuteness, their obliquity, the suitableness of the circumstances in which they consist, to the places in which those circumstances occur, and the circuitous references by which they are traced out) demonstrates that they have not been produced by meditation or by any fraudulent contrivance. But coincidences from which these causes are excluded, and which are too numerous and close to be accounted for by accidental concurrences of fiction, must necessarily have truth for their foundation."† The same learned writer also justly remarks, that " no advertency is sufficient to guard against slips and contradictions when circumstances are multiplied."‡ Hence it is observed in courts of justice, that witnesses who come to tell a concerted story are always reluctant to enter into particulars, and perpetually resort to shifts and evasions to gain time for deliberation and arrangement, before they reply

* *Per* Mr. Baron Rolfe, in Reg. *v.* Rush, Norfolk Sp. Ass. 1849.

† Paley's Evid. p. ii. c. vii.; Whately's Rhet. p. i. c. ii. s. 4; Greenleaf's Ex., *ut supra*, 39.

‡ Horæ Paulinæ, c. i.

directly to a course of examination likely to bring discredit upon their testimony.

It must nevertheless be admitted that history and experience supply abundant evidence that it would be most erroneous in the abstract to decide a matter of fact by numbers, and that there have been extraordinary cases of false charges, most artfully and plausibly supported by connected trains of feigned circumstances.

But considering the circumstances of the class of persons most frequently subjected to accusation for alleged crime,—deprived of personal freedom, often friendless, and still more frequently destitute of pecuniary resources and professional aid,—their imperfect means of knowing all the facts proposed to be proved, or the manner in which they are attempted to be connected,—the alleged facility of disproof is often more imaginary than real. Lord Eldon thus forcibly expressed himself on this question : " I have frequently thought that more effect has been given, than ought to have been given, in what is called the summing-up of a Judge on a trial, to the fact, that there has not been the contradiction on the part of the defence, which it is supposed the witnesses for the accusation might have received. . . . It may often happen that, in the course of a trial, circumstances are proved which have no bearing on the real question at issue ; and it may also happen, that facts are alleged and sworn to by witnesses, which it is impossible for the accused party to contradict ; circumstances may be stated by witnesses which are untrue ; yet they may not be contradicted, because the party injured by them, not expecting that that which never had any existence would be attempted to be proved, cannot be prepared with opposing witnesses. So also, in cases in which an individual witness speaks to occurrences at which no other person was present but himself, there it may be absolutely impossible to contradict him."[*]

Many of the disadvantages under which prisoners on trial are necessarily placed have been removed or diminished by the provisions of the Stats. 6 & 7 Will. IV., c. 114, ss. 3 and 4, and 22 & 23 Vict. c. 33, s. 3, which give to persons held to bail or committed to prison *a right* to require copies of the examination of the witnesses upon whose evidence they have been held to bail or committed, on payment of a moderate charge, and at the time of trial to inspect the depositions returned into Court.[†] The argument founded on the means afforded of disproof may consequently now be urged with more justice and effect than formerly, though still a party charged with crime has not of right any means of knowing any facts which may have been discovered in the interval before trial,[‡] or where an indictment is found without previous commitment. There are moreover many cases which do not afford the alleged facility of disproof in any degree; where, even admitting the truth of the testimony, the supposed presumption of guilt is nothing more than a mistaken conclusion from facts which afford no warrant for the inference of guilt; in such circumstances, to attempt disproof is to attempt to grapple with a shadow, —to require it, to exact an impossibility.[§]

[*] 3 Hansard's Parl. Deb., 2nd series, 1445.

[†] None of these enactments appear to apply to the case of commitment by the Coroner upon a verdict of murder. Of course, when the depositions are returned into the Court before which the trial is to be had, the Court has power by its general jurisdiction to order copies to be given.

[‡] Rex *v.* Greenacre, 8 C. & P. 32; Reg. *v.* Walford, *ib.* 767; Reg. *v.* Connor, 1 Cox, C. C. 233.

[§] Rex *v.* Looker, Rex *v.* Downing, and Rex *v.* Thornton, *supra.*

(3) The preceding considerations imply the necessity of consistency and general harmony in the testimony of the different witnesses.   All human events must necessarily form a coherent whole ; and actual occurrences can never be mutually inconsistent. If one of two witnesses depose that he saw an individual at London, and the other that he saw him at York at or near the same precise moment, the accounts are absolutely irreconcileable, and one or other of them must by design or by inadvertence be untrue.   A diversity ought always to excite caution and a scrupulous regard to the capacity, situation, and disposition of the witnesses, and especially to the possibility of confusion from some mental emotion.   " We are frequently mistaken," said Lord Chief Baron Pollock, " even as to what we may suppose we see ; and still oftener are we mistaken as to that which we suppose we hear."* Lord Clarenden relates, that in the alarm created by the Fire of London, so terrified were men with their own apprehensions, that the inhabitants of a whole street ran in a great tumult one way, upon the rumour that the French were marching at the other end of it.†   The same noble historian has also given another anecdote relating to that great calamity, too instructive as applicable to this subject to be omitted.   A servant of the Portuguese ambassador was seized by the populace and pulled about, and very ill-used, upon the accusation of a substantial citizen, who was ready to take his oath that he saw him put his hand in his pocket, and throw a fireball into a house, which immediately burst into flames.   The foreigner, who could not speak English, heard these charges interpreted to him with amazement.   Being

* In Reg. *v.* Manning and wife, *ut supra.*
† 3 Life and Continuation, 91, Oxford ed., 1827.

asked what it was that he pulled out of his pocket, and what it was he threw into the house, he answered, that he did not think he had put his hand into his pocket, but that he remembered very well that as he walked in the street he saw a piece of bread upon the ground, which he took up and laid upon a shelf in the next house, according to the custom of his country; which, observes a learned writer,* is so strong, that the King of Portugal himself would have acted with the same scrupulous regard to general economy. Upon searching the house, which was in view, the bread was found just within the door, upon a board as described; and the house on fire was two doors beyond it, the citizen having erroneously concluded it to be the same; "which," says Lord Clarendon, "was very natural in the fright that all men were in."†

But *variations* in the relations by different persons of the same transaction or event, in respect of unimportant circumstances, are not necessarily to be regarded as indicative of fraud or falsehood, provided there be substantial agreement in other respects. True strength of mind consists in not allowing the judgment, when founded upon convincing evidence, to be disturbed because there are immaterial discrepancies which cannot be reconciled. When the vast inherent differences in individuals with respect to natural faculties and acquired habits of accurate observation, faithful recollection, and precise narration, and the important influence of intellectual and moral culture, are duly considered, it will not be thought surprising that entire agreement is seldom found amongst a number of witnesses as to all the collateral incidents of the same principal event. Lord Ellenborough said that the general

* 3 Wooddeson's Lect. on the Laws of England, Lect. 53.
† 3 Clarendon's Life and Continuation, 86.

accordance of all material circumstances rather confirmed by minute diversity than weakened the general credit of the whole, and gave it the advantage which belongs to an artless and unartificial tale ; and that minute variances exclude the idea of any uniform contrivance and design in the variation, for where it is an artful and prepared story, the parties agree in the minutest facts as well as in the most important.*   " I know not," says Paley, " a more rash or unphilosophical conduct of the understanding than to reject the substance of a story by reason of some diversity in the circumstances with which it is related. The usual character of human testimony is substantial truth under circumstantial variety. That is what the daily experience of courts of justice teaches. When accounts of a transaction come from the mouths of different witnesses, it is seldom that it is not possible to pick out apparent or real inconsistencies between them. These circumstances are studiously displayed by an adverse pleader, but oftentimes with little impression upon the minds of the Judges. On the contrary, a close and minute agreement induces the suspicion of confederacy and fraud."†

Instances of discrepancy as to the minor attendant circumstances of historical events are numberless. Lord Clarendon relates that the Marquis of Argyle was condemned to be *hanged*, and that the sentence was performed the *same day*. Burnet, Woodrow, and Echard, writers of good authority, who lived near the time, state that he was *beheaded*, though condemned to be hanged, and that the sentence was pronounced on Saturday and carried into effect on the Monday following.‡ Charles II.,

* Rex *v.* Lord Cochrane and others, Gurney's Rep. 456.
† Paley's Ev. p. iii. c. i.
‡ Comp. 2 Life and Continuation, 266, and Paley's Ev. p. iii. c. 1.

after his flight from Worcester, has been variously stated to have embarked at Brighthelmstone, and at New Shoreham.* Clarendon states that the royal standard was erected about six o'clock of the evening of the 25th of August, "a very stormy and tempestuous day;" whereas other contemporary historians variously state that it was erected on the 22nd and the 24th of that month.† By some historians the death of the Parliamentary leader Pym, is stated to have taken place in the month of May, 1643;‡ while by others it is said to have occurred in the following year. To come nearer to our own times, the author of a celebrated biographical memoir relates, that after the Rebellion of 1745, three lords were executed at Tower-hill: whereas it is well known that *two* only underwent that doom, the third, Lord Nithsdale, having by the heroic self-devotion of his wife effected his escape the night before his intended execution.§ It is remarkable that contemporary and early writers have stated the lady in question to have been his mother. Such discrepancies never excite a serious doubt as to the truth of the principal facts with which they are connected; unless they can be traced to the operation of prejudice or some other sinister motive.‖

* 6 Hist. of Reb. 541 ; 11 Lingard's Hist. of Eng. c. 1.

† 3 Hist. of Reb. 190; 1 Rushworth's Coll. i. p. iii. 783 ; Mem. of Ludlow, 15.

‡ Whitelock's Memorials, 66 ; Baker's Chron. 570 b ; 4 Hist. of Reb. 436 ; 7 Hume's Hist. 510, ed. 1818 ; 1 Godwin's Hist. of the Comm. 17.

§ Coxe's Mem. of Walpole, 73.

‖ See in 4 Clarendon's Hist. 436, a remarkable instance of historical dishonesty. He states that Pym died of a loathsome disease, *morbus pediculosus*, evidently with the design of propagating the notion that it was "a mark of divine vengeance" (7 Hume's Hist. 510) ; whereas he must have known that his corpse was exposed to public view for several days before it was interred, in confutation of this calumnious statement. (Ludlow's Mem. 31.)

U

Still less are mere *omissions* to be considered as necessarily casting discredit upon testimony which stands in other respects unimpeached and unsuspected. Omissions are generally capable of explanation by the consideration that the mind may be so deeply impressed with, and the attention so riveted to, a particular fact, as to withdraw attention from concomitant circumstances, or prevent it from taking note of what is passing. It has been justly remarked, that "upon general principles, affirmative is better than negative evidence. A person deposing to a fact, which he states he saw, must either speak truly, or must have invented his story, or it must have been sheer delusion. Not so with negative evidence; a fact may have taken place in the very sight of a person who may not have observed it; and if he did observe it, may have forgotten it."* The meteor called the Northern Lights is not recorded to have been seen in the British Islands before the commencement of the last century.† Negative evidence is therefore regarded as of little or no weight when opposed to the positive affirmative evidence of persons of unimpeachable credit. Sometimes however the non-relation of particular facts amounts to the *suppressio veri*, which in point of moral guilt may be equal to positive mendacity, and destructive of all claim to testimonial credit.‡

* Sir Herbert Jenner, in Chambers *v.* the Queen's Proctor, 2 Curt. 415.
† Whately's Introd. Less. on Christ. Ev. 45.
‡ Grafton, who was printer to Queen Elizabeth, in his Chronicles, published in 1562, in writing the history of King John, has made no mention of Magna Charta ; perhaps he considered that his silence might be deemed complimentary to that arbitrary princess.

SECTION 3.

CASES IN ILLUSTRATION OF THE FORCE OF CIRCUMSTANTIAL EVIDENCE.

MANY remarkable cases of this nature have been given in the preceding pages, in application to the exemplification of some specific doctrine or object; to these will now be added, as an appropriate commentary upon this discussion of the scientific principles which govern the reception and estimate of circumstantial evidence, some of the most curious and instructive examples of the force of a cumulation of moral and mechanical facts which are to be found in the annals of criminal jurisprudence.

(1) In the autumn of 1786 a young woman, who lived with her parents in a remote district in Kirkcudbright, was one day left alone in the cottage, her parents having gone out to the harvest-field. On their return home a little after mid-day they found their daughter murdered, with her throat cut in a most shocking manner. The circumstances in which she was found, the character of the deceased, and the appearance of the wound, all concurred in excluding any presumption of suicide; while the surgeons who examined the wound were satisfied that it had been inflicted by a sharp instrument, and by a person who must have held the instrument in his left hand. Upon opening the body the deceased appeared to have been some months gone with child; and on examining the ground about the cottage, there were discovered the footsteps of a person who had seemingly been running hastily from the cottage, by an indirect road through a quagmire or bog in which there were stepping-stones. It appeared, however, that the person

in his haste and confusion had slipped his foot and stepped into the mire, by which he must have been wet nearly to the middle of the leg. The prints of the footsteps were accurately measured, and an exact impression taken of them; and it appeared that they were those of a person who must have worn shoes the *soles* of which had been newly mended, and which, as is usual in that part of the country, had iron knobs or nails in them. There were discovered also, along the track of the footsteps, and at certain intervals, drops of blood; and on a stile or small gateway near the cottage, and in the line of the footsteps, some marks resembling those of a hand which had been bloody. Not the slightest suspicion at this time attached to any particular person as the murderer, nor was it even suspected who might be the father of the child of which the girl was pregnant. At the funeral a number of persons of both sexes attended, and the stewart-depute thought it the fittest opportunity of endeavouring if possible to discover the murderer; conceiving rightly that to avoid suspicion, whoever he was, he would not on that occasion be absent. With this view he called together after the interment the whole of the men who were present, being about sixty in number. He caused the shoes of each of them to be taken off and measured; and one of the shoes was found to resemble, pretty nearly, the impression of the footsteps near to the cottage. The wearer of the shoe was the schoolmaster of the parish; which lead to a suspicion that he must have been the father of the child, and had been guilty of the murder to save his character. On a closer examination however of the shoe, it was discovered that it was pointed at the toe, whereas the impression of the footstep was round at that place.

The measurement of the rest went on, and after going through nearly the whole number, one at length was discovered which corresponded exactly with the impression in dimensions, shape of the foot, form of the sole, and the number and position of the nails. William Richardson, the young man to whom the shoe belonged, on being asked where he was the day the deceased was murdered, replied, seemingly without embarrassment, that he had been all that day employed at his master's work, a statement which his master and fellow-servants, who were present, confirmed. This going so far to remove suspicion, a warrant of commitment was not then granted; but some circumstances occurring a few days afterwards, having a tendency to excite it anew, the young man was apprehended and lodged in jail. Upon his examination he acknowledged that he was *left-handed;* and some scratches being observed on his cheek, he said he had got them when pulling nuts in a wood a few days before. He still adhered to what he had said of his having been on the day of the murder employed constantly at his master's work, at some distance from the place where the deceased resided; but in the course of the inquiry it turned out, that he had been absent from his work about half an hour (the time being distinctly ascertained) in the course of the forenoon of that day; that he called at a smith's shop, under the pretence of wanting something, which it did not appear he had any occasion for; and that this smith's shop was in the way to the cottage of the deceased. A young girl, who was some hundred yards from the cottage, said that about the time the murder was committed (and which corresponded to the time that Richardson was absent from his fellow-servants) she saw a person ex-

actly with his dress and appearance running hastily toward the cottage, but did not see him return, though
he might have gone round by a small eminence which
would intercept him from her view, and which was the
very track where the footsteps had been traced. His
fellow-servants now recollected that in the forenoon of
that day they were employed with Richardson in driving their master's carts; and that when passing by a
wood, which they named, he said that he must run to
the smith's shop and would be back in a short time.
He then left his cart under their charge; and having
waited for him about half an hour, which one of the servants ascertained by having at the time looked at his
watch, they remarked on his return that he had been
longer absent than he said he would be, to which he
replied that he stopped in the wood to gather some
nuts. They observed at this time one of his stockings
wet and soiled, as if he had stepped into a puddle; on
which they asked where he had been. He said he had
stepped into a marsh, the name of which he mentioned;
on which his fellow-servants remarked, " that he must
have been either mad or drunk if he had stepped into
that marsh, as there was a footpath which went along
the side of it." It then appeared, by comparing the
time he was absent with the distance of the cottage
from the place where he had left his fellow-servants,
that he might have gone there, committed the murder,
and returned to them. A search was then made for the
stockings he had worn that day, which were found concealed in the thatch of the apartment where he slept,
and appeared to be much soiled, and to have some
drops of blood on them. The last he accounted for by
saying, first, that his nose had been bleeding some days

before; but it being observed that he had worn other stockings on that day, he said he had assisted in bleeding a horse; but it was proved that he had not assisted, and had stood at such a distance that the blood could not have reached him. On examining the mud or sand upon the stockings, it corresponded precisely with that of the mire or puddle adjoining to the cottage, which was of a very particular kind, none other of the same kind being found in that neighbourhood. The shoemaker was then discovered who had mended his shoes a short time before, and he spoke distinctly to the shoes of the prisoner, which were exhibited to him, as having been those he had mended. It then came out that Richardson had been acquainted with the deceased, who was considered in the county as of weak intellect, and had on one occasion been seen with her in a wood, in circumstances that led to a suspicion that he had had criminal intercourse with her; and on being taunted with having such connection with one in her situation, he seemed much ashamed and greatly hurt. It was proved further, by the person who sat next to him when his shoes were measuring, that he trembled much, and seemed a good deal agitated; and that in the interval between that time and his being apprehended he had been advised to fly, but his answer was, " Where can I fly to ?"   On the other hand, evidence was brought to show that, about the time of the murder, a boat's crew from Ireland had landed on that part of the coast, near to the dwelling of the deceased; and it was said that some of the crew might have committed the murder, though their motives for doing so it was difficult to explain, it not being alleged that robbery was their purpose, or that anything was missing from the cottages in the neighbourhood. The prisoner was tried at Dumfries, in the spring of 1787, and the jury by a great plurality of voices found him guilty. Before his execution he confessed that he was the murderer ; and said it was to hide his shame that he committed the deed, knowing that the girl was with child by him. He mentioned also to the clergyman who attended him, where the knife would be found with which he had perpetrated the murder ; and it was found accordingly in the place he described, under a stone in a wall, with marks of blood upon it.*

The casual discovery of circumstances which indicated the existence of a powerful *motive* to commit the deed,— the facts, that it had been committed by a *left-handed* man, as the prisoner was, thus narrowing the range of inquiry, and that there was an interval of absence which afforded the prisoner the necessary *opportunity* of committing the crime,—his false assertion that he had not been absent from his work on that day, contradicted as it was by witnesses who saw him on the way to and in the vicinity of the scene of the murder, amounting to an admission of the relevancy and weight of that circumstance if uncontradicted,—the discovery of his footsteps, near the spot,—his agitation at the time of the admeasurement and comparison of his shoes with the impressions,—the discovery of his secreted stockings, spotted with blood, and soiled with mire peculiar to the vicinity of the cottage,—the scratches on his face,—his various contradicted statements,—all these particulars combine

---

* Rex *v.* Richardson, Burnett's C. L. *ut supra*, 524. This case is also concisely stated in the Memoirs of the Life of Sir Walter Scott (iv. 52, 2nd ed.); and it supplied one of the most striking incidents in ' Guy Mannering.'

to render this a most satisfactory case of conviction, and to exemplify the high degree of assurance which circumstantial evidence is capable of producing.

(2) A man named Patch had been received by Mr. Isaac Blight, a ship-breaker, near Greenland Dock, into his service in the year 1803. Mr. Blight having become embarrassed in his circumstances in July 1805, entered into a deed of composition with his creditors; and in consequence of the failure of this arrangement he made a colourable transfer of his property to the prisoner. It was afterwards agreed between them, that Mr. Blight was to retire nominally from the business, which the prisoner was to manage, and the former was to have two-thirds of the profits, and the prisoner the remaining third, for which he was to pay £1250. Of this amount, £250 was paid in cash, and a draft was given for the remainder upon a person named Goom, which would become payable on the 16th of September; the prisoner representing that he had received the purchase-money of an estate and lent it to Goom. On the 16th of September the prisoner represented to Mr. Blight's bankers that Goom could not take up the bill, and withdrew it, substituting his own draft upon Goom, to fall due on the 20th of September. On the 19th of September Mr. Blight went to visit his wife at Margate, and the prisoner accompanied him as far as Deptford, and then went to London, and represented to the bankers that Goom would not be able to face his draft, but that he had obtained from him a note which satisfied him, and therefore they were not to present it. The prisoner boarded in Mr. Blight's house, and the only other inmate was a female servant, whom, about eight o'clock on the same evening (the 19th), he sent out to procure some oysters for his supper. During

her absence a gun or pistol ball was fired through the shutter of a parlour fronting the Thames, where the family, when at home, usually spent their evenings. It was low water, and the mud was so deep that any person attempting to escape in that direction must have been suffocated; and a man who was standing near the gate of the wharf, which was the only other mode of escape, heard the report, but saw no person. From the manner in which the ball had entered the shutter, it must have been discharged by some person who was close to the shutter; and the river was so much below the level of the house, that the ball, if it had been fired from thence, must have reached a much higher part than that which it struck. The prisoner declined the offer of the neighbours to remain in the house with him that night. On the following day he wrote to inform Mr. Blight of this transaction, stating his hope that the shot had been accidental, that he knew of no person who had any animosity against him, that he wished to know for whom it was intended, and that he should be happy to hear from him, but much more so to see him. Mr. Blight returned home on the 23rd of September, having previously been to London to see his bankers on the subject of the £1000 draft. Upon getting home, the draft became the subject of conversation, and Mr. Blight desired the prisoner to go to London and not to return without the money. Upon his return from London the prisoner and Mr. Blight spent the evening in the *back* parlour, a different one from that in which the family usually sat. About eight o'clock the prisoner went from the parlour into the kitchen, and asked the servant for a candle, complaining that he was disordered. The prisoner's way from the kitchen was through an outer door which fastened by a spring lock, and across a paved court in front of the house, which was enclosed by palisadoes, and through a gate over a wharf, in front of that court, on which there was the kind of soil peculiar to premises for breaking up ships, and then through a counting-house. All of these doors, as well as the door of the parlour, the prisoner left open, notwithstanding the state of alarm excited by the shot. The servant heard the privy-door slam, and almost at the same moment saw the flash of a pistol at the door of the parlour where the deceased was sitting, upon which she ran and shut the outer door and gate. The prisoner immediately afterwards rapped loudly at the door for admittance, with his clothes in disorder. He evinced great apparent concern for Mr. Blight, who was mortally wounded and died on the following day. From the state of the tide, and from the testimony of various persons who were on the outside of the premises, no person could have escaped from them. In consequence of this event Mrs. Blight returned home, and the prisoner, in answer to an inquiry about the draft which had made her husband so uneasy, told her that it was paid, and claimed the whole of the property as his own. Suspicion soon fixed upon the prisoner, and in his sleeping-room was found a pair of stockings rolled up like clean stockings, but with the feet plastered over with the sort of soil found on the wharf, and a ramrod was found in the privy. The prisoner usually wore boots, but on the evening of the murder he wore shoes and stockings. It was supposed that, to prevent alarm to the deceased or the female servant, the murderer must have approached without his shoes, and afterwards gone on the wharf to throw away the pistol into the river. All the prisoner's

statements as to his pecuniary transactions with Goom
and his right to draw upon him, and the payment of the
bill, turned out to be false. He attempted to tamper
with the servant-girl as to her evidence before the coroner, and urged her to keep to one account; and before
that officer he made several inconsistent statements as to
his pecuniary transactions with the deceased, and equi-
vocated much as to whether he wore boots or shoes
on the evening of the murder, as well as to his ownership of the soiled stockings, which however were clearly
proved to be his, and for the soiled state of which he
made no attempt to account. The prisoner suggested
the existence of malicious feelings in two persons with
whom the deceased had been on ill terms; but they had
no motive for doing him any injury, and it was clearly
proved that upon both occasions of attack they were at
a distance.

The prisoner's motive was to possess himself of the
business and property of his benefactor; and to all appearance his falsehoods and duplicity were on the point
of being discovered. His apparent incaution on the
evening of the murder could be accounted for after the
preceding alarm, by no other supposition than that it was
the result of premeditation, and intended to afford facilities for the execution of his dark purposes. The direction of the first ball through the shutter, excluded the
possibility that it had been fired from any other place
than the deceased's own premises; and by a singular
concurrence of circumstances, it was clearly proved that
no person escaped from the premises after either of the
shots, so that suspicion was necessarily restricted to the
persons on the premises. The occurrence of the first
attack during the temporary absence of the servant (that

absence contrived by the prisoner himself),—the discovery of a ramrod in the very place where the prisoner
had been, and of his soiled stockings folded up so as to
evade observation,—his interference with one of the witnesses,—his falsehoods respecting his pecuniary transactions with Goom and with the deceased,—and his
attempts to exonerate himself from suspicion by impli-
cating other persons,—all these cogent circumstances of
presumption tended to show not only that the prisoner
was the only person who had any motive to destroy the
deceased, but that the crime could have been committed
by no other person; and while all the facts were naturally explicable upon the hypothesis of his guilt, they
were incapable of any other reasonable solution. The
prisoner was convicted and executed.*

(3) A respectable farmer, who had been at Stourbridge market on the 18th of December, left that place
on foot a little after four in the afternoon, to return
home, a distance of between two and three miles. About
half a mile from his own house he was overtaken by a
man, who inquired the road for Kidderminster; and
they walked together for two or three hundred yards,
when the stranger drew behind and shot him in the
back, and then robbed him of about eleven pounds in
money and a silver watch. After lingering ten days, he
died of the wound thus received. The wounded man
noticed that the pistol was long and very bright, and
that the robber had on a dark-coloured great-coat, which
reached down to the calves of his legs. Several circumstances of correspondence with the description given
by the deceased, conspired to fix suspicion upon the

* Surrey Spring Ass. 1806, *coram* L. C. B. Macdonald. Gurney's
Short-hand Report.

prisoner, who for about fourteen months had worked as a carpenter at Ombersley, seventeen miles from Stourbridge. It was discovered that he had been absent from that place from the 17th to the 22nd of December; that on the 23rd he had taken two boxes, one containing his working-tools and the other his clothes, to Worcester, and there delivered them to a carrier, addressed to John Wood, at an inn in London, to be left till called for, the name by which he was known being William Howe; and that on the 25th he finally left Ombersley, and went to London. Upon inquiry at the inn to which the boxes were directed, it was found that a person answering the description of the prisoner had removed them in a mealman's cart to the Bull in Bishopsgate Street, and that on the 5th of January they had been removed from thence in a cooper's cart. Here all trace of the boxes seemed cut off; but on the 12th of January the police officers succeeded in tracing them to a widow woman's house, in a court in the same street; when, upon examining the box which contained the prisoner's clothes, they found a screw-barrel pistol, a pistol-key, a bullet-mould, a single bullet, a small quantity of gunpowder in a cartridge, and a fawn-skin waistcoat; which latter circumstance was important, as the prisoner was seen in Stourbridge on the day of the murder, dressed in a waistcoat of that kind. By remaining concealed in the woman's house the police were enabled to apprehend the prisoner, who called there the following night. Upon his apprehension, he denied that he had ever been at Stourbridge, or heard of the deceased being shot; and he accounted for changing his name at Worcester, by stating that he had had a difference with his fellow work-people, and afterwards that he did it to prevent his wife, whom he had determined to leave, from being able to follow him.   On being asked where he was on the 18th of December, he said he believed at Kidderminster, a town about six miles from Stourbridge.   Upon the prisoner's subsequent examination before the magistrates, he stated that he was at Kidderminster on the 17th of December, and at Stourbridge on the 18th, (the day of the murder,) but that he was not out of the latter town from the time of his arrival there, at one o'clock in the afternoon, until half-past seven the following morning; that in the afternoon he went to look about the town for lodgings, and ultimately went to his lodgings about six o'clock in the evening. The account which the prisoner thus gave of himself was proved to be a tissue of falsehoods.   He had been seen by several witnesses between four and five in the afternoon of the day in question, on the road leading from Stourbridge toward, and not far from, the spot where the deceased was shot, and about half past five he was seen going in great haste in the opposite direction, toward Stourbridge.   He afterwards called at two public-houses at Stourbridge,—at the first of them about six o'clock, and at the other about nine the same evening; at both of which the attack and robbery were the subjects of conversation, in which the prisoner joined; and he was distinctly spoken to as having worn a fawn-skin waistcoat.   On the 21st of December the prisoner sold a watch of which the deceased had been robbed, at Warwick, stating it to be a family watch.   But the most conclusive circumstance was, that a letter was sent by the prisoner while in gaol to his wife, who, being herself unable to read, had got a neighbour to read it to her; which contained a direction to remove some things concealed in a rick near Stourbridge; where, upon search being made, were discovered a glove, containing three bullets, and a screw-barrel pistol, the fellow to that found in the prisoner's box. A gunmaker deposed that the bullet extracted from the wound had been discharged from a screw-barrel pistol, such as that produced, and that that bullet and the bullet found in the prisoner's box had been cast in the same mould.

The prisoner's denial, on his apprehension, that he had ever been at Stourbridge, or heard of the act, though he had been seen near the spot about the time when the shot was fired, denoted a consciousness of the fatal effect of any evidence tending to establish the fact of his presence there. The discovery of a fawn-skin waistcoat in his possession, corresponding with that worn by him when seen at Stourbridge on the evening of the murder, —his possession and disposal of the deceased's watch within three days after he had delivered it to his murderer,—his false statement that it was a family watch,— the correspondence between the weapon found in the rick and that found in the prisoner's box, and between the bullet extracted from the wound and that found in the same box, and the peculiarity that the deceased had been killed by a wound from a screw-barrelled pistol,—all these circumstances placed the guilt of the prisoner beyond any reasonable doubt, and there was no possibility of referring them to casual and accidental coincidence, or of explaining them upon any hypothesis compatible with his innocence. He was convicted, and before his execution confessed his guilt.*

(4) Three men, named Smith, Varnham, and Timms, were tried before Mr. Justice Coltman, at the Norfolk Spring Assizes, 1837, for the murder of Hannah Mans-

* Stafford Spring Ass. 1813, *coram* Mr. Justice Bayley.

field, on Tuesday the 3rd of January preceding. The deceased, who was about forty years of age, lived alone in a cottage at Denver, on the border of a common, at a distance from the turnpike-road leading from Hilgay through Denver to Downham, and remote from any other house, except an adjoining cottage under the same roof, occupied by a labourer and his family. The deceased had acquired some repute as a fortune-teller, for which purpose she kept by her some money, which she called her bright money; and she possessed a quantity of plate, consisting of cream-jugs, table- and tea-spoons, sugar-tongs, salt-cellars, and a silver tankard, which she kept in a corner cupboard and had frequently boastfully displayed. She spent the evening preceding the murder at her neighbour's house, which she left about half-past eleven; her neighbour's wife, being engaged in washing, did not go to bed till one o'clock, when she disturbed her husband, who, as he lay awake, about two o'clock, heard a noise in the deceased's cottage, but hearing nothing further, went to sleep again. About ten o'clock the following morning the poor woman was found dead in her cottage, with her throat cut from ear to ear; the cottage-door had been split open by some violent effort, and the cottage had been robbed of her money and treasure. The footsteps of two men were traced from the turnpike-road towards the deceased's house, and from the house into the stack-yard, and back again to the foot-path, and across the common to a run of water, and thence to the turnpike-road: one of the footsteps was very large, and peculiarly shaped and nailed, there being four nailmarks in the centre of the heel, in a line from back to front, and two on each side; and there were nailmarks also in the waist of the heel, between the sole

x

and the heel, and the sole was very full of nailmarks.
The prisoner Timms's shoes exactly corresponded with
these marks ; the other footstep was a smaller one, and
full of such marks. The large footmark proceeding from
the house had marks of blood, and the smaller footstep
was on the other side of the path, and the centre of the
path was so hard and beaten that a third person might
have walked on it without leaving any impression. Only
the larger footstep was traced to the stack-yard, but both
footsteps were traced in a direction toward and from the
house. There was also the footstep of a third person,
who appeared to have been stationed for the purpose of
watching the back door of the adjoining cottage. The
three prisoners had worked in the neighbourhood as ex-
cavators, a few months before the murder ; and about
twelve months previously, the prisoner Smith, in company with two other men, had called at the adjoining
cottage, and asked if Hannah Mansfield was at home,
supposing that to be her cottage, stating that he had lost
some tools, about which he wished to consult her. They
had been loitering at various low public-houses in the
neighbourhood of the deceased's cottage for several days
preceding the murder, and left one of those public-houses
about two miles from her residence, where they had
spent the evening, about eleven o'clock on the night of
the murder. Three men, corresponding in appearance
with the prisoners, one of whom was identified as the
prisoner Timms, were met on the following morning
about three o'clock, a mile from the deceased's house,
walking very fast along the road from Denver to Downham ; and about half-past eight the same morning the
same three men were seen at Leverington, fourteen miles
from Denver, apparently fatigued, and the pocket of one

of them stuffed with something bulky. At Sutton St. Edmund's, about twenty miles from Denver, the prisoners stopped at a public-house to refresh themselves, and one of them paid away a very bright and unworn sixpence and shilling, of the year 1817. After having staid some hours, they proceeded to Whaplode Drove, where they remained at a public-house for several days, and fell into company with a shoemaker, who made two pairs of boots for Varnham and Smith, for which Timms paid in a half-sovereign, a half-guinea, and a sixpence. Varnham cut the tops from his old boots, and the landlord's wife burned the soles, and threw the clates upon an ash-heap, where they were afterwards found by a police-officer, and they exactly fitted one of the impressions made in the snow near the cottage. While sitting by the fireside one evening at this public-house, the prisoner Smith laid hold of the bottom of his pocket, which seemed heavy, and a bundle contained in a silk handkerchief dropped out, from which some teaspoons, a pair of sugar-tongs, and some glass fell on the floor; the glass was broken, the other things he hastily collected and replaced. On the following day the prisoner Timms called upon the shoemaker, who had been present on the previous evening, professedly to talk about the boots which he had to make, and took occasion to remark, that "he need not say anything about what he had seen, as it might get the landlord into a scrape, though for themselves they did not care about it, as they had got the things from Lisbon." On the Saturday following the prisoners were traced to Whittlesea, where they offered for sale to a gunmaker a mass of molten silver, upwards of two pounds weight, which the prisoner Timms said had consisted of spoons, salt-cellars, and elegant things fit for any table,

—a description corresponding with the deceased's plate; and they offered to purchase a pair of pistols. The silver was cut by the person to whom it was offered into six or seven pieces, and offered by him for sale to another person; but not having succeeded in disposing of it, they gave his wife in return for his trouble a small strip of it, weighing about an ounce, and three keys, which were afterwards identified as having belonged to the deceased. The prisoners were then traced to and apprehended at Doncaster. To the officers they gave false accounts of themselves. Stains of blood were found upon some parts of the clothes of all the prisoners, and the clothes of two of them appeared to have been washed in order to remove stains. On the person of Smith were found several pounds in money, a picklock key, lucifer matches, and a knife on which was some coagulated blood; and on the person of Timms was found, wrapped up in a piece of linen, a mass or wedge of molten silver. With several of their fellow-prisoners Smith and Varnham conversed upon the subject of this cruel action in language of disgusting coarseness and brutality; which implied guilty knowledge of and participation in the crime, since they expressed confidence of security if their companions remained silent, as nobody had seen them go to the house.

The knowledge which the prisoners possessed of the locality of the deceased's cottage, and of her character and circumstances,—their presence in the vicinity at so suspicious an hour, in the inclement season of mid-winter, so close upon the time when the deceased was murdered,—their subsequent wanderings, apparently without any object,—their profuse expenditure of money,—their apparently wanton destruction of valuable articles of apparel, unaccountable except on the supposition that they were the pregnant evidences of guilt,—their possession of so much money and molten silver when apprehended,—the correspondence of the shoe-marks about the cottage with the shoes of two of the two prisoners, —and the possession of the deceased's keys,—the concurrence of these otherwise inexplicable facts could not be rationally accounted for except by the conclusion of the guilt of the prisoners, who made a full confession, and two of whom, Smith and Timms, were executed.[*]

A foreigner, named Courvoisier, was tried at the Central Criminal Court (June 1840) for the murder of Lord William Russell, an elderly gentleman, seventy-five years of age, a widower, who lived in Norfolk Street, Park Lane. The deceased's family consisted of the prisoner, who had been in his service as valet about five weeks, and of a housemaid and cook, who had lived with him three years, beside a coachman and groom who did not live in the house. On the 6th of May the female servants went to bed as usual, and the housemaid on going to bed lighted a fire and set a rush-light in her master's bedroom, which presented its usual appearance; the prisoner remained sitting up to warm his bed. The housemaid rose about half-past six on the following morning, and on going downstairs knocked, as usual, at the prisoner's door. At her master's door she noticed the warming-pan, which was usually taken downstairs; on going into a back drawing-room she found the drawers of her master's desk open, his bunch of keys lying on the carpet, and a screw-driver lay on a chair. In the hall his Lordship's cloak was found neatly folded up, together with a bundle, containing a variety

* Rex v. Smith, Varnham, and Timms.

of valuable articles, most of them portable, such as a thief would ordinarily put in his pocket instead of deliberately packing up. In the dining-room she found several articles of plate scattered about. The street-door, though shut, was unfastened, but the testimony of the police who passed the house many times in the night rendered it very unlikely that any person had left it in that direction. Alarmed by these appearances, the housemaid called the prisoner, and found him dressed, though only a few moments had elapsed since she had knocked at his door, which was a much shorter time than he usually took to dress. They went together downstairs; and after examining the state of the dining-room and the prisoner's pantry, where the cupboard and drawers were all found opened, they proceeded to their master's bed-room, where he was found with his throat cut, in a manner which must have produced instant death. His Lordship usually placed his watch and rings on his dressing-table; but they had been taken away, and his note-cases, in one of which the prisoner stated that he had seen a £10 and a £5 note a few days before, were open and emptied of their contents. A book was found on the floor, and his Lordship's spectacles lay upon it, and there was a candlestick about four or five feet from the bed, with a candle burned to the socket. These articles appeared to have been so placed, to create the impression that his Lordship had been murdered while reading; but he was not accustomed to read in bed, and only so much of the rush-light was burned as would have been consumed in about an hour and a half, though the candle was completely burned away. The prisoner stated that he left his master reading. Upon the door of the prisoner's pantry, leading

to a back area, were marks as if it had been broken
into, and the prisoner suggested that the thieves had
entered by that door; but they appeared to have been
made from within, and none of them had been made
by the application of sufficient force to break open the
door; the bolts appeared not to have been shot at the
time, and the socket of one of them had been wrenched
off when the door was open. The marks on this door
appeared to have been made with a bent poker found in
the pantry. It was clear that no person had entered the
premises from the rear, since in one direction they could
have been approached only by passing over a wall covered with dust, which would have retained the slightest impression; and on the other, the party must have
passed over some tiling which was so old and perished
as necessarily to have been damaged by the passing of
any person over it; while from the testimony of the
police it was equally clear that no person had escaped
through the front door. For several days the missing
articles could not be found, and the case appeared to be
wrapped in impenetrable mystery; but at length, upon
a stricter search, his Lordship's rings and Waterloo
medal, five sovereigns, and a £10 note, the latter of
which had been removed from his note-case, were found
concealed behind the skirting-board in the prisoner's
pantry; and beneath the leaden covering of a sink was
found his Lordship's watch, and several other articles
were also found in other parts of the same room. But
a quantity of plate which had been stolen still remained
undiscovered, notwithstanding the most diligent efforts
to discover it; and its non-production was the only circumstance which gave any apparent countenance to the
possibility that the house had been robbed on the night

of the murder, by parties who had escaped. The mystery was cleared up however in a very extraordinary manner, during the progress of the trial. About a fortnight before the murder, the prisoner had left a parcel in the care of an hotel-keeper with whom he had formerly lived as waiter, whose curiosity was excited to examine its contents by reading in a newspaper a suggestion that, as the prisoner was a foreigner, he had probably left the plate at one of the foreign hotels in London. The parcel was found to contain the missing plate. The prisoner had been known in this situation only by his Christian name, which circumstance accounted for the fact that suspicion had not been sooner excited by the account of the murder and robbery which had appeared in the daily journals. This discovery, in conjunction with the simulated appearances of external violence and robbery, and the conclusive evidence that the premises had not been entered from without, made it certain that the robbery of the plate and the murder had been committed by one of the inmates; while the manner and place of concealment, and the artless and satisfactory account given by the female servants, rendered it equally clear that the prisoner and he alone could have been the perpetrator of this cruel action. He made a confession of his guilt, and was executed pursuant to his sentence.*

It is scarcely possible, in the absence of unimpeachable direct evidence, to conceive of any grounds of moral assurance and judgment more satisfactory and conclusive than those afforded by such combinations of facts as were presented in the foregoing cases.

* Sessions Papers, 1840 ; 2 Townsend's St. Tr. 211.

Section 4.

CONCLUSION.

The rules of evidence are the practical maxims of legal and philosophic sagacity and experience, matured and methodized by a succession of wise men, as the best means of discriminating truth from error, and of contracting as far as possible the dangerous power of judicial discretion. They have their origin in man's nature, as an intellectual and a moral being; and "are founded" (to use the language of one of the most eloquent of advocates,) " in the charities of religion, in the philosophy of nature, in the truths of history, and in the experience of common life."* Such rules must of necessity be substantially the same, in all cases and in every civilized country ; and the inviolable observance of them is indispensable to social security and happiness. To disregard them, under whatever circumstances or pretext, is to subject to the sport of chance those fundamental rights which it is the object of social institutions to secure.

The design of this Essay has been to investigate the foundations of our faith in circumstantial evidence, to ascertain its limits and its just moral effect, and to illustrate and confirm the reasonableness of the practical rules which have been established in order to prevent the unauthorized assumption of facts, and to secure to relevant facts their proper weight. It has been maintained that circumstantial evidence is inherently of a different and inferior nature from direct and positive testimony; but that nevertheless such evidence, although not invariably so, is most frequently superior in proving power to the average strength of direct evidence; and that, under the

* 29 St. Tr. 966.

safeguards and qualifications which have been stated, it affords a secure ground for the most important judgments in cases where direct evidence is not to be obtained.

It must however be conceded, that " with the wisest laws, and with the most perfect administration of them, the innocent may sometimes be doomed to suffer the fate of the guilty; for it were vain to hope that from any human institution all error can be excluded."* But certainty has not always been attained even in those sciences which admit of demonstration ; still less can unfailing assurance be invariably expected in investigations of moral and contingent truth. Nor can any argument against the validity and sufficiency of circumstantial evidence as a means of arriving at moral certainty be drawn from the consideration that it has occasionally led to erroneous convictions, which does not equally apply as an objection against the validity and sufficiency of moral evidence of every kind ; and it is believed that a far greater number of mistaken sentences have taken place in consequence of false and mistaken direct and positive testimony, than from erroneous inferences drawn from circumstantial evidence. " Admitting," said Mr. Justice Story, " the truth of such cases, are we, then, to abandon all confidence in circumstantial evidence, and in the testimony of witnesses ? Are we to declare that no human testimony to circumstances or to facts is worthy of belief, or can furnish a just foundation for a conviction ? That would be to subvert the whole foundations of the administration of public justice."†

These considerations ought not therefore to produce

* Romilly's Obs. on the C. L. of Engl. 74.
† Wharton's C. L. of the U. S. 343.

an unreasonable and indiscriminate scepticism ; the legitimate consequence of such reflections should be to inspire a salutary caution in the reception and estimate of circumstantial evidence, and to render the legislator especially wary how he authorizes, and the magistrate how he inflicts, punishment of a nature which admits neither of reversal nor mitigation. Would that the total abolition of such punishment were compatible with the paramount claims of social security! It is indispensable, however, under every system, to the very existence of society, that the tribunals should act upon circumstantial evidence. Infallibility belongs not to man ; and even his strongest degree of moral assurance must be accompanied by the possible danger of mistake; but after just effect has been given to sound practical rules of evidence, there will remain no other source of uncertainty or fallacy, than that general liability to error, which is necessarily incidental to all investigations founded upon moral evidence, and from which no conclusion of the human judgment in relation to questions of contingent truth, whether based upon direct or circumstantial evidence, can be absolutely and entirely exempt.

Note to Page 116.

[I am indebted to M. D. Hill, Esq., Q.C., the learned Recorder of Birmingham, for the particulars of a remarkable case, in which he was retained as counsel for a prisoner accused of shooting at a young woman, and in which the intended victim was prepared to swear that she recognized the prisoner by the flash of the gun which was fired at her. The trial, which was to have taken place at the Derby Spring Assizes, 1840, was prevented by the suicide of the prisoner, after the business of the Assizes had begun; but Mr. Hill was present at a series of experiments made with a view to test the possibility of the alleged recognition, and the conclusion he drew was "that all stories of recognition from the flash of gun or pistol must be founded upon a fallacy." There were many circumstances in the case calculated to produce a strong impression on the young woman's mind that the prisoner was her assailant, and she doubtless mistook the impression so created for ocular demonstration.—Ed.]

INDEX.

THE END.

A
Catalogue

OF

LAW WORKS

PUBLISHED BY

MESSRS. BUTTERWORTH,

Law Booksellers and Publishers

TO THE QUEEN'S MOST EXCELLENT MAJESTY

AND TO

H.R.H. THE PRINCE OF WALES.

" Now for the Laws of England (if I shall speak my opinion of them
" without partiality either to my profession or country), for the matter and
" nature of them, I hold them wise, just and moderate laws: they give to God,
" they give to Cæsar, they give to the subject what appertaineth. It is true
" they are as mixt as our language, compounded of British, Saxon, Danish,
" Norman customs. And surely as our language is thereby so much the richer,
*" so our laws are likewise by that mixture the more complete."—*LORD BACON.

1868.

7, FLEET STREET, LONDON, E.C.

Index to Catalogue.

Coote's & Tristram's Probate Practice.—5th Edition.

8vo., 24s. cloth.

THE PRACTICE of the COURT of PROBATE, in Common Form Business. By HENRY CHARLES COOTE, F.S.A., Proctor in Doctors' Commons, &c., &c. Also a Treatise on the Practice of the Court in Contentious Business, by THOMAS H. TRISTRAM, D.C.L., Advocate in Doctors' Commons, and of the Inner Temple. Fifth Edition, with great Additions, and including all the Statutes, Rules, Orders, &c., to the present time ; together with a Collection of Original Forms and Bills of Costs.

"The profession will be glad to welcome the publication of this most valuable work. When the monopoly which the proctors and advocates enjoyed in Doctors' Commons was abolished, and the practice in probates and letters of administration was thrown open to the general profession, the uninitiated derived greater benefit and instruction from this book than from any other which was published for their guidance. It has become an acknowledged necessity in the library of every practitioner. Since the publication of the last edition, new rules have been promulgated for the Court of Probate, other regulations have been made by acts of parliament and an order in council, and the practice of the Court has in some respects been altered and settled. These changes have been attended to. A more useful book than this we do not know, and we need not say more than that in this edition the authors have done all in their power to increase its utility and secure its completeness."—*Law Magazine and Review.*

"A fifth edition in so short a time is a success that few law books can boast, and it is well deserved. Mr. Coote as a proctor possesses that intimate acquaintance with the minutiæ of practice which experience only can supply: and Dr. Tristram's education as an advocate enables him to treat of the jurisdiction of the Probate Court, the law which it administers, and the principles established for the administration of that law, with a mastery of his subject that has made this production of the united labours of two such competent men the accepted text book of the Probate Court. Having noticed its successive editions as they appeared, it remains only to say that it brings down the statutes and cases to the present time."—*Law Times.*

"We must not omit to praise the complete character of the Appendix, which, occupying more than half the whole work, presents us with the statutes, the orders in council, rules and fees, tables of costs and forms, and leaves nothing to be desired by the proctor or solicitor either in the routine of common form or in the stages of suits."—*Law Journal.*

Hunt on Boundaries and Fences.

Post 8vo., 9s. cloth.

THE LAW RELATING to BOUNDARIES and FENCES. By ARTHUR JOSEPH HUNT, of the Inner Temple, Esq., Barrister at Law.

"Among other matters discussed are the rights of property on the sea shore ; navigable and private rivers ; the duties of mine owners with regard to boundaries ; the rights and liabilities of landlords and tenants as to fences, hedges and ditches, and the liability to make and repair the same ; the duty to fence land adjoining roads ; the law relating to trees and hedges on the boundaries of property, &c. The second chapter of Mr. Hunt's work, which relates to fences generally, is especially worthy of perusal, as cases are repeatedly arising between adjoining proprietors. Too much praise cannot be given to the modesty of an author, who, following the example of early text writers, constructs his work on the so-called utterances of the Judges, and does not, like some writers, place too much reliance upon his own *ipse dixit*. With these remarks we take leave of Mr. Hunt's book, recommending it as a work containing a great deal of information in a small compass, and one on which no small amount of time, labour and research must necessarily have been bestowed."—*Law Times.*

"Mr. Hunt has done good service by collecting and arranging, in a clear and convenient manner, a large amount of information which lies scattered through the old text books, the reports and the statutes, and to which there has hitherto been no clue. Mr. Hunt appears to have ransacked the American as well as the English treatises and reports: but his work is not a mere compilation: he has investigated for himself and stated the results concisely and clearly."—*Jurist.*

"The law of boundaries and fences, is, in the work before us, treated with great ability, and as the language is clear, and, as far as may be, free from technicalities, it will be found useful beyond the limits of the legal profession."—*Athenæum.*

"This is a very useful work as a common place book on the subject of which it treats."—*Law Magazine.*

"This is a concise and well-written book on a small but not unimportant subject, and displays considerable care both in arrangement and detail. It will be seen that the author very carefully and completely dissects his subject, and then very succinctly treats of the parts."—*Solicitors' Journal.*

Dixon's Law of Partnership.

1 vol. 8vo., 22s. cloth.

A TREATISE on the LAW of PARTNERSHIP. By JOSEPH DIXON, of Lincoln's Inn, Esq., Barrister at Law. Editor of "Lush's Common Law Practice."

"It is with considerable gratification that we find the subject treated by a writer of Mr. Dixon's reputation for learning, accuracy and painstaking. Mr. Lindley's view of the subject is that of a philosophical lawyer, Mr. Dixon's is purely and exclusively practical from beginning to end. We imagine that very few questions are likely to come before the practitioner which Mr. Dixon's book will not be found to solve. Having already passed our opinion on the way in which the work is carried out, we have only to add that the value of the book is very materially increased by an excellent marginal summary, and a very copious index."—*Law Magazine and Review.*

"Mr. Dixon has done his work well. The book is carefully and usefully prepared."—*Solicitors' Journal.*

"Mr. Dixon enters into all the conditions of partnerships at common law, and defines the rights of partners among themselves; the rights of the partnership against third persons; the rights of third persons against the partnership; and the rights and liabilities of individuals, not actually partners, but liable to be treated by third persons as partners."—*The Times.*

"We heartily recommend to practitioners and students Mr. Dixon's treatise as the best exposition of the law we have read, for the arrangement is not only artistic, but conciseness has been studied without sacrifice of clearness. He sets forth the principles upon which the law is based as well as the cases by which its application is shown. Hence it is something more than a digest, which too many law books are not: it is really an essay."—*Law Times.*

"Mr. Dixon's manual on the law of partnership will be an acceptable addition to the shelves of our law libraries, whilst from its portable size it will be equally useful as a companion in court. He has evidently bestowed upon this book the same conscientious labour and painstaking industry for which we had to compliment him some months since when reviewing his edition of Lush's 'Practice of the Superior Courts of Law,' and, as a result, he has produced a clearly written and well arranged manual upon one of the most important branches of our mercantile law."—*Law Journal.*

"The law of partnerships at common law, as it is established by the latest decisions, will be found concisely stated in these pages. The matter is well arranged and the work is carefully executed."—*Athenæum.*

Hallilay's Law Examination Reporter.

8vo. in Numbers at 6d., by Post 7d., every Term on the Morning of the Second Day after the Examination.

THE LAW EXAMINATION REPORTER. Containing all the Questions and Answers at the Examinations of Law Students at the Incorporated Law Society.

Contents of No. I.—HIL. TERM, 1866.—Notice to Readers—How to Study—The Examiners—Examination Questions and Answers.

Contents of No. II.—EAST. TERM, 1866.—Notice to Readers—What to Study for Pass or Honors—The Examiners—Examination Questions and Answers.

Contents of No. III.—TRIN. TERM, 1866.—My first Criminal Client—Important Bills in Parliament—The Examiners—Examination Questions and Answers.

Contents of No. IV.—MICH. TERM, 1866.—On Memory, its Abuse and its Aids—Result of the past, intermediate and final Examinations—The Examiners—Examination Questions and Answers.

Contents of No. V.—HIL. TERM, 1867.—Sketches at a Police Court—Reviews of New Books—Observations on the Michaelmas Term's Questions—The Examiners—All the Hilary Term's Questions and Answers.

Contents of No. VI.—EAST. TERM, 1867.—The Preliminary Examinations and the Judges' Dispensations—Observations on the Hilary Term's Equity Questions—The Examiners—All the Easter Term's Questions and Answers.

Contents of VII.—TRIN. TERM, 1867.—Notice to Readers—The Rejected and the Reason—Examination and Legal News—The Examiners—Intermediate Examination Questions—Final Examination Questions and Answers.

Contents of No. VIII.—MICH. TERM, 1867.—New Statutes—Result of Past Examinations—New Prizes—Law Societies—Reviews of Books—The Examiners—The Intermediate Questions—All the Michaelmas Term's Examination Questions and Answers.

Contents of No. IX.—HIL. TERM, 1868.—Notice to Readers—Proposed Amalgamation of the Bar and the Attornies—New Statutes and Rules—Correspondence—Moot Points—Reviews of New Books—Intermediate Examination Questions—The Examiners—Final Examination Questions and Answers for Hilary.

Contents of No. X.—EAST. TERM, 1868.—Hints to Young Attorneys—Reviews of Books—Intermediate Questions and Answers—All the Easter Term's Final Questions and Answers.

Contents of No. XI.—TRIN. TERM, 1868.—What to do after Passing—Answers to Moot Points—Reviews—Intermediate Questions and Answers—Trinity Term's Final Questions and Answers.

Davis's Law of Registration and Elections.

One small 12mo vol.,   cloth.

MANUAL OF THE LAW AND PRACTICE OF REGISTRATION AND ELECTIONS. The Reform, Registration and Election Acts, with Notes and Introduction. By JAMES EDWARD DAVIS, Esq., Barrister at Law, Author of "Manual of Practice and Evidence in the County Courts," &c.

Davis's Law of Master and Servant.

12mo. 6s. cloth.

THE MASTER AND SERVANT ACT, 1867 (30 & 31 Vict. c. 141), with an Introduction, copious Notes, Tables of Offences, and Forms of Proceedings, prepared expressly for this Work. By JAMES E. DAVIS, Esq., Barrister at Law, Stipendiary Magistrate, Stoke-upon-Trent.

*** Besides the Act and copious Notes, Introduction, and a variety of Forms of Summons, Orders, Convictions, Recognizances, &c., specially prepared for this work, Tables have been framed classifying all the offences within the jurisdiction of Justices. It is hoped that this will be found useful, not only to Magistrates and their Clerks, but to the Legal Profession generally, for in consequence of the new Act not describing the offences, but merely referring to a schedule of seventeen former Acts, it is very difficult to say what cases are or are not within the purview of the new Act. The decisions of the Superior Courts, so far as they are applicable to the present law, are also given.*

"Mr. Davis has remedied as far as possible a great practical defect in the Act by a Table of Offences to which its provisions apply. The notes are full and to the point, and the Forms will be found highly useful to those who have to administer the Act. The name of Mr. Davis is a sufficient guarantee that the work is done well."—*Law Magazine and Review.*

"We are glad to see that the question has been treated so ably and carefully as it is in the present volume. His experience as stipendiary magistrate of Stoke-upon-Trent render his suggestions as to the practice and procedure to be employed in working out its provisions peculiarly valuable."—*Solicitors' Journal.*

"The task that Mr. Davis undertook in editing this new Master and Servant Act has been well performed, and indeed in a manner that probably no one who did not enjoy the exceptional advantages for the purpose that Mr. Davis does could have executed so satisfactorily."—*Irish Law Times.*

"With such a manual before them as that of Mr. Davis, magistrates and practitioners will have little difficulty in fully comprehending the law and knowing how to apply it. We therefore recommend this edition to them."—*Gloucester Journal.*

"The edition of the act which Mr. Davis, the stipendiary magistrate at Stoke-upon-Trent, has just published, will prove of great use as a clue to this legislative labyrinth. In this little work so much of the statutes referred to as is required to make the new law intelligible is quoted at full length, and Mr. Davis has also added sundry tables of matters and things within the jurisdiction of justices under the Master and Servant Act, which remedy as far as possible the omissions of the measure itself."—*Saturday Review.*

"This will be found a useful little work for all who have occasion to inquire into master and servant laws as affected by the statute of last session. This book is calculated to be especially serviceable to magistrates and justices of the peace. and they undoubtedly will find it very useful. It is written by one of themselves, and is therefore likely to be particularly adapted to their wants."—*Law Journal.*

"He has been enabled to present in this volume a lucid interpretation of the recent act, an interpretation the necessity for which will be appreciated from the fact that the act of 1867 has been based on a number of statutes to which it refers merely in a schedule. This book summarizes the state of the law before the passing of the act, and points out the changes which have been effected thereby. It also contains copious notes and forms, with tables of offences, by means of which and the comments of the writer the existing state of the law and the necessity for further amendments will be clearly understood."—*Observer.*

"Mr. Davis has performed a good service by publishing that act with an introduction and notes for the guidance of magistrates, lawyers and others. His exposition of the act is clear and full, making everything as to its application plain enough for the guidance even of those who are not of the legal profession."—*Edinburgh Courant.*

"Any unhappy man who may wish to make use of the statute of 1867 might therefore have to undertake a most laborious hunt through the statutes at large, if he were not saved from that dire necessity by a compilation such as that which is now before us. Mr Davis has in this little volume collected a large amount of practical information."—*Athenæum.*

Davis's County Courts Practice and Evidence.—Third Edit.

One thick volume, Royal 12mo. 28s. cloth.

A MANUAL of the PRACTICE and EVIDENCE in ACTIONS and other PROCEEDINGS in the COUNTY COURTS, including the PRACTICE in BANKRUPTCY, with an Appendix of Statutes and Rules. By JAMES EDWARD DAVIS, of the Middle Temple, Esq., Barrister at Law. Third Edition, considerably enlarged.

*** *This is the only work on the County Courts which gives Forms of Plaints and treats fully of the Law and Evidence in Actions and other Proceedings in these Courts.*

"It is undoubtedly the best book on the Practice of the County Courts, and the appearance of a third edition proves that such is the opinion of the Profession."—*Law Times.*

"This is the third edition of a text-book which is well known in both branches of the Legal Profession. From a small beginning it has gradually grown into a bulky volume of 829 pages, and now contains an inexhaustive exposition of the Law and Practice relating to the County Courts. The second part of this manual contains a valuable digest of the Law of Evidence, as applicable to the Procedure of the County Courts. In this particular, it certainly excels all the other text-books on the subject. The importance of this part of the work cannot be too highly estimated. The chapters on the County Practice in Bankruptcy display the usual care and ability of the author, and give a completeness to a work which has hitherto been deservedly popular in the Profession."—*Law Magazine.*

"This is a greatly enlarged edition of Davis's County Courts Practice, a work well enough known as to need no introduction to the legal public, or at any rate to that portion of it concerned with proceedings in the County Courts. The edition before us follows in its main features the second edition of the book, but it is to that second edition as the full-blown rose to the bud, not merely in quantity but in quality of matter. We can heartily and safely recommend the book for the perusal of all intending practitioners in any County Court."—*Solicitors' Journal.*

Davis's County Courts Act, 1867.

Royal 12mo., 12s. cloth.

THE COUNTY COURTS ACT, 1867, and the provisions of the Common Law Procedure Act, 1854, relating to Discovery, Attachment of Debts, and Equitable Defences (applied by Orders in Council to the County Courts). Edited, with Notes and Introduction and a Chapter on Costs, together with all the New County Court Rules, Orders and Forms, by J. E. DAVIS, Esq., Barrister at Law.

*** *This edition may be used either as an Appendix to the third edition of "Davis's Practice and Evidence in the County Courts," or as an independent work.*

"It is almost impossible, within the narrow limits of a review to do justice to this admirable work. Mr. Davis is known to the profession as a singularly learned, able and clear writer: and although the present volume makes no claim to the same literary rank as the well-known County Courts Manual, it will certainly add to the author's reputation. The Act of 1867 has been the parent of several works; but, in our judgment, the one of Mr. Davis, for general purposes, certainly bears the palm. We agree with Mr. Davis that a thorough knowledge of the jurisdiction of the County Courts is 'absolutely essential for all lawyers;' and to all lawyers we heartily commend this last work of an able and erudite writer."—*Law Magazine and Review.*

"Mr. Davis has good title to come before the public with a book on the New County Court Act, inasmuch as he has already occupied the ground by his Manual on the Practice and Evidence and other Proceedings in the County Courts, and might feel himself called upon to complete his former treatise by adding what was rendered necessary by the changes of the law, as he justly says the best way to acquire a thorough knowledge and comprehension of the jurisdiction and practice of the County Courts is to treat the new law as supplemental to the former law. We may add that this treatise is arranged very clearly, and the practitioner can in a moment find the information which he may require. The book is admirably printed, and there is a good index to the whole volume."—*Law Journal.*

"This volume contains a preface, an introductory chapter, the act itself, annotated, a chapter on costs, the order in council, all the new rules, forms and orders, &c., and a full index. The principal feature which attracted our attention is the chapter on costs, no other treatise on the act which has yet appeared having dealt with this important subject specifically. It would be unfair to extract, even in an abridged form, this valuable addition to the law literature of the County Courts, and we would recommend our readers to obtain Mr. Davis's volume, even though they already possess any of the treatises published on the new act. The whole work is done in Mr. Davis's usually thorough and efficient manner, and the book is got up in Messrs. Butterworths' best style."—*Law Times.*

"The form of this work is adapted to render clear the actual practical effect of the new Act. Mr. Davis treats us to an analysis in his introductory Chapter. The Act itself is very carefully annotated with a view to practically applying it. Following the Act is a Chapter on Costs, which will be found very valuable. The book contains the whole of the rules, forms and orders, and is worth the 12s. which is asked for it."—*County Courts Chronicle.*

Davis's County Courts Equitable Jurisdiction.

Royal 12mo., *5s.* cloth.

THE ACT to confer on the COUNTY COURTS a LIMITED JURISDICTION in EQUITY, 28 & 29 Vict. cap. 99, with the New Rules and Forms, including those of 28th May, 1866; also Introductory Chapters, Copious Notes and a Full Index. By JAMES EDWARD DAVIS, Esq., of the Middle Temple, Barrister at Law.

Hunter's Suit in Equity.—Fourth Edition.

Post 8vo. 10s. cloth.

AN ELEMENTARY VIEW of the PROCEEDINGS IN A SUIT IN EQUITY. With an Appendix of Forms. By SYLVESTER J. HUNTER, B.A., of Lincoln's Inn, Barrister at Law. Fourth Edition, by G. W. LAWRANCE, M.A., of Lincoln's Inn, Barrister at Law.

" It is now ten years since Mr. Hunter's modest and unpretending volume first saw the light, and few we imagine have been the students of equity practice during those years who have not been indebted to its pages for their first initiation into the mysteries of the Court of Chancery. Within the compass of three hundred pages the reader (as far as is possible without the result of practical experience) may obtain an accurate idea of the various incidental proceedings leading up to and following the decree, while the several stages of the suit are all carefully illustrated by forms referred to in the text and collected together in an appendix at the end of the volume. We will only add that we are glad to find this little work is in such good hands, and while it continues to receive from time to time Mr. Lawrance's careful revision, we venture to predict for it a long-lived success and many future editions."—*Law Journal.*

" An outline, after this fashion, of a suit in equity is contained in Mr. Hunter's little volume, and that it has been found to perform its province is proved by its arrival at a fourth edition. Mr. Lawrance has added a chapter on the equitable jurisdiction of the county courts."—*Law Times.*

" This book has now maintained for so long a time the position of a standard manual for the use of law students, that there is little for us to say respecting its general scope. The work is intended for beginners, and the design is excellently carried out. Everything is there which ought to be placed before the learner, and yet the book is not encumbered with references and details which would serve merely to embarrass him; the arrangement is also very clear. Since the issue of the first edition in 1858, two successive editions besides the present have been prepared by Mr. Lawrance, the present editor, a sufficient guarantee that the book has answered the purpose for which it was intended."—*Solicitors' Journal.*

Kerr's Action at Law.—Third Edition.

12mo., 13s. cloth.

AN ACTION AT LAW: being an Outline of the Jurisdiction of the Superior Courts of Common Law, with an Elementary View of the Proceedings in Actions therein. By ROBERT MALCOLM KERR, Barrister at Law; now Judge of the Sheriff's Court of the City of London. Third Edition.

" There is considerable merit in both works (John William Smith's and Malcolm Kerr's); but the second (Kerr) has rather the advantage, in being more recent, and published since the Common Law Procedure Act, 1860."—*Jurist.*

" Mr. Kerr's book is more full and detailed than that of Mr. John William Smith, and is therefore better adapted for those who desire to obtain not merely a general notion but also a practical acquaintance with Common Law Procedure."—*Solicitors' Journal.*

" As a Third Edition the volume needs no description and permits no criticism. Enough to say that its present appearance will amply sustain the reputation it had already acquired."—*Law Times.*

" This is just the book to put into a Student's hand when he enters the legal profession. We have had occasion more than once to recommend it to the notice of our junior brethren."—*Leguleian.*

Lush's Common Law Practice.—Third Edit. by Dixon.

2 vols. 8vo., 46s. cloth.

LUSH'S PRACTICE of the SUPERIOR COURTS of COMMON LAW at WESTMINSTER, in Actions and Proceedings over which they have a common Jurisdiction: with Introductory Treatises respecting Parties to Actions; Attornies and Town Agents, their Qualifications, Rights, Duties, Privileges and Disabilities; the Mode of Suing, whether in Person or by Attorney in Formâ Pauperis, &c. &c. &c.; and an Appendix, containing the authorized Tables of Costs and Fees, Forms of Proceedings and Writs of Execution.   Third Edition.   By JOSEPH DIXON, of Lincoln's Inn, Esq., Barrister at Law.

"This is an excellent edition of an excellent work. We think that Mr. Dixon has been wise in basing his work on the original edition of the Practice, and not upon the second edition published in the year 1856. The last nine years alone have produced a very large number of new cases, and even had the text of the second edition been followed, much must have been altered or re-written. The responsibility, moreover, for any imperfections would have been divided between three writers, and the result of their united labours would probably have not been very satisfactory. As Mr. Lush's heavy professional engagements made it impossible for him to remodel his book himself, the best course was that it should be re-edited at first hand and not indirectly. Literary patchwork is always objectionable. To edit an author is a task requiring great skill, but to edit an author's edition is still more difficult. We congratulate Mr. Dixon on the judgment he has displayed in selecting the proper alternative. He has effected a most successful 'restoration.' As far as the great changes in the law permit, he has re-produced the original work. He has adopted Mr. Lush's arrangement, and only made those alterations and additions which recent legislation has rendered indispensable. The whole work, which contains altogether 1,183 pages, concludes with a copious index, entirely re-written and very considerably enlarged. Mr. Dixon has made very few retrenchments in Mr. Lush's work. Nearly all his alterations have been by way of addition. The forms of declarations, pleas, &c., contained in the first part of the original work, have been, we think, wisely omitted. Their place is rather in a treatise on pleading than in one of practice. Altogether, both in what he has omitted and what he has added, Mr. Dixon has been guided by sound discretion. We trust that the great and conscientious labours he has undergone will be rewarded. He has striven to make his work "thorough," and because he has done so we take pleasure in heartily recommending it to every member of both branches of the profession."—*Solicitors' Journal.*

" Lush's Practice is what Tidd's Practice was in our days of clerkship, and what Archbold's Practice was in our early professional days—the practice in general use, and the received authority on the subject. It was written by Mr. Lush when he was only a junior rising into fortune and fame. His practical knowledge, his clearness and industry, were even then acknowledged, and his name secured for his work an immediate popularity, which experience has confirmed and extended. But the work was, in its turn, productive of considerable advantage to the author, it largely increased the number of his clients. When new editions were called for, Mr. Lush was too occupied with briefs to find time for the preparation of books, and hence the association of his name with that of Mr. Dixon as editor, and by whom the new edition has been produced. Mr. Dixon reminds us that twenty-five years have passed since Mr. Lush made his appearance as an author, and vast indeed have been the changes the law has since witnessed. So numerous are they, that the editor has found it the most convenient course to ignore, as it were, the second edition, to take the text of the original work as it came fresh from Mr. Lush's pen, and to mould that to the present practice. He is thus enabled to assure the reader, that for every alteration in, or addition to, the text, he alone is responsible. The index is very copious and complete. Under Mr. Dixon's care Lush's Practice will not merely maintain, it will largely extend its reputation."—*Law Times.*

"The profession cannot but welcome with the greatest cordiality and pleasure a third edition of their old and much valued friend ' Lush's Practice of the Superior Courts of Law.' Mr. Dixon, in preparing this edition, has gone back to the original work of Mr. Justice Lush, and, as far as the legislative changes and decisions of the last twenty-five years would allow, reproduced it. This adds greatly to the value of this edition, and at the same time speaks volumes for Mr. Dixon's conscientious labour."—*Law Journal.*

Rouse's Practical Conveyancer.—Third Edition.

Two vols. 8vo., 30s. cloth.

THE PRACTICAL CONVEYANCER, giving, in a mode combining facility of reference with general utility, upwards of Four Hundred Precedents of Conveyances, Mortgages and Leases, Settlements, and Miscellaneous Forms, with (not in previous editions) the Law and numerous Outline Forms and Clauses of WILLS and Abstracts of Statutes affecting Real Property, Conveyancing Memoranda, &c. By ROLLA ROUSE, Esq., of the Middle Temple, Barrister at Law, Author of "The Practical Man," &c. Third Edition, greatly enlarged.

"The best test of the value of a book written professedly for practical men is the practical one of the number of editions through which it passes. The fact that this well-known work has now reached its third shows that it is considered by those for whose convenience it was written to fulfil its purpose well."—*Law Magazine.*

"This is the third edition in ten years, a proof that practitioners have used and approved the precedents collected by Mr. Rouse. In this edition, which is greatly enlarged, he has for the first time introduced Precedents of Wills, extending to no less than 116 pages. We can accord unmingled praise to the conveyancing memoranda showing the practical effect of the various statutory provisions in the different parts of a deed. If the two preceding editions have been so well received, the welcome given to this one by the profession will be heartier still."—*Law Times.*

"So far as a careful perusal of Mr. Rouse's book enables us to judge of its merits, we think that as a collection of precedents of general utility in cases of common occurrence it will be found satisfactorily to stand the application of the test. The draftsman will find in the Practical Conveyancer precedents appropriate to all instruments of common occurrence, and the collection appears to be especially well supplied with those which relate to copyhold estates. In order to avoid useless repetition and also to make the precedents as simple as possible, Mr. Rouse has sketched out a number of outline drafts so as to present to the reader a sort of bird's-eye view of each instrument and show him its form at a glance. Each paragraph in these outline forms refers, by distinguishing letters and numbers, to the clauses in full required to be inserted in the respective parts of the instrument, and which are given in a subsequent part of the work, and thus every precedent in outline is made of itself an index to the clauses which are necessary to complete the draft. In order still further to simplify the arrangement of the work, the author has adopted a plan (which seems to us fully to answer its purpose) of giving the variations which may occur in any instrument according to the natural order of its different parts."—*Law Journal.*

"That the work has found favor is proved by the fact of our now having to review a third edition. This method of skeleton precedents appears to us to be attended with important advantages. Space is of course saved, but besides this there is the still more important consideration that the draftsman is materially assisted to a bird's-eye view of his draft. Everyone who has done much conveyancing work knows how thoroughly important, nay, how essential to success, is the formation of a clear idea of the scope and framework of the instrument to be produced. To clerks and other young hands a course of conveyancing under Mr. Rouse's auspices is, we think, calculated to prove very instructive. To the solicitor, especially the country practitioner, who has often to set his clerks to work upon drafts of no particular difficulty to the experienced practitioner, but upon which they the said clerks are not to be quite trusted alone, we think to such gentlemen Mr. Rouse's collection of Precedents is calculated to prove extremely serviceable. We repeat, in conclusion, that solicitors, especially those practising in the country, will find this a useful work."—*Solicitors' Journal.*

Fisher's General Law of Mortgage.—Second Edition.

Two vols. royal 8vo., 55s. cloth.

THE LAW of MORTGAGE, and other Securities upon Property. By WILLIAM RICHARD FISHER, of Lincoln's Inn, Esq., Barrister at Law. Second Edition, very considerably enlarged.

"Whatever may have been the merits of the papers recently submitted to the Digest of Law Commissioners by other competitors, we think the profession will feel more than satisfied at the selection of Mr. Fisher as the successful candidate on the subject of Mortgage. The appearance of his full and elaborate treatise on this subject simultaneously with the announcement of the Commissioners' decision, gives, as it were, a material guarantee of Mr. Fisher's competency for undertaking that department of the work which we presume will be assigned to him. The second edition of this book, comprised in two volumes of royal octavo, has little beyond its paternity to identify it with the original volume which appeared in 1856. If we speak of the author's first essay as merely tentative and meagre and partial, it is only to draw particular attention to the very complete arrangement and copious detail of the edition now before the public. . . . These chapters taken together evince that laborious research and accuracy which, more than any other qualification, is required of a text writer, and we doubt not that the excellence of the work will receive its due appreciation at the hands of the profession. A word in conclusion is due to the clearness and simplicity which pervades Mr. Fisher's writing. If his language is too often bold and devoid of grace it is never obscure, and we think that the absence of attractive composition will not in these days be accounted a demerit in a treatise designed solely for professional purposes, which possesses the essential qualities of accurate learning and lucid arrangement."—*Law Journal.*

"The second edition of Mr. Fisher's work has expanded from one into two volumes; from a work which dealt only with those parts of the law of mortgage, which embrace the equitable remedies of mortgagors and mortgagees, into an exhaustive treatise upon securities affecting property. The treatise of Mr. Fisher is a valuable exposition of the existing law; but if he would build himself a reputation more lasting and more worthy than a mere compiler, he will, in his appointment under the Digest Commission, deal with the law of mortgage in a new and bold manner. . . . How great, how laborious a task like this would be no one probably knows better than Mr. Fisher. But no one is more qualified to take it in hand. If he does take it in hand—if he completes it conscientiously—he will do his country great service, and he will gain for himself enduring fame."—*Law Magazine.*

Coote's Admiralty Practice.—Second Edition.

8vo., 16s. cloth.

THE PRACTICE of the HIGH COURT of ADMIRALTY of ENGLAND: also the Practice of the Judicial Committee of Her Majesty's Most Honorable Privy Council in Admiralty Appeals, with Forms and Bills of Costs. By HENRY CHARLES COOTE, F.S.A., one of the Examiners of the High Court of Admiralty, Author of "The Practice of the Court of Probate," &c. Second Edition, almost entirely re-written.

"Mr. Coote, being an Examiner of the Court, may be considered as an authoritative exponent of the points of which he treats. His treatise is, substantially considered, everything that can be desired to the practitioner."—*Law Magazine.*

"The book before us is a second and enlarged edition of a work on the Practice of the Admiralty Court, written by the author some ten years ago. It is, however, a great improvement on its predecessor, being much fuller and more systematically arranged, and containing greater facilities for reference. The first part of the book is a treatise on the practice of the Court, which appears to us to be very carefully done, and to go thoroughly into the subject. The second part is a similar treatise on the practice of the Judicial Committee of the Privy Council in Admiralty matters, written on the same system as the former part. The appendix contains a large number of common forms and precedents of pleadings used in the Court of Admiralty, together with bills of costs. Altogether Mr. Coote has done his work very carefully and completely, and we think his labours will be duly appreciated by Admiralty practitioners."—*Solicitors' Journal.*

"The first edition of this excellent work was produced for the purpose of illustrating the practice of the High Court of Admiralty, just then subordinated to the 'Rules of 1859' drawn up by the late distinguished judge. Since then several important changes have been carried out, both in the matter of an extended jurisdiction and of practice. These changes it has been Mr. Coote's object to incorporate in the present edition of his work. In addition he has increased the utility of his book by a chapter on the practice of the Judicial Committee of the Privy Council in Admiralty Appeals, and by a copious set of Admiralty precedents, in which it is the author's hope and belief that no necessary common form has been omitted. The present edition appears very seasonably, and will, we doubt not, prove very acceptable to that portion of the legal profession practising in the Court of Admiralty."—*Shipping and Mercantile Gazette.*

Stephen's Commentaries.—Sixth Edition.

4 vols. 8vo., £4 : 4s. cloth.

Mr. SERJEANT STEPHEN'S NEW COMMENTARIES ON THE LAWS OF ENGLAND, partly founded on Blackstone. The Sixth Edition, prepared for the press, by JAMES STEPHEN, LL.D., of the Middle Temple, Barrister-at-Law, Registrar in Bankruptcy, formerly Recorder of Poole, and late Professor of English Law at King's College, London.

Stephen's Questions.

Nearly ready. 8vo., 10s. 6d. cloth.

QUESTIONS FOR LAW STUDENTS on the SIXTH EDITION of Mr. SERJEANT STEPHEN'S NEW COMMENTARIES on the LAWS of ENGLAND. By JAMES STEPHEN, LL.D., of the Middle Temple, Barrister at Law.

Sir T. E. May's Parliamentary Practice.—Sixth Edition.

One very thick volume, 8vo., 35s. cloth.

A TREATISE on the LAW, PRIVILEGES, PROCEEDINGS and USAGE of PARLIAMENT. By Sir THOMAS ERSKINE MAY, K.C.B., of the Middle Temple, Barrister at Law ; Clerk Assistant of the House of Commons. Sixth Edition, Revised and Enlarged.

CONTENTS :—Book I. Constitution, Powers and Privileges of Parliament.—Book II. Practice and Proceedings in Parliament.—Book III. The Manner of Passing Private Bills, with the Standing Orders in both Houses, and the most recent Precedents.

"The high reputation and the proved practical utility of Sir T. Erskine May's work, render it unnecessary for us to say anything as to its merits. The present edition has been carefully revised and considerably enlarged. It comprises every alteration in the Law and Practice of Parliament, and all material precedents relating to public and private business from the date of the former edition down to the end of the session of 1867, and many even of the last session, including the latest orders concerning committees and referees on private bills. Sir T. Erskine May deserves the best thanks of all who are interested in parliamentary proceedings, for the care and attention he has bestowed in preparing this edition of his valuable work."—Law Magazine.

"We hail with satisfaction a new edition of this admirable work. The politician, the lawyer, the parliamentary agent and the educated gentleman, will find here a teacher, a guide, a digest of practice and a pleasing companion. To legal readers, the first portion of this work is of the most value. We may advert to the great care with which the author has noted up and incorporated in this new edition all the changes and events of importance since the publication of the fifth edition. From un-fragmentary excerpts, it is plain that the author has taken pains to add all novel matter bearing on the subject matter, and to maintain for the work that character for accuracy and completeness which it has already acquired."—Law Journal.

"Six editions in twenty-four years attest the estimation in which this great work is held by the members of successive Parliaments, by the promoters of private bills, and by constitutional lawyers. It is an exhaustive treatise on that most lawless of all law the Law of Parliament. Since the publication of the last edition considerable changes have been made in the Standing Orders of both Houses, and these have been embodied in the present edition. We may point to the words sixth edition upon the title page as the best possible testimony to its practical value, for all who are in any way concerned in the Law and Practice of Parliament."—Law Times.

"Perhaps no work has achieved a greater reputation among lawyers than May's Parliamentary Practice. Since the first publication in 1844, a succession of editions have been called for, and now, after an interval of four years since the issue of the fifth, a sixth edition has been found necessary. The work is too well-known to need the repetition of any description of its scope, and we will therefore merely add that it is extremely useful to the parliamentary lawyer, in fact the only work in which he can obtain every information on matters of practice ; and is moreover a work from which the lay reader may learn very much as to the history and constitution of English Parliamentary Government."—Solicitors' Journal.

Barry's Practice of Conveyancing.

8vo., 18s. cloth.

A TREATISE on the PRACTICE of CONVEYANCING.

By W. WHITTAKER BARRY, Esq., of Lincoln's Inn, Barrister at Law, late Holder of the Studentship of the Inns of Court, and Author of "A Treatise on the Statutory Jurisdiction of the Court of Chancery."

CONTENTS:—

"The author of this valuable treatise on conveyancing has most wisely devoted a considerable part of his work to the practical illustration of the working of the recent Statutes on Registration of Title—and for this, as well as for other reasons, we feel bound to strongly recommend it to the practitioner as well as the student. The author has proved himself to be a master of the subject, for he not only gives a most valuable supply of practical suggestions, but criticises them with much ability, and we have no doubt that his criticism will meet with general approval."—*Law Magazine*.

"The author introduces a work which will be found a very acceptable addition to the law library, and to supply a want which we think has hitherto been felt. It contains, in a concise and readable form, the law relating to almost every point likely to arise in the ordinary every day practice of the conveyancer, with references to the various authorities and statutes to the latest date, and may be described as a manual of practical conveyancing."—*Law Journal*.

"This treatise supplies a want which has long been felt. There has been no treatise on the Practice of Conveyancing issued for a long time past that is adequate for the present requirements. Mr. Barry's work is essentially what it professes to be, a treatise on the Practice of Conveyancing, in which the theoretical rules of real property law are referred to only for the purpose of elucidating the practice. Mr. Barry appears to have a very accurate insight into the practice in every department of our real property system. Although we cannot boast, like Duval, of having ever read abstracts of title with pleasure, we have certainly read Mr. Barry's chapter on abstracts and numerous other parts of his work with very considerable satisfaction on account of the learning, great familiarity with practice, and power of exposition of its author. The treatise, although capable of compression, is the production of a person of great merit and still greater promise."—*Solicitors' Journal*.

"Readers who recal the instruction they gathered from this treatise when published week by week in the pages of the Law Times, will be pleased to learn that it has been reproduced in a handsome volume, which will be a welcome addition to the law library. It will be remembered that the papers so contributed by Mr. Barry were remarkable for the precision with which the law was stated, and being addressed to law students this was a characteristic of primary importance. The Author's design was to do for the *practice* of conveyancing what Mr. Joshua Williams has done for its principles, to describe it simply, clearly and succinctly, recollecting that he was only laying the foundation and not crowning the edifice. A work the substance of which is so well known to our readers, needs no recommendation from us, for its merits are patent to all, from personal acquaintance with them. The information that the treatise so much admired may now be had in the more convenient form of a book, will suffice of itself to secure a large and eager demand for it."—*Law Times*.

"The work is clearly and agreeably written, and ably elucidates the subject in hand."—*Justice of the Peace*.

"Mr. Barry has the rare faculty of being very comprehensible to his readers; he has his subjects so well in hand, that he is able to condense them without in any way leaving it perceptible that too little has been done; and so well has he laid out his table of contents, that it becomes at once an elaborate index, by which any point can be at once found; and the legal reader will understand this when we say that the index or table of contents extends to no less than eighteen closely-printed pages. The work is the most important and best treatise on conveyancing that now exists, and the student can have no better authority than Mr. Barry to get himself well up in conveyancing. Nor can the legal practitioner, and especially country solicitors, find a safer book of reference in practice than Mr. Barry's very valuable treatise."—*News of the World*.

"We must content ourselves with the statement that the present is a work of very great ability. There is no modern work which deals with precisely the same subject, and we have no doubt whatever that this will prove a book of very great value, both to the practitioner and to the student-at-law."—*Athenæum*.

Lewis's Introduction to Equity Drafting.

Post 8vo., 12s. cloth.

PRINCIPLES of EQUITY DRAFTING; with an Appendix of Forms. By HUBERT LEWIS, B.A., of the Middle Temple, Barrister at Law; Author of "Principles of Conveyancing," &c.

*** This Work, intended to explain the general principles of Equity Drafting, as well as to exemplify the Pleadings of the Court of Chancery, will, it is hoped, be useful to lawyers resorting to the New Equity Jurisdiction of the County Courts.

" We have little doubt that this work will soon gain a favorable place in the estimation of the profession. It is written in a clear attractive style, and is plainly the result of much thoughtful and conscientious labour."—*Law Magazine and Review.*

" Mr. Lewis's work is likely to have a much wider circle of readers than he could have anticipated when he commenced it, for almost every page will be applicable to County Court Practice, should the bill, in any shape or under any title, be retained in the new jurisdiction,—without it we fear that equity in the County Courts will be a mass of uncertainty,—with it every practitioner must learn the art of equity drafting, and he will find no better teacher than Mr. Lewis."—*Law Times.*

" This will, we think, be found a very useful work, not only to students for the bar and solicitors practising in the County Courts, as anticipated by the author, but also to the equity draftsman."—*Law Journal.*

Lewis's Introduction to Conveyancing.

8vo., 18s. cloth.

PRINCIPLES of CONVEYANCING explained and illustrated by Concise Precedents; with an Appendix on the effect of the Transfer of Land Act in modifying and shortening Conveyances. By HUBERT LEWIS, B.A., late Scholar of Emmanuel College, Cambridge, of the Middle Temple, Barrister at Law.

" The preface arrested our attention, and the examination we have made of the whole treatise has given us (what may be called a new sensation) pleasure in the perusal of a work on Conveyancing. We have, indeed, read it with pleasure and profit, and we may say at once that Mr. Lewis is entitled to the credit of having produced a very useful, and, at the same time, original work. This will appear from a mere outline of his plan, which is very ably worked out. The manner in which his dissertations elucidate his subject is clear and practical, and his expositions, with the help of his precedents, have the best of all qualities in such a treatise, being eminently judicious and substantial. Mr. Lewis's work is conceived in the right spirit. Although a learned and goodly volume, it may yet, with perfect propriety, be called a 'handy book.' It is besides a courageous attempt at legal improvement; and it is, perhaps, by works of such a character that law reform may be best accomplished."—*Law Magazine and Review.*

"It was still felt that a work explanatory and illustrative of conveyancing precedents remained a *desideratum*. Mr. Lewis proposes to supply this want in the work now before us. The book will be of the greatest use to those who have some antecedent knowledge of real property law, but who have not had much experience in the preparation of conveyances. 'How to do it' might well be the motto of the author, and certainly no ordinary lawyer can peruse Mr. Hubert Lewis's book without making himself much more competent to prepare and understand conveyancing than he was before. On the whole we consider that the work is deserving of high praise, both for design and execution. It is wholly free from the vice of book making, and indicates considerable reflection and learning. Mr. Lewis has, at all events, succeeded in producing a work to meet an acknowledged want, and we have no doubt he will find many grateful readers amongst more advanced, not less than among younger, students. In an appendix, devoted to the Land Transfer Act of last session, there are some useful and novel criticisms on its provisions."—*Solicitors' Journal.*

"Mr. Lewis has contributed a valuable aid to the law student. He has condensed the practice of conveyancing into a shape that will facilitate its retention by the memory, and his precedents are usefully arranged as a series of progressive lessons which may be used as either illustrations or exercises."—*Law Times.*

" We have long felt the want of a book of this kind. It is a work of no ordinary difficulty, but, judging from a first perusal, it could not have fallen into better hands. The great object in compiling a book of this nature is to make it practically useful, and in this Mr. Lewis has been generally successful. The perusal of the work has given us much pleasure, it shows a thorough knowledge of the various subjects treated of, and is clearly and intelligibly written. Students will now not only be able to become proficient draftsmen, but, by carefully studying Mr. Lewis's dissertations, may obtain an insight into the hitherto neglected principles of conveyancing."—*Legal Examiner.*

Tudor's Leading Cases on Real Property, &c.—Second Edition.

One thick vol. royal 8vo., 42s. cloth.

A SELECTION OF LEADING CASES on the LAW RELATING to REAL PROPERTY, Conveyancing, and the Construction of Wills and Deeds ; with Notes. By OWEN DAVIES TUDOR, Esq., of the Middle Temple, Barrister at Law. Author of " A Selection of Leading Cases in Equity." Second Edition.

" The Second Edition is now before us, and we are able to say that the same extensive knowledge and the same laborious industry as have been exhibited by Mr. Tudor on former occasions characterize this later production of his legal authorship ; and it is enough at this moment to reiterate an opinion that Mr. Tudor has well maintained the high legal reputation which his standard works have achieved in all countries where the English language is spoken, and the decisions of our Courts are quoted."—*Law Magazine and Review.*

" The work before us comprises a digest of decisions which, if not exhaustive of all the principles of our real property code, will at least be found to leave nothing untouched or unelaborated under the numerous legal doctrines to which the cases severally relate. To Mr. Tudor's treatment of all these subjects, so complicated and so varied, we accord our entire commendation. There are no omissions of any important cases relative to the various branches of the law comprised in the work, nor are there any omissions or defects in his statement of the law itself applicable to the cases discussed by him. We cordially recommend the work to the practitioner and the student alike, but especially to the former."—*Solicitors' Journal.*

" This and the other volumes of Mr. Tudor are almost a law library in themselves, and we are satisfied that the student would learn more law from the careful reading of them than he would acquire from double the time given to the elaborate treatises which learned professors recommend the student to peruse, with entire forgetfulness that time and brains are limited, and that to do what they advise would be the work of a life. Smith and Mr. Tudor will together give them such a knowledge of law as they could not obtain from a whole library of text books, and of law that will be useful every day, instead of law that they will not want three times in their lives. At this well the practising lawyer might beneficially refresh his memory by a draught, when a leisure hour will permit him to study a leading case. No law library should be without this most useful book."—*Law Times.*

Benham's Student's Examination Guide.

12mo. 3s. cloth.

THE STUDENT'S GUIDE to the PRELIMINARY EXAMINATION for ATTORNEYS and SOLICITORS, and also to the Oxford and Cambridge Local Examinations and the College of Preceptors; to which are added numerous Suggestions and Examination Questions, selected from those asked at the Law Institution. By JAMES ERLE BENHAM, of King's College, London.

" The book is artistically arranged. It will become a useful guide and instructor not only to law students but to every student who is preparing for a preliminary examination."—*Law Journal.*

" The book is written in a clear and agreeable style, and will no doubt be found useful by the class of readers for whom it is intended."—*Law Magazine and Review.*

" Mr. Benham has produced a very useful manual for the aid of intending candidates at the solicitors' preliminary examinations and the Oxford and Cambridge local examinations. He gives many suggestions on all the subjects of examination and full information thereon."—*Law Examination Reporter.*

" It is certainly a useful guide to that curious *olla podrida* expected from the candidate. There are persons who can never learn to swim without first feeling the confidence which an artificial aid gives them, and to those who are nervous at facing the troubles of dates and arithmetic it may be well to have a systematized mode of ' cram' suggested in a distinct and accurate manner."—*London Review.*

" A useful little treatise by Mr. James Erle Benham, intended to supply to students about to encounter the examination which precedes entering into articles of clerkship the necessary information as to subjects of study."—*Star.*

" He has succeeded in producing a book which will doubtless prove useful to those students who desire to prepare themselves for examination without the assistance of a tutor. The sets of examination papers appear to be judiciously selected and are tolerably full."—*Irish Law Times.*

Latham on the Law of Window Lights.

Post 8vo., 10s. cloth.

A TREATISE on the LAW of WINDOW LIGHTS. By Francis Law Latham, of the Inner Temple, Esq., Barrister at Law.

"This is not merely a valuable addition to the law library of the practitioner, it is a book that every law student will read with profit. It exhausts the subject of which it treats."—*Law Times.*

"His arrangement is logical, and he discusses fully each point of his subject. The work, in our opinion, is both perspicuous and able, and we cannot but compliment the author on it."—*Law Journal.*

"A treatise on this subject was wanted, and Mr. Latham has succeeded in meeting that want."—*Athenæum.*

"Mr. Latham is evidently one of those authors who like to have a complete skeleton of their subject elaborated before putting pen to paper; and the consequence is, that this little work is one which we have much pleasure in recommending to the profession. The sequence of discussion is well ordered, and the author's plan well adhered to; and although the text comprises less than 250 octavo pages, the subject is quite exhaustively treated. To solicitors the volume will, we think, be particularly serviceable. Armed with the work we have now reviewed, the practitioner will be in a fair way to cope successfully with the most *exigent* client who comes to consult him about his windows."—*Solicitors' Journal.*

"This subject has acquired a general commercial interest, and a clear concise work upon it is, at this time, very opportune. Mr. Latham's treatise on the Law of Window Lights appears to supply in a convenient form all the information which, in a general way, may be required. The text throughout is lucid and is well supported by precedents."—*Building News.*

"The ancient light question, owing to the demand for enlarged buildings within the area of our large towns, becomes more important every day, and Mr. Latham has done well in providing a new treatise on the subject, and setting forth some of the more recent decisions of our courts. It is well arranged and clearly written. We recommend the book."—*Builder.*

Tudor's Charitable Trusts.—Second Edition.

Post 8vo., 18s. cloth.

THE LAW OF CHARITABLE TRUSTS; with the Statutes to the end of Session 1862, the Orders, Regulations and Instructions, issued pursuant thereto; and a Selection of Schemes. By Owen Davies Tudor, Esq., of the Middle Temple, Barrister-at-Law; Author of "Leading Cases in Equity;" "Real Property and Conveyancing;" &c. Second Edition.

"Mr. Tudor in the present edition of his work has struck out beyond his original intention, and has made it a complete compendium of the law of charities. In carrying out this intention his object appears to have been to produce a practical and concise summary of this branch of the law. No living writer is more capable than Mr. Tudor of producing such a work: his Leading Cases in Equity, and also on the Law of Real Property, have deservedly earned for him the highest reputation as a learned, careful and judicious text-writer. The main feature of the work is the manner in which Mr. Tudor has dealt with all the recent statutes relating to this subject: we have only to add that the index is very carefully compiled."—*Solicitors' Journal.*

"Mr. Tudor's excellent little book on Charitable Trusts. It is indeed no longer a little book but a bulky one of some 650 pages. Mr. Tudor however is a singular painstaking author, his books, as the profession well knows, are models of industry and care, and hence their popularity. This second edition has collected the cases decided since the issue of the first, and their number is surprising—upwards of one thousand. Mr. Tudor has made his work complete by the introduction of several schemes for the settlement of charities, so that it is in all respects the text-book for the lawyer, as well as a hand-book for reference by trustees and others engaged in the management of charities."—*Law Times.*

"The account of the Law of Mortmain and the statutes respecting charitable bequests in their bearing on the different religious orders is full and definite, and the duties of trustees are explained in a clear and straightforward way. Altogether this work must be exceedingly useful, not to say indispensable, to all persons who are connected with charitable trusts whether as founders, managers or trustees."—*English Churchman.*

"To this second edition large additions are made, and it is now a complete compendium of the Law of Charities."—*Clerical Journal.*

"To all who have occasion to look into the nature and origin of those trusts, together with the several Acts of Parliament which affect or govern them, Mr. Tudor's work will be found of great value, more especially as in this second and improved edition all the more recent cases have been carefully collated."—*Bell's Messenger.*

Mosely's Handy-Book for Articled Clerks.

12mo., 7s. cloth.

A PRACTICAL HANDY-BOOK of ELEMENTARY LAW,

designed for the use of Articled Clerks, with a Course of Study and Hints on Reading for the Intermediate and Final Examinations. By M. S. MOSELY, Solicitor, Clifford's Inn Prizeman, M. T. 1867.

CONTENTS :—

PREFACE.—INTRODUCTORY REMARKS.—CHAP. I.—THE FIRST YEAR.—Introduction to the office—What may be learned by copying a Draft—Explanation of technical terms—The profession, and its subdivisions—Conveyancing; Equity; Common Law; Bankruptcy Law —Office work and office routine—Course of reading for the first year—Practical hints on reading—System of self-examination. CHAP. II.—THE SECOND YEAR.—Practical view of the ordinary routine of Conveyancing—Investigation of Titles—Purchases—Leases—Mortgages—Settlements—Wills—Course of reading for the second year—Introduction to the Statute-law—General analysis of the Statutes at large, preliminary to their study. CHAP. III. THE THIRD YEAR.—Office work—Suggestions for acquiring a knowledge of the Details of Common-law practice—The Courts—Nisi Prius business—The Brief and its preparation—Marshalling the Evidence—General rules of Evidence—A short practical view of the ordinary steps in an Action, with examples—Course of reading for the third year : the Intermediate Examination—Points to be attended to in reading for it—Method of answering the Examiners' questions—The Statue-law (*continued*). CHAP. IV.—THE FOURTH YEAR.—The County Courts—Method of acquiring a knowledge of Practice—Hints on Advocacy—Course of reading for the fourth year. CHAP. V.—THE LAST YEAR.—Assignment of Articles— The town agent's office—London professional life—Attendance at Chambers—Rules of Pleading—General view of points to be attended to during the last year under Articles— Course of reading for the fifth year : *Résumé* of old books—Analysis of Case-law. CHAP. VI. The final Examination—Practical suggestions on reading for the Examination—Notes and Commonplace-book—The Examiners' standard —" Coaches," their advantages and disadvantages—Reading for honours—Routine of the Examination—Admission—Conclusion. APPENDIX. —(A.) Practical directions for Examination and Admission. —(B.) List of standard books on special subjects.

" This useful little book is intended for the use of articled clerks during the period of their articles. The style of this book is peculiar : it is an exaggeration of the style adopted by Mr. Haynes in his admirable 'Outlines of Equity.' The author seems to think the adoption of such a style the only way to make the study of the law popular, and we are not prepared to say he is wrong."—*Law Magazine and Review.*

"'The design of this little book is to combine instruction, advice and amusement, if anything amusing can be extracted from the routine of a solicitor's office and the studies of articled clerks. The book will certainly be found useful by any articled clerk, for it contains much information which it is sometimes very troublesome to find, and the facetiousness of Mr. Mosely's manner will doubtless help to grease the course of a rough and uneasy subject."—*Law Journal.*

" There are few who read this book with care who will not readily admit that on many intricate points of law their notions have become much clearer than before their acquaintance with it. Both parts are well worked out, and will be found useful ; but in the second division of each chapter the law student will find most valuable information, as there Mr. Mosely not only marks out the course of reading which he recommends for each year, but also carefully analyses the contents of each book, and points out those chapters and subjects which it will be most advantageous for the student to master at the first reading, and those which he ought to defer till a second perusal and a wider experience have made him more competent to understand them. The style is remarkably good, and, considering the subject, free from technical expressions."— *Irish Law Times.*

Ingram's Law of Compensation for Lands, &c.

Post 8vo. 10s. cloth.

COMPENSATION to LAND and HOUSE OWNERS :

being a Treatise on the Law of the Compensation for Interests in Lands, &c. payable by Railway and other Public Companies ; with an Appendix of Forms and Statues. By THOMAS DUNBAR INGRAM, of Lincoln's Inn, Esq., Barrister at Law.

" We say at once that it is a work of great merit. It is a concise, clear and complete exposition of the law of compensation applicable to the owners of real property and railway and other companies."—*Law Magazine.*

" Whether for companies taking land or holding it, Mr. Ingram's volume will be a welcome guide. With this in his hand the legal adviser of a company, or of an owner and occupier whose property is taken, and who demands compensation for it, cannot fail to perform his duty rightly."—*Law Times.*

Tomkins' Institutes of Roman Law.

Part I. royal 8vo. (to be completed in Three Parts) 12s. cloth.

THE INSTITUTES OF THE ROMAN LAW. PART I.

The Sources of the Roman Law and its external History to the decline of the Eastern and Western Empires. By FREDERICK TOMKINS, M.A., D.C.L., Barrister-at-Law, of Lincoln's Inn.

"This work promises to be an important and valuable contribution to the study of the Roman Law."—*Law Magazine.*

"Of all the works on the Roman Law we believe this will be the best suited to law students. Mr. Tomkins gives us a simple English history of Roman Law, arranged most lucidly with marginal notes, and printed in a form calculated for easy reading and retention in the memory. We welcome the book of Mr. Tomkins. It is calculated to promote the study of Roman Law; and both at the Universities and in the Inns of Court it is a work which may safely and beneficially be employed as a text book."—*Law Times.*

"This work is pronounced by its author to be strictly elementary. But in regard to the labour bestowed, the research exercised, and the materials brought together, it seems to deserve a more ambitious title than that of an elementary treatise. The chapter on legal instruction, detailing the systems of legal education pursued in the various epochs of Rome, reflects great credit on the author, and so far as we know is purely original, in the sense that no preceding English writer has collated the matter therein contained."—*Law Journal.*

"Mr. Tomkins has chosen his subject wisely in at least one respect, there can be no doubt that a good introductory treatise on the Roman law is sorely needed at present. The present part is only an instalment. But the present part is unquestionably both valuable in itself and of good promise for the future. We know of no other book in which anything like the same amount of information can be acquired with the same ease. We shall look with great interest for the publication of the remainder of this treatise. If the second part is as well executed as the first and bears a due proportion to it, we think the work bids fair to become the standard text book for English students."—*Solicitors' Journal.*

Christie's Crabb's Conveyancing.—Fifth Edit. by Shelford.

Two vols. royal 8vo., 3l. cloth.

CRABB'S COMPLETE SERIES of PRECEDENTS in CONVEYANCING and of COMMON and COMMERCIAL FORMS in Alphabetical Order, adapted to the Present State of the Law and the Practice of Conveyancing; with copious Prefaces, Observations and Notes on the several Deeds. By J. T. CHRISTIE, Esq., Barrister-at-Law. The Fifth Edition, with numerous Corrections and Additions, by LEONARD SHELFORD, Esq., of the Middle Temple, Barrister-at-Law.

From the Law Times.

"The preparation of it could not have been confided to more able hands than those of Mr. Shelford, the veteran authority on real property law. With the industry that distinguishes him he has done ample justice to his task. In carefulness we have in him a second Crabb, in erudition Crabb's superior; and the result is a work of which the original author would have been proud, could it have appeared under his own auspices. It is not a book to be quoted, nor indeed could its merits be exhibited by quotation. It is essentially a book of practice, which can only be described in rude outline and dismissed with applause, and a recommendation of it to the notice of those for whose service it has been so laboriously compiled."

From the Solicitors' Journal.

"The collection of precedents contained in these two volumes are all that could be desired. They are particularly well adapted for Solicitors, being of a really practical character. They are moreover free from the useless repetitions of common forms that so much increase the bulk and expense of some collections that we could name. We know not of any collection of conveyancing precedents that would make it so possible for a tyro to put together a presentable draft at an exigency, or which are more handy in every respect, even for the experienced draftsman. Mr. Shelford has proved himself in this task to be not unworthy of his former reputation. To those familiar with his other works it will be a sufficient recommendation of this."

From the Law Magazine and Review.

"To this important part of his duty—the remodelling and perfecting of the Forms—even with the examination which we have already been able to afford this work, we are able to affirm, that the learned editor has been eminently successful and effected valuable improvements."

From the Law Chronicle.

"It possesses one distinctive feature in devoting more attention than usual in such works to forms of a commercial nature. We are satisfied from an examination of the present with the immediately preceding edition that Mr. Shelford has very considerably improved the character of the work, both in the prefaces and in the forms. On the whole the two volumes of Crabb's Precedents, as edited by Mr. Leonard Shelford, will be found extremely useful in a solicitor's office, presenting a large amount of real property learning, with very numerous precedents: indeed we know of no book so justly entitled to the appellation of 'handy' as the fifth edition of Mr. Crabb's Precedents."

Rouse's Copyhold Manual.—-Third Edition.

12mo., 10s. 6d. cloth.

THE COPYHOLD ENFRANCHISEMENT MANUAL, giving the Law, Practice and Forms in Enfranchisements at Common Law and under Statute, and in Commutations; with the Values of Enfranchisements from the Lord's various Rights: the Principles of Calculation being clearly explained, and made practical by numerous Rules, Tables and Examples. Also all the Copyhold Acts, and several other Statutes and Notes. Third Edition. By ROLLA ROUSE, Esq., of the Middle Temple, Barrister at Law, Author of "The Practical Conveyancer," &c.

" This new edition follows the plan of its predecessor, adopting a fivefold division:—1. The Law. 2. The Practice, with Practical Suggestions to Lords, Stewards and Copyholders. 3. The Mathematical consideration of the Subject in all its Details, with Rules, Tables and Examples. 4. Forms. 5. The Statutes, with Notes. Of these, we can only repeat what we have said before, that they exhaust the subject; they give to the practitioner all the materials required by him to conduct the enfranchisement of a copyhold, whether voluntary or compulsory."—*Law Times.*

" When we consider what favor Mr. Rouse's Practical Man and Practical Conveyancer have found with the profession, we feel sure the legal world will greet with pleasure a new and improved edition of his copyhold manual. The third edition of that work is before us. It is a work of great practical value, suitable to lawyers and laymen. We can freely and heartily recommend this volume to the practitioner, the steward and the copyholder."—*Law Magazine.*

" Now, however, that copyhold tenures are being frequently converted into freeholds, Mr. Rouse's treatise will doubtless be productive of very extensive benefit; for it seems to us to have been very carefully prepared, exceedingly well composed and written, and to indicate much experience in copyhold law on the part of the author."—*Solicitors' Journal.*

Wills on Evidence.—Fourth Edition.

8vo., 10s. cloth.

AN ESSAY on the PRINCIPLES of CIRCUMSTANTIAL EVIDENCE. Illustrated by numerous Cases. By the late WILLIAM WILLS, Esq. Fourth Edition, edited by his Son, ALFRED WILLS, Esq., Barrister at Law.

Shelford's Succession Duties.—Second Edition.

12mo., 16s. cloth.

THE LAW relating to the PROBATE, LEGACY and SUCCESSION DUTIES in ENGLAND, IRELAND and SCOTLAND, including all the Statutes and the Decisions on those Subjects: with Forms and Official Regulations. By LEONARD SHELFORD, Esq., of the Middle Temple, Barrister-at-Law. The Second Edition, with many Alterations and Additions.

"The book is written mainly for solicitors. Mr. Shelford has accordingly planned his work with careful regard to its practical utility and daily use."—*Solicitors' Journal.*

" The treatise before us on the charges which the State levies on the devolution of property by death has been one of the most useful and popular of his productions, and being now the text book on the subject nothing remains but to make known its appearance to our readers. Its merits have been already tested by most of them."—*Law Times.*

" The work, although called a new edition, is in great part entirely new. On the whole Mr. Shelford's book appears to us to be the best and most complete work on this extremely intricate subject."—*Law Magazine.*

Woolrych on Sewers.—Third Edition.

8vo., 12s. cloth.

A TREATISE of the LAW of SEWERS, including the DRAINAGE ACTS. By HUMPHRY W. WOOLRYCH, Serjeant at Law. Third Edition, with considerable Additions and Alterations.

" Two editions of it have been speedily exhausted, and a third called for. The author is an accepted authority on all subjects of this class."—*Law Times.*

" This is a third and greatly enlarged edition of a book which has already obtained an established reputation as the most complete discussion of the subject adapted to modern times. Since the treatise of Mr. Serjeant Callis in the early part of the 17th century, no work filling the same place has been added to the literature of the Profession. It is a work of no slight labour to digest and arrange this mass of legislation; this task, however, Mr. Serjeant Woolrych has undertaken, and an examination of his book will, we think, convince the most exacting that he has fully succeeded. No one should attempt to meddle with the Law of Sewers without its help."—*Solicitors' Journal.*

Grant's Law of Corporations in General.

Royal 8vo., 26s. boards.

A PRACTICAL TREATISE on the LAW of CORPORATIONS in GENERAL, as well Aggregate as Sole; including Municipal Corporations; Railway, Banking, Canal, and other Joint-Stock and Trading Bodies; Dean and Chapters; Universities; Colleges; Schools; Hospitals; with *quasi* Corporations aggregate, as Guardians of the Poor, Churchwardens, Churchwardens and Overseers, etc.; and also Corporations sole, as Bishops, Deans, Canons, Archdeacons, Parsons, etc. By JAMES GRANT, Esq., of the Middle Temple, Barrister at Law.

J. Chitty, jun's. Precedents in Pleading.—Third Edition.

Complete in One Vol. Royal 8vo., 38s. cloth.

J. CHITTY, JUN's. PRECEDENTS in PLEADING; with copious Notes on Practice, Pleading and Evidence. Third Edition. By the late TOMPSON CHITTY, Esq., and by LEOFRIC TEMPLE, R. G. WILLIAMS, and CHARLES JEFFERY, Esquires, Barristers at Law. (Part 2 may, for the present, be had separately, price 18s. cloth, to complete sets.)

" To enter into detailed criticism and praise of this standard work would be quite out of place. In the present instance the matter has fallen into competent hands, who have spared no pains. This valuable and useful work is brought down to the present time, altered in accordance with the cases and statutes now in force. Great care has been expended by the competent editors, and its usefulness, as heretofore, will be found not to be confined to the chambers of the special pleader, but to be of a more extended character. To those who knew the work of old no recommendation is wanted, to those younger members of the profession who have not that privilege we would suggest that they should at once make its acquaintance."—*Law Journal.*

" The value of this practical work has greatly increased in the practical hands of the editors. It is framed solely with the view of being a safe and ready guide for the practitioner in the art of pleading. The notes are concise and suggestive, and almost every precedent is accompanied by a list of the cases supporting it. The precedents themselves give abundant proof of the learning and care that have been devoted to them. We hope that the remainder will soon be published. When it is finished the work will, without doubt, be the best and most complete work on pleading in our libraries."—*Law Magazine.*

" A book almost as well known to the profession as " Tidd " was has been republished, we might almost say rewritten, and adapted to the requirements of modern pleading. Few there are for whom assistance will not be found by reference to these pages, which serve yet another useful purpose, by helping the lawyer to pick holes in his adversary's pleadings, as well as properly to frame his own. Nor is the volume useful in the Superior Courts only; practitioners in the County Courts will find it a valuable adviser in the preparation of pleadings, such as they are."—*Law Times.*

Scriven on Copyholds.—Fifth Edition by Stalman.

Abridged in 1 vol. royal 8vo., £1 : 10s. cloth.

A TREATISE ON COPYHOLD, CUSTOMARY FREE-HOLD and ANCIENT DEMESNE TENURE, with the Jurisdiction of Courts Baron and Courts Leet. By JOHN SCRIVEN, Serjeant at Law. Fifth Edition, containing references to Cases and Statutes to 1867. By HENRY STALMAN, of the Inner Temple, Esq., Barrister at Law.

" No lawyer can see or hear the word 'copyhold' without associating with it the name of Scriven, whose book has been always esteemed not merely the best but the only one of any worth. Until a commutation of the tenure for a fixed rent-charge, after the manner of a tithe commutation, is compelled by the legislature, this treatise will lose none of its usefulness to the solicitors in the country."—*Law Times.*

" It would be wholly superfluous to offer one word of comment on the general body of the work. Scriven on Copyholds has for exactly half a century been not only a standard work but one of unimpeachable authority, and in its pages the present generation has learned all that is known of copyhold and customary tenures. All that is necessary to say is, that in the present edition of Scriven on Copyholds Mr. Stalman has omitted what it was useless to retain, and inserted what it was necessary to add. Until copyholds have disappeared utterly, it is at least certain that Scriven on Copyholds by Stalman will hold undisputed sway in the profession."—*Law Journal.*

Browning's Divorce and Matrimonial Causes Practice.

Post 8vo., 8s. cloth.

THE PRACTICE and PROCEDURE of the COURT for DIVORCE and MATRIMONIAL CAUSES, including the Acts, Rules, Orders, copious Notes of Cases and Forms of Practical Proceedings, with Tables of Fees and Bills of Costs. By W. ERNST BROWNING, Esq., of the Inner Temple, Barrister-at-Law.

" After a careful study of this work, we unhesitatingly recommend it as well to the student as to the legal practitioner."—*Law Magazine and Review.*

" If the future editions are edited with the same care and ability that have been bestowed upon this, it will probably take its place as *the* Practice of the Divorce Court."—*Jurist.*

"We ought not to omit noticing the very useful precedents of bills of costs which it contains. These alone are sufficient to obtain a good circulation for this manual."—*Solicitors' Journal.*

" Mr. Browning's little volume will doubtless become *the* practice of the Divorce Court." —*Law Times.*

Brandon's Law of Foreign Attachment.

8vo., 14s. cloth.

A TREATISE upon the CUSTOMARY LAW of FOREIGN ATTACHMENT, and the PRACTICE of the MAYOR'S COURT of the CITY OF LONDON therein. With Forms of Procedure. By WOODTHORPE BRANDON, Esq., of the Middle Temple, Barrister-at-Law.

Moseley on Contraband of War.

Post 8vo., 5s. cloth.

WHAT IS CONTRABAND OF WAR AND WHAT IS NOT. Comprising all the American and English Authorities on the Subject. By JOSEPH MOSELEY, Esq., B.C.L., Barrister at Law.

Oke's Magisterial Synopsis.—Tenth Edition.

Dedicated by permission to the Right Hon. Lord Cairns, Lord Chancellor.

Two vols., 8vo. cloth.

THE MAGISTERIAL SYNOPSIS: a Practical Guide for Magistrates, their Clerks, Attornies and Constables; Summary Convictions and Indictable Offences, with their Penalties, Punishments, Procedure, &c., being Alphabetically and Tabularly arranged. By GEORGE C. OKE, Chief Clerk to the Lord Mayor of London. Tenth Edition.

Opinion of Lord Chancellor Westbury.

"*Upper Hyde Park Gardens, October 30th,* 1862.

"'The Lord Chancellor presents his compliments to Mr. Oke, and thanks him very much for the valuable present of his most excellent and elaborate works, the 'Magisterial Synopsis' and 'Magisterial Formulist,' which, in the opinion of the Lord Chancellor, will be of great public service.

"To George C. Oke, Esq., &c., &c., &c., Mansion House, London."

Opinions of the late Lord Chancellor Campbell.

" I congratulate you on the great success of your valuable Synopsis, and I shall be well pleased to be Dedicatee of successive editions while you desire that I should have this honour."—*Letter to Mr. Oke, dated April 6th,* 1858.

"*Stratheden House, May 24th,* 1858.

" My dear Sir,—I thank you for the copy of your new edition which you have had the goodness to send me, and I am glad to hear of the increased circulation of the Work.

" Your instructions as to cases under 20 & 21 Vict. c. 43, will be particularly useful.

" I remain, yours faithfully,

" George C. Oke, Esq."   " CAMPBELL."

" I am aware that the Lord Mayor has at present an able assistant in the person of a gentleman of the name of Oke, Author of the 'Magisterial Synopsis,' a very enterprising, able and learned man."—*The Lord Chancellor (Campbell) in the House of Lords, February 23rd,* 1860.

Oke's Turnpike Laws.—Second Edition.

12mo., 18s. cloth.

THE LAWS of TURNPIKE ROADS; comprising the whole of the General Acts; the Acts as to the Union of Trusts, for facilitating Arrangements with their Creditors; the Interference of Railways and other Public Works with Roads, their Non-repair, and enforcing Contributions from Parishes (including the Acts as to South Wales Turnpike Roads), &c. &c.; practically arranged, with Cases, Notes, Forms, &c. &c. By GEORGE C. OKE, Author of "*The Magisterial Synopsis.*" Second Edition.

" In the 'Synopsis' Mr. Oke is unique; the plan was perfectly original, and he has no competitor. In the Turnpike Law he is himself a competitor with others, who had previously possession of the field. Nevertheless, so well has he executed his design that his volume has fairly taken precedence in the esteem of the profession, because he has written it with the same industrious research and painstaking correction which distinguished the ' Synopsis.' "—*Law Times.*

" All Mr. Oke's works are well done, and his 'Turnpike Laws' is an admirable specimen of the class of books required for the guidance of magistrates and legal practitioners in country districts."—*Solicitors' Journal.*

Oke's Magisterial Formulist.—Fourth Edition.

One thick volume, 8vo., 38s. cloth.

The MAGISTERIAL FORMULIST: being a complete Collection of Forms and Precedents for practical use in all Cases out of Quarter Sessions, and in Parochial Matters, by Magistrates, their Clerks, Attornies and Constables: with an Introduction, Explanatory Directions, Variations and Notes. By GEORGE C. OKE, Author of "The Magisterial Synopsis." Fourth Edition, enlarged and improved.

*** This new edition is brought down to the close of the last Session of Parliament (1867). It is much enlarged and improved, and contains the Forms under the Master and Servant Act, 1867, and the magisterial legislation of the last six years.

"The publication of a new edition of this most useful collection of forms has been urgently called for. Mr. Oke's works are so well known to all who are concerned in the administration of magisterial law, that we need say no more than that the present edition seems to have been prepared with his usual care. On a reference to a very full index at the end of the book, we have been unable to detect the omission of any subject in the place where it might be expected to be found, and such forms as the author has had to draw, and not merely to transcribe, appear well executed."—*Solicitors' Journal.*

"Mr. Oke has had many predecessors in his office of Chief Clerk to the Lord Mayor of London of skill, learning and reputation, but it would be impossible to name any one of such officers who has rendered such signal services to the administration of the law by the justices as the author of the book before us. It is indeed difficult to offer any remarks of moment upon a work which has gone through three editions, and has been acknowledged as complete by all who has had occasion to use it. But time alone, and the mass of new legislation which it has brought with it, have made the revision of the book necessary. The important changes and extensions of the law administered by the magistrates since the session of 1861 have justified and demanded a new edition, and in that new edition we believe will be found the same qualities of accuracy and completeness which distinguished its three predecessors. No clerk to justices, and no justice who is anxious to discharge his onerous functions successfully, should be without the 'Magisterial Formulist' and the 'Magisterial Synopsis;' and it need scarcely be added that those members of the profession who are brought in contact with business in petty sessions will derive great assistance from them."—*Law Journal.*

"This work is too well known to need eulogy. It is in universal use in magistrates' courts; it has been out of print for some time, and a new edition was urgently required. We believe that Mr. Oke purposely delayed it that it might be made contemporaneous, or nearly so, with the Synopsis. The contents are brought down to the end of last year, and consequently it includes all the forms required by the new statutes and decisions of the six years that have elapsed since the publication of the third edition. They have been arranged under divers new titles, and especially the modes of describing indictable offences have been much enlarged. It is a book that has been known so long, and so extensively, that no further description of it is needed now." *Law Times.*

Chadwick's Probate Court Manual.

Royal 8vo., 12s. cloth.

EXAMPLES of ADMINISTRATION BONDS for the COURT of PROBATE; exhibiting the Principle of various Grants of Administration, and the correct Mode of preparing the Bonds in respect thereof; also Directions for preparing the Oaths, arranged for practical utility. With Extracts from the Statutes; also various Forms of Affirmation prescribed by Acts of Parliament, and a Supplemental Notice, bringing the work down to 1865. By SAMUEL CHADWICK, of Her Majesty's Court of Probate.

"We undertake to say that the possession of this volume by practitioners will prevent many a hitch and awkward delay, provoking to the lawyer himself and difficult to be satisfactorily explained to the clients."—*Law Magazine and Review.*

"Mr. Chadwick's volume will be a necessary part of the law library of the practitioner, for he has collected precedents that are in constant requirement. This is purely a book of practice, but therefore the more valuable. It tells the reader what *to do*, and that is the information most required after a lawyer begins to practise."—*Law Times.*

Grant's Law of Banking.—Second Edition by Fisher.

8vo. 21s. cloth.

GRANT'S LAW of BANKERS and BANKING and BANKS OF ISSUE, Limited and Chartered, and Winding-up; Directors, Managers and Officers; and the Law as to Cheques, Circular Notes or Letters of Credit, Bank Notes, Exchequer Bills, Coupons, Deposits, &c. (Appendix contains the Bank Notes Issue Bill, and Reasons for Bill, and Official Bank Returns.) Second Edition. By R. A. FISHER, Esq., of the Middle Temple, Barrister-at-Law.

"The present editor has very much increased the value of the original work, a work whose sterling merits had already raised it to the rank of a standard text-book."—*Law Magazine.*

"No man in the profession was more competent to treat the subject of Banking than Mr. Grant. This volume appears opportunely. To all engaged in the litigations, as well as to all legal advisers of Bankers, Mr. Grant's work will be an invaluable assistant. It is a clear and careful treatise on a subject not already exhausted, and it must become *the* text-book upon it."—*Law Times.*

"A Second Edition of Mr. Grant's well-known treatise on this branch of the law has been called for and very ably supplied by Mr. Fisher."—*Law Times, Second Notice.*

"The learning and industry which were so conspicuous in Mr. Grant's former work are equally apparent in this. The book supplies a real want, which has long been felt both by the profession and by the public at large."—*Jurist.*

"We commend this work to our readers. It is at once practical and intelligible, and is of use alike to the unprofessional as well as the professional reader. No bank, whether a private concern or a joint-stock company, should be without it."—*Money Market Review.*

Parkinson's Common Law Chamber Practice.

12mo., 7s. cloth.

A HANDY BOOK FOR THE COMMON LAW JUDGES' CHAMBERS. By GEO. H. PARKINSON, Chamber Clerk to the Hon. Mr. Justice Byles.

"For this work Mr. Parkinson is eminently qualified."—*Jurist.*

"It is extremely well calculated for the purpose for which it is intended. So much work is now done in Common Law Chambers by junior clerks that such a little treatise is much wanted. Mr. Parkinson has performed his task skilfully and with care."—*Solicitors' Journal.*

"The practice in Chambers has become sufficiently important to call for a treatise devoted to it, nor could a more competent man for the task have presented himself than Mr. Parkinson, whose great experience as well as intelligence have long placed him in the position of an authority on all matters appertaining to this peculiar but very extensive branch of Common Law Practice."—*Law Times.*

"There is much that would prove very useful to the practitioner in Mr. Parkinson's compilation, and which, so far as we are aware, is not to be found in any other book collected with equal conciseness."—*Law Magazine and Review.*

Lushington's Naval Prize Law.

Royal 8vo., 10s. 6d. cloth.

A MANUAL of NAVAL PRIZE LAW. By GODFREY LUSHINGTON, of the Inner Temple, Esq., Barrister at Law.

Lovesy's Law of Arbitration (Masters and Workmen).

12mo. 4s. cloth.

(*Dedicated, by permission, to Lord St. Leonards.*)

THE LAW of ARBITRATION between MASTERS and WORKMEN, as founded upon the Councils of Conciliation Act of 1867 (30 & 31 Vict. c. 105), the Masters and Workmen Act (5 Geo. 4, c. 96), and other Acts, with an Introduction and Notes. By C. W. LOVESY, Esq., of the Middle Temple, Barrister at Law.

"Where the adoption of this act is contemplated, a better handbook could not be provided for the guidance of masters and men than this edition of the act (which has been carefully and intelligently noted by Mr. Lovesy), as being printed in a convenient form for use and provided with an excellent index."—*Law Times*.

"The professed object of the author has been to give the substance of the two statutes in a popular form, and in that endeavour he seems to have succeeded."—*Law Journal*.

"We think the duty has been well performed by Mr. Lovesy. He has given us a clear and concise statement of the effect of the five statutes aforesaid, and we think his little book will be found extremely useful."—*Solicitors' Journal*.

"I think you have bestowed much attention upon the late statute and added some useful notes."—*Lord St. Leonards*.

"In a plain familiar style, such as may be readily comprehended by those for whose benefit he writes, the author has given the substance of the several statutes relating to this subject, and the notes which he has introduced will considerably facilitate the attainment of his object. The book is not exclusively addressed to the legal world; all those who come within the comprehensive terms of employers and employed may refer to it with advantage, and we sincerely trust that the publication of this useful work will be the means of decreasing some of the existing difficulties."—*Justice of the Peace*.

Smith's Bar Education.

8vo., 9s. cloth.

A HISTORY of EDUCATION for the ENGLISH BAR, with SUGGESTIONS as to SUBJECTS and METHODS of STUDY. By PHILIP ANSTIE SMITH, Esq., M.A., LL.B., Barrister-at-Law.

Trower's Church Building Laws.

Post 8vo. 8s. cloth.

THE LAW of the BUILDING of CHURCHES, PAR-
SONAGES, and SCHOOLS, and of the Division of Parishes and Places.
By CHARLES FRANCIS TROWER, M.A., of the Inner Temple, Esq., Barrister
at Law, late Fellow of Exeter College, Oxford, and late Secretary of Pre-
sentations to Lord Chancellor Westbury.

" A good book on this subject is calculated to be of considerable service both to lawyers, clerics and laymen, and, on the whole, after taking a survey of the work before us, we may pronounce it a useful work. It contains a great mass of information of essential import, and those who, as parishioners, legal advisers, or clergy-men, are concerned with glebes, endowments, district chapelries, parishes, ecclesiastical com-missions, and such like matters, about which the public, and notably the clerical public, seem to know but little, but which it is needless to say are matters of much importance."—*Solicitors' Journal.*

" The questions discussed make the work a most valuable legal guide to the clergy. Mr. Trower proposes by this volume to assist the clergy and the lawyers in their dealing with this subject. His book is just the one we could wish every clergyman to possess, for if it was in the hands of our readers they would be saved the trouble of asking us very many questions."—*Clerical Journal.*

" Mr. Trower brings his professional research to the rescue. In a well-arranged volume this gentleman points out concisely and intelligibly how the difficulties which usually beset parties in such matters may be avoided."—*Oxford University Herald.*

" The learned author of this lucid volume has done his best to summarise the several acts of par-liament that bear upon ecclesiastical structures, and to explain their meaning. On all the topics germane to its title this volume will be found a handy book of ecclesiastical law, and should on that account be made widely known among the clergy. The production is worthy of its author, and will, we hope, shortly establish itself in the good esteem of the clerical and general public."—*Church Mail.*

" Mr. Trower aims very successfully at giving a complete account of the present state of the law, and rendering it as nearly as possible in-telligible, and we hope that it may prove useful to all church building clergy and laity. It is a compact and handy treatise, very clearly written, well arranged, easy of reference, and, besides a good table of contents, it has an elaborate index. It is a book we are glad to have and to recom-mend."—*Literary Churchman.*

" Not only has Mr. Trower performed this work, but he has performed it in a thoroughly satisfac-tory manner, giving us a volume which will set many minds at rest, and prevent, it may be, many a parish squabble, or its natural complement a law suit. We recommend all our clerical readers to peruse the book with attention from beginning to end, and at once to give it a place in their libraries."—*Church Opinion.*

" Mr. Trower has, as we have said, supplied this need ; and done so fairly well. On the sub-jects of these acts, viz.—church building, par-sonage building, school building (including in the word ' building' augmenting and repairing) and erecting districts or sub-parishes—he has pro-duced a very useful and concise practical guide."—*Guardian.*

" This book will be a boon to many a puzzled and bewildered clergyman. Mr. Trower deserves the gratitude of all those who wish for a guide through that ' labyrinth of ambiguity,' which our unecclesiastical method of ecclesiastical legis-lation has built up. We commend the book to every clergyman."—*Churchman.*

" We welcome Mr. Trower's book as a valuable and useful manual of the obscurest and most dis-creditable portion of the statute book."—*Record.*

" Mr. Trower took upon himself a task by no means inviting, but one which the author—evidently looking upon it as a labour of love—has performed in a manner which does justice to the subject and credit to his own reputation as a scholar and lawyer."—*Builder.*

Drewry's Equity Pleader.

12mo., 6s. cloth.

A CONCISE TREATISE on the PRINCIPLES of EQUITY
PLEADING ; with Precedents. By C. STEWART DREWRY, of the Inner
Temple, Esq., Barrister at Law.

" It will be found of great utility as intro-ductory to the more elaborate treatises, or to refresh the memory after the study of the larger books."—*Law Times.*

" Keeping in view Mr. Drewry's design, namely, to produce a work on Equity Plead-ing for the information of students, he has successfully accomplished his professed ob-ject."—*Law Chronicle.*

" As an introduction to pleadings as they now subsist in the Equity Courts the book is well timed."—*Law Magazine and Law Review.*

Goldsmith's Equity.—Fifth Edition.

Post 8vo., 16s. cloth.

THE DOCTRINE and PRACTICE of EQUITY : or, a Concise Outline of Proceedings in the High Court of Chancery. Designed principally for the Use of Students. By G. GOLDSMITH, Esq., M.A., Barrister-at-Law. Fifth Edition, including all the alterations made in pursuance of the late acts and the orders thereon to the present time.

"A volume designed for the law student. Hence such a volume as Mr. Goldsmith has published is a perennial, and, while addressed principally to the student, it may be profitably read by the practitioner. Five editions attest the approval of those who have experienced the benefit of its instructions. It has grown in bulk with each successive appearance, as Mr. Goldsmith discovered what were the wants of his readers, and a continued succession of new topics has been added. It is now an extremely comprehensive sketch of the history, jurisdiction and practice of our Courts of Equity—a summary of what could be obtained only by hard reading of Reeve and Spence and Ayckbourn and Drewry. It commences with an historical outline : then it states the principles of equity jurisprudence ; then it shows their application to the various subject matters that fall within its jurisdictions ; and finally, it presents a clear and very instructive sketch of the procedure by which those jurisdictions are enforced."—*Law Times.*

"The excellencies of each ('Smith's Manual' and 'Hunter's Suit') appear to be successfully combined in Mr. Goldsmith's Treatise. Though professedly an elementary work, its merits are greater than its pretensions. Professing to accomplish a limited task, that task has been well done. The knowledge in haste and by piecemeal acquired, remains long ill digested, perhaps through life, crude and unready. This manual seeks to prevent such a result by introducing to the learner a plain summary of the doctrines of equity, together with a sketch of the practice in the Chancery Courts. We cordially recommend Mr. Goldsmith's Treatise to those for whom it is designed."—*The Law Magazine and Review.*

"It contains a great deal of miscellaneous information, and if a student were confined to the selection of one book on equity, both for its doctrine and practice, he could hardly do better than choose the one before us."—*The Solicitors' Journal.*

"It is eminently a student's book, and as such has we believe been appreciated. We recollect consulting a former edition a dozen years ago, and we are glad to see that it is still in favour. The Work contains evidence of originality, and freedom from hackneyed phraseology. It is not intended to lay before the student the system of Equity jurisprudence, but it is intended as a pioneer for the studies that should follow, and it is well suited to that end. It will certainly impress the student with a notion of Equity principles and practice, and it will so far familiarize him with the subject, that he will more readily catch hold of its ramifications when he studies it more deeply."—*The Leguleian and Articled Clerks' Magazine.*

Petersdorff's Abridgment of the Common Law.—New Ed.

6 vols., Royal 8vo., 7l. 7s. cloth.

A CONCISE, PRACTICAL ABRIDGMENT of the COMMON AND STATUTE LAW, as at present administered in the Common Law, Probate, Divorce and Admiralty Courts, excluding all that is obsolete, overruled or superseded : comprising a Series of Condensed Treatises on the different Branches of the Law, with detailed Directions, Forms and Precedents ; an Alphabetical Dictionary of Technical Law Terms and Maxims, and a Collection of Words that have received a Special Judicial Construction ; the whole illustrated by References to the principal Cases in Equity, and in the Scotch, American and Irish Reports, and the most eminent text writers. By CHARLES PETERSDORFF, Serjeant-at-Law, assisted by CHARLES W. WOOD, Esq., and WALKER MARSHALL, Esq., Barristers-at-Law.

"Mr. Serjeant Petersdorff has brought to a close his labours upon this great and useful work. It is a complete dictionary of the law as it exists at the present day, and is also an index to every law library. We noticed the plan and object of this work at some length on the completion of the first volume. Now that the sixth has been published, we have nothing to add, except that the execution seems to be in the best style of this laborious jurist and professional writer."—*Times.*

Glen's Law of Highways.—Second Edition.

Post 8vo., 20s. cloth.

The LAW of HIGHWAYS: comprising the Highway Acts 1835, 1862 and 1864; the South Wales Highway Act; the Statutes and Decisions of the Courts on the subject of Highways, Bridges, Ferries, &c., including the Duties of Highway Boards, Surveyors of Highways, the Law of Highways in Local Board of Health Districts; Highways affected by Railways, and Locomotives on Highways. With an Appendix of Statutes in force relating to Highways. By W. CUNNINGHAM GLEN, Esq., Barrister at Law. Second Edition.

"Altogether we may confidently venture to confirm the statement in the preface that it may now fairly claim to be recognized as a standard authority on the law of highways by those who are engaged officially or otherwise in the administration of that branch of the law. It is so as we from personal knowledge can affirm, and, we may add, that it is received by them as a trustworthy guide in the discharge of their onerous duties."—*Law Times.*

"The present edition of Mr. Glen's work contains a great deal of valuable matter which is entirely new. To those interested in the law of highways this manual as it now appears will be found a safe and efficient guide."—*Law Magazine.*

"Mr. Glen has an established reputation in the legal profession as a careful and laborious writer, and this new edition of his new work on highway law will convince those who refer to it that he has neglected no topic likely to be useful to those whose duties require them to have a knowledge of this particular branch of the law. This work aspires above others which profess merely to be annotated reprints of acts of parliament. It will be found to contain much information which might be looked for elsewhere in vain. The general law upon the subject is set forth with a care and lucidity deserving of great praise, and a good index facilitates reference, and renders this work the most complete on this important subject which has yet been published."—*Justice of the Peace.*

"Mr. Glen may well say that an entire revision of the first edition was necessitated by the recent statutes, and his second edition is a bulky volume of 800 pages. His work may be read with satisfaction by the general student as well as referred to with confidence by the practitioner. We need say nothing further of this second edition than that we think it likely to maintain fully the reputation obtained by its predecessor. It has the advantages, by no means unworthy of consideration, of being well printed and well indexed, as well as well arranged, and a copious index of statutes renders it a perfect compendium of the authorities bearing in any way on the law of highways."—*Solicitors' Journal.*

Fry's Specific Performance of Contracts.

8vo., 16s. cloth.

A TREATISE on the SPECIFIC PERFORMANCE of CONTRACTS, including those of Public Companies, with a Preliminary Chapter on the Provisions of the Chancery Amendment Act, 1858. By EDWARD FRY, B.A., of Lincoln's Inn, Esq., Barrister at Law.

"It will be seen what a masterly grasp the author has taken of his subject, and his treatment of the various parts of it equally exhibits the hand of a man who has studied the law as a science. He is skilful in the extraction of principles, precise in the exposition of them, apt in their application to the particular case, but in all he is thoroughly practical. The practitioner who uses it as a text book will find in it an adviser who will tell him not only what the law is, but how it may be enforced."—*Law Times.*

"Mr. Fry's work presents in a reasonable compass a large quantity of modern learning on the subject of contracts, with reference to the common remedy by specific performance, and will thus be acceptable to the profession generally."—*Law Chronicle.*

"There is a closeness and clearness in its style, and a latent fulness in the exposition, which not only argue a knowledge of the law, but of those varying circumstances in human society to which the law has to be applied."—*Spectator.*

"Mr. Fry's elaborate essay appears to exhaust the subject, on which he has cited and brought to bear, with great diligence, some 1,500 cases, which include those of the latest reports."—*Law Magazine and Review.*

"Although a professional work, it is sufficiently popular in style to be serviceable to all persons engaged in commercial or joint-stock undertakings."—*The Times.*

"The law of specific performance is a growing law just now, and the characteristic which gives its special value to Mr. Fry's work is, that the recent cases are as well digested in his mind as the older ones. Mr. Fry's is one of the best specimens of the modern law book."—*The Economist.*

Oke's Game and Fishery Laws.—Second Edition.

12mo., 10s. 6d. cloth.

A HANDY-BOOK of the GAME and FISHERY LAWS; containing the whole Law as to Game, Licences and Certificates, Poaching Prevention, Trespass, Rabbits, Deer, Dogs, Birds and Poisoned Grain throughout the United Kingdom, and Private and Salmon Fisheries in England. Systematically arranged, with the Acts, Decisions, Notes, Forms, Suggestions, &c., &c. By GEORGE C. OKE, Author of "*The Magisterial Synopsis*," &c. &c. Second Edition.

⁎ This Edition includes Chapters on the Scotch and Irish Game Laws, Property in Game, Suggestions for Amendment of the Laws, the Poaching Prevention Act, 1862, the Poisoned Grain Prohibition Act, 1863, &c. &c.

"The first edition having enjoyed a rapid sale, a second has enabled Mr. Oke greatly to enlarge his design and to add the very important statutes which have been passed since the publication of the first edition. Its size is doubled, a tabular list of the penalties has been appended, and the index made extremely copious and complete. This is now really what it is termed, a Handy Book of the Game and Fishery Laws, and gives all the information that can be required by the sportsman or his legal adviser."—*Law Times.*

"This treatise has come out at a very seasonable time, casting the light of English law on recent statutes for the protection of game by land or water, and will be found invaluable to all connected with those laws."—*Perthshire Courier.*

"The work is carefully composed, and contains a full index."—*Solicitors' Journal.*

"Care and Industry are all that can be shown in such productions, and these qualities are generally shown in the present works. Mr. Oke's book takes a somewhat larger range than Mr. Paterson's, as it embraces the late statute relating to the Salmon Fisheries."—*Athenæum.*

"The plan of Mr. Oke's Handy Book is a very plain and useful one ⁎ ⁎ It will be a most acceptable addition to the country gentleman's library, and presents a most intelligible guide to the existing English laws on game and fish, brought down to the present time."—*The Field.*

"To sportsmen, as well as to those magistrates and professional gentlemen who are concerned in the administration of the Game Laws, Mr. Oke's digest and interpretation of the various statutes will prove of great assistance."—*Stamford Mercury.*

"Mr. Oke makes the laws easily comprehended in all their bearings, so that the person requiring information will find it at once, and that in a condensed form. ⁎ ⁎ It is a work that every sportsman would find useful, now that the season is before him and he is anxious to know how the law stands under the recent acts of parliament."—*Bell's New Messenger.*

"We recommend justices, landlords and others whom it behoves to be well acquainted with the Game Laws, to supply themselves with a copy of this work; they will find every requisite information in a small space and in an intelligible form."—*Cambridge Chronicle.*

Glen's Poor Law Board Orders.—Sixth Edition.

Post 8vo. 18s. cloth.

The GENERAL, CONSOLIDATED, and other ORDERS of the POOR LAW COMMISSIONERS and the POOR LAW BOARD: with explanatory Notes elucidating the Orders, Tables of Statutes, Cases and Index to the Orders and Notes. By W. CUNNINGHAM GLEN, Esq., Barrister at Law. Sixth Edition.

Smith's Practice of Conveyancing.

Post 8vo., 6s. cloth.

AN ELEMENTARY VIEW of the PRACTICE of CONVEYANCING in SOLICITORS' OFFICES; with an Outline of the Proceedings under the Transfer of Land and Declaration of Title Acts, 1862, for the use of Articled Clerks. By EDMUND SMITH, B.A., late of Pembroke College, Cambridge. Attorney and Solicitor.

Powell on Evidence.—Third Edition by Cutler & Griffin.

12mo., 15s. cloth.

THE PRINCIPLES and PRACTICE of the LAW of EVIDENCE. By EDMUND POWELL, M.A., Barrister at Law. Third Edition by JOHN CUTLER, B.A., of Lincoln's Inn, Barrister at Law, Professor of English Law and Jurisprudence, and Professor of Indian Jurisprudence ; and EDMUND FULLER GRIFFIN, B.A., of Lincoln's Inn, Barrister at Law.

"We have very great pleasure in noticing this edition of a work with which we have long been familiar. It was certainly a good idea to make the book useful to the equity practitioner. It was a still better idea to adapt the Anglo-Indian rules of evidence, which must assist materially those who are studying in England for the Indian bar, or preparing for the Indian civil service. Mr. Cutler, being Professor of Indian Jurisprudence at King's College, has executed this latter branch of the work with the ability which was to be expected from him, and we can heartily recommend this excellent edition of Mr. Powell's book as likely to prove of very wide utility."—*Law Times.*

"To put before students in an attractive and concise form the principles of the laws of evidence the authors have achieved a success. The treatise before us has with great care and skill incorporated the principles of evidence observed in equity, and also the salient rules adopted in the Anglo-Indian courts. While we think that the sphere of this treatise must be confined to the education of students, we have no hesitation in asserting that within that sphere the book is a great success, and we cordially recommend the volume to students both for the English bar and for the Indian bar. Its simplicity and perspicuity render it also a valuable aid to members of the Indian civil service."—*Law Journal.*

"This is a new edition of a work which we fancy has scarcely been as well known as it deserves. It has not of course the pretensions to completeness of Mt. Pitt Taylor's book, nor possibly has it so much merit as an original and scientific treatise as Mr. Best's, at the same time it is probably more useful than either for ready reference in court on ordinary points. The present volume is of handy size, is moderately cheap, and its contents are remarkably well arranged, so that anything it contains can be rapidly found. We think this will be enough to make the work useful to practitioners on circuit, at quarter sessions, and especially in county courts where access to a library is not usually to be had and it is inconvenient or impossible to take many or large books. To students and young barristers also the book will be useful, not only for reading at home, as more practical than Best and less detailed than Taylor, but also for taking with them into court."—*Solicitors' Journal.*

"This is a good edition of a very useful work. The book itself we have always considered as well adapted for the student and convenient for the practitioner. It explains principles clearly, and illustrates them without overloading them by the cases quoted. The work is more practical in its object than that of Mr. Best, and treats the subject in a more succinct manner than Mr. Pitt Taylor. There could be no better introduction to the study of the law of evidence than Mr. Powell's book, whilst it is perfectly suitable for ordinary reference, and the care that has been bestowed on it by the present editors will, we think, considerably enhance its value. The law has been brought down to the close of last year, and the principles of the law of evidence followed by the Court of Chancery have been incorporated in the work, and the rules of evidence adopted by the Anglo-Indian courts have been referred to, the chief part of the Indian Evidence Act being in the appendix. This last feature of the work will render it very valuable for those who are studying for the Indian civil service, and will not be without interest for all who wish to understand thoroughly the principles of the law of evidence."—*Law Magazine and Review.*

"We are glad to see a new edition of Mr. Powell's work on the law of evidence. It was no doubt an act of some temerity on Mr. Powell's part when he first gave the legal public the fruits of his labours on this subject in the face of such exhaustive treatises as Taylor, Phillips, Starkie, and Roscoe. But that such a work was wanted, and is appreciated by the profession, is evidenced by the sale of two editions, and the production of a third. Mr. Powell's plan is well known. It is to state fundamental principles and illustrate them by leading cases, and he has brought to bear on his task powers of arrangement, of brevity and clearness of expression seldom met with. The present edition is ably edited by Mr. Cutler and Mr. Griffin, who have, in addition to the previous text, added the principles and practice of the law of evidence adopted by the Court of Chancery, and other important matter, and brought down the law to the present time. The book will be found a most useful addition to the lawyer's library, and to those practising, or about to practise, in the county courts it is almost a necessity."—*Law Examination Reporter.*

. *Although in this work the most important decisions only are quoted, and as a rule but one authority is given for each proposition, yet there are upwards of 400 cases cited therein which do not appear in the table of cases prefixed to the latest edition of "Taylor on Evidence."*

Wigram on Extrinsic Evidence as to Wills.

Fourth Edition.   8vo., 11s. cloth.

AN EXAMINATION OF THE RULES OF LAW respecting the Admission of EXTRINSIC EVIDENCE in Aid of the INTERPRETATION OF WILLS. By the Right Hon. Sir JAMES WIGRAM, Knt. The Fourth Edition, prepared for the press with the sanction of the learned Author, by W. KNOX WIGRAM, M.A., of Lincoln's Inn, Esq., Barrister-at-Law.

" In the celebrated treatise of Sir James Wigram, the rules of law are stated, discussed and explained in a manner which has excited the admiration of every judge who has had to consult it."—*Lord Kingsdown, in a Privy Council Judgment, July 8th, 1858.*

Williams's Common Law Pleading and Practice.

8vo., 12s. cloth.

An INTRODUCTION to PRACTICE and PLEADING in the SUPERIOR COURTS of LAW, embracing an outline of the whole proceedings in an Action at Law, on Motion, and at Judges' Chambers; together with the Rules of Pleading and Practice, and Forms of all the principal Proceedings. By WATKIN WILLIAMS, Esq., of the Inner Temple, Barrister at Law.

" For the Student especially the book has features of peculiar value, it is at the same time scientific and practical, and throughout the work there is a judicious union of general principles with a practical treatment of the subject, illustrated by forms and examples of the main proceedings."—*Jurist.*

Bainbridge on Mines and Minerals.—Third Edition.

8vo., cloth.

A TREATISE on the LAW of MINES and MINERALS. By WILLIAM BAINBRIDGE, Esq., F.G.S., of the Inner Temple, Barrister at Law. Third Edition, carefully revised, and much enlarged by additional matter relating to manorial rights—rights of way and water and other mining easements—the sale of mines and shares—the construction of leases—cost book and general partnerships—injuries from undermining and inundations—barriers and working out of bounds. With an Appendix of Forms and Customs and a Glossary of English Mining Terms.

" When a work has reached three editions, criticism as to its practical value is superfluous. We believe that this work was the first published in England on the special subject of mining law—others have since been published—but we see no reason in looking at the volume before us to believe that it has yet been superseded."—*Law Magazine.*

" Mr. Bainbridge was we believe the first to collect and publish, in a separate treatise, the Law of Mines and Minerals, and the work was so well done that his volume at once took its place in the law library as the text book on the subject to which it was devoted. This work must be already familiar to all readers whose practice brings them in any manner in connection with mines or mining, and they well know its value. We can only say of this new edition that it is in all respects worthy of its predecessors."—*Law Times.*

" After an interval of eleven years we have to welcome a new edition of Mr. Bainbridge's work on mines and minerals. It would be entirely superfluous to attempt a general review of a work which has for so long a period occupied the position of the standard work on this important subject. Those only who, by the nature of their practice, have learned to lean upon Mr. Bainbridge as on a solid staff, can appreciate the deep research, the admirable method, and the graceful style of this model treatise. Therefore we are merely reduced to the inquiry, whether the law has, by force of statutes and of judicial decisions, undergone such development, modification, or change since the year 1856 as to justify a new edition? That question may be readily answered in the affirmative, and the additions and corrections made in the volume before us furnish ample evidence of the fact. It may be also stated that this book, being priced at 30s., has the exceptional character of being a cheap law publication."—*Law Journal.*

Civil Service Examinations.

8vo., 1s. sewed.

ON REPORTING CASES for their PERIODICAL EXAMINATIONS by Selected Candidates for the Civil Service of India: Being a Lecture delivered on Wednesday, June 12, 1867, at King's College, London. By JOHN CUTLER, B.A., of Lincoln's Inn, Barrister at Law, Professor of English Law and Jurisprudence and Professor of Indian Jurisprudence at King's College, London.

Davis's Criminal Law Consolidation Acts.

12mo., 10s. cloth.

THE NEW CRIMINAL LAW CONSOLIDATION ACTS, 1861; with an Introduction and practical Notes, illustrated by a copious reference to Cases decided by the Court of Criminal Appeal. Together with alphabetical Tables of Offences, as well those punishable upon Summary Conviction as upon Indictment, and including the Offences under the New Bankruptcy Act, so arranged as to present at one view the particular Offence, the Old or New Statute upon which it is founded, and the Limits of Punishment; and a full Index. By JAMES EDWARD DAVIS, Esq., Barrister-at-Law.

"This is a carefully prepared edition of the New Criminal Law Consolidation Acts, and will be found extremely useful for practical purposes. The name of Mr. Davis will be a sufficient guarantee that the work has been done in a lawyer-like manner. There can be no doubt that Mr. Davis's edition of the New Criminal Statutes will prove very serviceable both to magistrates and the profession."—*Law Magazine and Review.*

Powell's Law of Inland Carriers.—Second Edition.

8vo., 14s. cloth.

THE LAW OF INLAND CARRIERS, especially as regulated by the Railway and Canal Traffic Act, 1854. By EDMUND POWELL, Esq., of Lincoln College, Oxon, M.A., and of the Western Circuit, Barrister at Law, Author of "Principles and Practice of the Law of Evidence." Second Edition, almost re-written.

"The treatise before us states the law of which it treats ably and clearly, and contains a good index."—*Solicitors' Journal.*

"Mr. Powell's writing is singularly precise and condensed, without being at all dry, as those who have read his admirable Book of Evidence will attest. It will be seen, from our outline of the contents, how exhaustively the subject has been treated, and that it is entitled to be, that which it aspires to become, the text book on the Law of Carriers."—*Law Times.*

"The subject of this treatise is not indeed a large one, but it has been got up by Mr. Powell with considerable care, and contains ample notice of the most recent cases and authorities."—*Jurist.*

"The two chapters on the Railway and Canal Traffic Act, 1856, are quite new, and the recent cases under the provisions of that statute are analyzed in lucid language."—*Law Magazine.*

Phillips on the Law of Lunacy.

Post 8vo., 18s. cloth.

THE LAW CONCERNING LUNATICS, IDIOTS and PERSONS of UNSOUND MIND. By CHARLES PALMER PHILLIPS, M.A., of Lincoln's Inn, Esq., Barrister at Law, and Secretary to the Commissioners of Lunacy.

"Mr. C. P. Phillips has in his very complete, elaborate and useful volume presented us with an excellent view of the present law as well as the practice relating to lunacy."—*Law Magazine and Review.*

"The work is one on which the author has evidently bestowed great pains, and which not only bears the mark of great application and research, but which shows a familiarity with the subject."—*Justice of the Peace.*

Cutler on English, Roman, Hindu and Mahommedan Law.
On the Study of the English, Roman, Hindu and Mahommedan Legal
Systems, with especial regard to their salient points of Agreement and
Difference: being a Lecture delivered at King's College, London. By
JOHN CUTLER, B.A., of Lincoln's Inn, Barrister at Law, Professor of
English Law and Jurisprudence, and Professor of Indian Jurisprudence,
at King's College, London. 8vo. 1s. sewed.

A General Catalogue of all Modern Law Works now on Sale by
Messrs. BUTTERWORTH, with a Chronological List of all the Reports from
the earliest Period to the present Time, and an Index of Subjects for convenience of Reference: intended as a Guide to Purchasers. 8vo. 1s. sewed.
(*Gratis to Purchasers.*)

Sharkey's Hand Book of the Practice of Election Committees.
With an Appendix of Forms and Precedents. By P. BURROWES SHARKEY,
Solicitor and Parliamentary Agent. Second Edition. 12mo. 10s. 6d. cloth.

Hamel's International Law, in connexion with Municipal Statutes
relating to the Commerce, Rights and Liabilities of the Subjects of Neutral
States pending Foreign War; considered with reference to the Case of the
Alexandra, seized under the provisions of the Foreign Enlistment Act. By
FELIX HARGRAVE HAMEL, Barrister at Law. Post 8vo. 3s. boards.

Francillon's Lectures, Elementary and Familiar, on English Law.
FIRST and SECOND SERIES. By JAMES FRANCILLON, Esq., County Court
Judge. 2 vols. 8vo. 8s. each, cloth

Pearce's Guide to the Inns of Court and Chancery; with
Notices of their Ancient Discipline, Customs and Entertainments; an
Account of the Eminent Men of Lincoln's Inn, the Inner Temple, the
Middle Temple, and Gray's Inn, &c.; together with the Regulations as to
the Admission of Students, Keeping Terms, Call to the Bar, &c. By
ROBERT R. PEARCE, Esq., of Gray's Inn, Barrister at Law. 8vo. 8s. cloth.

Bristowe's Local Government Act, 1858, 21 & 22 Vict. c. 98;
with Notes; an Appendix of Cases decided upon the Public Health Act,
1848; and a copious Index. By S. B. BRISTOWE, Esq., of the Inner
Temple, Barrister-at-Law. 12mo. 2s. 6d. cloth.

The Laws of Barbados. (By Authority.) Royal 8vo. 21s. cloth.

Le Marchant's Report of Proceedings of the House of Lords
on the Claims to the Barony of Gardner, with an Appendix of Cases illustrative of the Law of Legitimacy. By Sir DENIS LE MARCHANT, of
Lincoln's Inn, Barrister at Law. 8vo. 18s. boards.

Norman's Treatise on the Law and Practice relating to Letters
Patent for Inventions as altered and amended by Statutes 15 & 16 Vict. c. 83,
and 12 & 13 Vict. c. 109. By JOHN PAXTON NORMAN, M.A., Barrister
at Law. Post 8vo., 7s. 6d., cloth.

Gray's Treatise on the Law of Costs in Actions and other Proceed-
ings in the Courts of Common Law at Westminster. By JOHN GRAY, Esq.,
of the Middle Temple, Barrister at Law. 8vo., 21s. cloth.

The South Australian System of Conveyancing by Registration
of Title. By ROBERT R. TORRENS and HENRY GAWLER, Esq., Barrister,
8vo., 4s. half cloth.

The Practice of the Ecclesiastical Courts, with Forms and Tables
of Costs. By H. C. COOTE, F.S.A., Proctor in Doctors' Commons, &c.
8vo. 28s. boards.

Baker's Compendium of the Statutes, Cases and Decisions affecting the Office of Coroner. By WILLIAM BAKER, Coroner of Middlesex. 12mo. 7s. cloth.

Brandt's Law, Practice and Procedure of Divorce and Matrimonial Causes; with Precedents. By WILLIAM BRANDT, Esq., Barrister at Law. 12mo. 7s. 6d. boards.

A Brief Memoir of Lord Lyndhurst. By William Sidney Gibson, Esq., M.A., Barrister at Law, of Lincoln's Inn. 8vo., 1s. sewed

A Memoir of Mr. Justice Talfourd. By a Member of the Oxford Circuit. Reprinted from the Law Magazine. 8vo., 1s. sewed.

A Report of the Bread Street Ward Scrutiny; with Introductory Observations, a Copy of the Poll, and a Digest of the Evidence, Arguments, and Decisions in each Case. By W. T. HALY, Esq., Barrister at Law. 12mo. 4s. boards.

Greening's Forms of Declarations, Pleadings and other Proceedings in the Superior Courts of Common Law, with the Common Law Procedure Act, and other Statutes; Table of Officers' Fees; and the New Rules of Practice and Pleading, with Notes. By HENRY GREENING, Esq., Special Pleader. Second Edition. 12mo. 10s. 6d. boards.

O'Dowd's Merchant Shipping Act, 1862. By JAMES O'DOWD, Esq., Barrister at Law and Assistant Solicitor for the Merchant Shipping Department of Her Majesty's Customs. 12mo. 7s. 6d. cloth.

Bowditch's Treatise on the History, Revenue Laws, and Government of the Isles of Jersey and Guernsey, to which is added the recent Acts as to Smuggling, Customs and Trade of the Isle of Man and the Channel Islands, Forms, Costs, &c. By J. BOWDITCH, Solicitor. 8vo. 3s. 6d. sewed.

Pulling's Practical Compendium of the Law and Usage of Mercantile Accounts: describing the various Rules of Law affecting them, at Common Law, in Equity, Bankruptcy and Insolvency, or by Arbitration. Containing the Law of Joint Stock Companies' Accounts, and the Legal Regulations for their Adjustment under the Winding-up Acts of 1848 and 1849. By ALEXANDER PULLING, Esq. of the Inner Temple, Barrister at Law. 12mo. 9s. boards.

Leigh's Abridgment of the Law of Nisi Prius. By P. Brady LEIGH, of the Inner Temple, Barrister at Law. 2 vols. 8vo. £2:8s. boards.

Warren's Manual of the Parliamentary Election Law of the United Kingdom, with reference to the Conduct of Elections, and the Registration Court. By SAMUEL WARREN, D.C.L., Q.C. One thick vol. royal 12mo. 25s. cloth.

Warren's Manual of the Law and Practice of Election Committees. By SAMUEL WARREN, D.C.L., Q.C. Royal 12mo., 15s. cloth.

Lewis's Election Manual for England and Wales, with the Statutes, Notes & Precedents. By C. E. LEWIS, Solicitor. 12mo., 5s. boards.

Judge Redfield's Law of Railways. 3rd Edition (Boston). 2 vols royal 8vo. £3:10s. cloth.

Judge Redfield's Law of Wills. 2nd Edition (Boston). 2 vols. royal 8vo. £3:12s. cloth.

Washburn's Law of Easements. (Boston.) 1 vol. royal 8vo. 22s. 6d. cloth.

Curtis's Law of Patents. (Boston.) 1 vol. royal 8vo. 22s. 6d. cloth.

A Complete Collection of the Treaties and Conventions, and Reciprocal Regulations, at present subsisting between Great Britain and Foreign Powers. By LEWIS HERTSLET, Esq. late Librarian and Keeper of the Papers, Foreign Office. Vols. 1 to 11, 8vo. £12:15s. boards.

Dr. Deane's Law of Blockade, as contained in the Judgments of Dr. Lushington and the Cases on Blockade decided during 1854. By J. P. DEANE, D.C.L., Advocate in Doctors' Commons. 8vo. 10s. cloth.

Drainage of Land: How to procure Outfalls by New Drains, or the Improvement of Existing Drains, in the Lands of an Adjoining Owner, under the Act of 24 & 25 Vict. cap. 133. By J. WM. WILSON, Solicitor. 8vo., 1s. sewed.

Sewell's Treatise on the Law of Sheriff, with Practical Forms and Precedents. By RICHARD CLARKE SEWELL, Esq., D.C.L., Barrister at Law. 8vo. 21s. boards.

The Law relating to Transactions on the Stock Exchange. By HENRY KEYSER, Esq., Barrister at Law. 12mo., 8s. cloth.

Sewell's Municipal Corporation Acts, 5 & 6 Will. 4, c. 76, and 6 & 7 Will. 4, cc. 103, 104, 105, with Notes, and Index. By R. C. SEWELL, Esq., Barrister at Law. 12mo. 9s. boards.

Indian Civil Code. The Indian Succession Act, 1865, with Intro- duction, Synopsis, and General Index. By EDWARD HYDE, M.A., of the Inner Temple, Barrister at Law. 8vo. 10s. cloth.

Phillimore's Commentaries on International Law. By the Right Hon. Sir ROBERT J. PHILLIMORE, Knt., now Judge of the High Court of Admiralty of England. 4 vols. 8vo. £5 cloth.

Extract from Pamphlet on "American Neutrality," by George Bemis (Boston, U.S.)

"Sir Robert Phillimore, the present Queen's Advocate, and author of the most comprehensive and systematic 'Commentary on International Law' that England has produced."

*** Vol. 2, price 22s., Vol. 3, price 32s., and Vol. 4, price 30s., may be had separately to complete sets.

A Legigraphical Chart of Landed Property in England from the time of the Saxons to the present Æra. By CHARLES FEARNE, Esq., Barrister at Law. On a large sheet, 6s. coloured.

Dwyer's Compendium of the Principal Laws and Regulations relating to the Militia of Great Britain and Ireland 12mo. 5s. 6d. cloth.

The Common Law of Kent; or the Customs of Gavelkind. With an Appendix concerning Borough English. By T. ROBINSON, Esq. THIRD EDITION, with Notes and References to modern Authorities, by JOHN WILSON, Esq. Barrister at Law. 8vo. 18s. boards.

The Marriage and Registration Acts, 6 & 7 Will. 4, caps. 85, 86; with Instructions, Forms, and Practical Directions for the Use of Officiating Ministers, Superintendent Registrars, Registrars. The Acts of 1837, viz. 7 Will. 4, c. 1, and 1 Vict. c. 22, with Notes and Observations; and a full Index. By JOHN SOUTHERDEN BURN, Esq., *Secretary to the Commission.* 12mo. 6s. 6d. boards.

A Treatise on the Law of Gaming, Horse-Racing, and Wagers. By FREDERIC EDWARDS, Esq., Barrister at Law. 12mo. 5s. cloth.

Hamel's Laws of the Customs, consolidated by direction of the Lords Commissioners of her Majesty's Treasury, under the Acts of 1853 and 1854; with a Commentary, containing Practical Forms, Notes of Decisions in Leading Customs Cases, Appendix of Acts, and a copious Index. By FELIX JOHN HAMEL, Esq., Solicitor for her Majesty's Customs. 1 vol. royal 8vo. 16s. cloth.

A Digest of Principles of English Law; arranged in the order of the Code Napoleon, with an Historical Introduction. By GEORGE BLAXLAND, Esq. Royal 8vo. £1 : 4s. boards.

The Law Student's Guide; containing an Historical Treatise on each of the Inns of Court, with their Rules and Customs respecting Admission, Keeping Terms, Call to the Bar, Chambers, &c., Remarks on the Jurisdiction of the Benchers, Observations on the Study of the Law, and other useful Information. By P. B. LEIGH, Esq. of Gray's Inn, Barrister at Law. 12mo. 6s. boards.

A Treatise on the Law of Commerce and Manufactures, and the Contracts relating thereto; with an Appendix of Treaties, Statutes, and Precedents. By JOSEPH CHITTY, Esq. Barrister at Law. 4 vols. royal 8vo. £6 : 6s. boards.

Sheppard's Touchstone of Common Assurances, being a Plain and Familar Treatise on Conveyancing, with Copious Notes, Table of Cases, and extensive Analytical Index. The Eighth Edition, by EDMOND GIBSON ATHERLEY, of Lincoln's Inn, Barrister at Law. 2 vols. royal 8vo. 10s. boards.

Anstey's Pleader's Guide ; a Didactic Poem, in Two Parts. The Eighth Edition. 12mo. 7s. boards.

Hardy's Catalogue of Lords Chancellors, Keepers of the Great Seal, and Principal Officers of the High Court of Chancery. By THOMAS DUFFUS HARDY, Principal Keeper of Records. Royal 8vo. 20s. cloth. (Only 250 copies printed.)

Smyth's Chronicle of the Law Officers of Ireland: containing Lists of the Lords Chancellors and Keepers of the Great Seal, &c., &c., from the earliest period. By C. J. SMYTH, B.A., of Lincoln's Inn. 12mo. 9s. cloth.

An Essay on Charitable Trusts, under the Charitable Trusts Act, 1853. By HENRY JOHN PYE, Esq. Post 8vo. 6d. sewed.

A Practical Treatise on Life Assurance; in which the Statutes, &c., affecting unincorporated Joint Stock Companies are briefly considered and explained. SECOND EDITION. By FREDERICK BLAYNEY, Esq., Author of "A Treatise on Life Annuities." 12mo. 7s. boards.

Pothier's Treatise on the Contract of Partnership : with the Civil Code and Code of Commerce relating to this Subject, in the same Order. Translated from the French. By O. D. TUDOR, Esq., Barrister. 8vo., 5s. cloth.

Browne's Practical Treatise on Actions at Law, embracing the subjects of Notice of Action ; Limitation of Actions; necessary Parties to and proper Forms of Actions, the Consequence of Mistake therein ; and the Law of Costs with reference to Damages. By R. J. BROWNE, Esq., of Lincoln's Inn, Special Pleader. 8vo., 16s. boards.

Archdeacon Hale's Essay on the Union between Church and State, and the Establishment by Law of the Protestant Reformed Religion in England, Ireland, and Scotland. By W. H. HALE, M.A., Archdeacon of London. 8vo. 1s. sewed.

"This is the production of a very able man, and will be read by lawyers as well as by divines with interest and advantage."—*Law Magazine.*

Burder *v.* **Heath. Judgment delivered on November 2, 1861,** by the Right Honorable STEPHEN LUSHINGTON, D.C.L., Dean of the Arches. Folio, 1s. sewed.

The Judgment of the Right Hon. Dr. Lushington, D.C.L., &c. &c. delivered in the Consistory Court of the Bishop of London, in the cases of Westerton against Liddell (clerk) and Horne and others, and Beale against Liddell (clerk) and Parke and Evans, on December 5th, 1855. Edited by A. F. BAYFORD, D.C.L. Royal 8vo. 2s. 6d. sewed.

The Judgment of the Dean of the Arches, also the Judgment of the PRIVY COUNCIL, in Liddell (clerk), and Horne and others against Westerton, and Liddell (clerk) and Park and Evans against Beal. Edited by A. F. BAYFORD, LL.D.: and with an elaborate analytical Index to the whole of the Judgments in these Cases. Royal 8vo., 3s. 6d. sewed.

The Case of Long *r.* **Bishop of Cape Town, embracing the opinions** of the Judges of Colonial Court hitherto unpublished, together with the decision of the Privy Council, and Preliminary Observations by the Editor. Royal 8vo., 6s. sewed.

Hamel's Law of Ritualism in the United Church of England and Ireland. With Practical Suggestions for Amendment of the Law, and a Form of Bill for that purpose. By F. HARGAVE HAMEL, Esq., of the Inner Temple, Barrister at Law. Post 8vo. 1s. sewed.

Archdeacon Hale's Inquiry into the Legal History of the Supre- macy of the Crown in Matters of Religion, with especial reference to the Church in the Colonies ; with an Appendix of Statutes. By W. H. HALE, M.A., Archdeacon of London. Royal 8vo. 4s. cloth.

" The archdeacon has shown that he possesses a legal mind in the good sense of the term."— *Law Magazine.*

The Judgment delivered by the Right Hon. Sir Robert Phillimore, D.C.L., Official Principal of the Court of Arches, in the Cases of Martin *v.* Mackonochie and Flamank *v* Simpson. Edited by WALTER G. F. PHIL-LIMORE, B.A., of the Middle Temple, Fellow of All Souls College, and Vinerian Scholar, Oxford. Royal 8vo. 2s. 6d. sewed.

Law Pamphlets.

The Privilege of Religious Confessions in English Courts of Justice considered in a Letter to a Friend. By EDWARD BADELEY, Esq., M.A., Barrister at Law. 8vo. 2s. sewed.

Neutrals and Belligerents: also The Trent and San Jacinto: Papers read at the Juridical Society. By CHARLES CLARK, Esq., Barrister at Law. 8vo. 1s. each, sewed.

On the Amendment of the Law of Evidence, in order to admit the Testimony of Parties in all Civil Suits, and of Defendants in Criminal Trials. By ALFRED WADDILOVE, D.C.L. 8vo. 6d. sewed.

Gibson's Letter to the Lord Chancellor on Bankruptcy Reform, 1867. Post 8vo. 1s. sewed.

Jamaica Riot.— The Case of George William Gordon. With Preliminary Observations on the Jamaica Riot of October 11, 1865. By B. T. WILLIAMS, Esq., M.A., Barrister at Law. 8vo. 2s. sewed.

Our Judicial System.— A Speech in the House of Commons, February 22, 1867. By SIR ROUNDELL PALMER, Q C., M.P. 8vo. 1s. sewed.

On the Necessity for Additional Common Law Judges.— A Paper read before the Metropolitan and Provincial Law Association, October, 1866. By J. ANDERSON ROSE. 8vo. 1s. sewed.

More Judges: Are they Wanted? By T. W. WHEELER, B.A., Barrister at Law. 8vo. 1s. sewed.

A Plan for the Formal Amendment of the Law of England. By THOMAS ERSKINE HOLLAND, M.A., Barrister at Law. 8vo. 1s. sewed.

A Digest of the Law: How Attainable. By R. MALCOLM KERR, LL.D., Advocate and Barrister at Law. 8vo. 1s. sewed.

Observations on County Courts and Local Municipal Courts as Courts for the Recovery of Small Debts. By WOODTHORPE BRANDON, Esq., Barrister at Law. 8vo. 6d. sewed.

Law Reports.

(Sets of the **Law Journal Reports** in all the Courts from 1823 to the present time, embracing both the Old and New Series, are constantly kept in stock, and estimates for the same, in capital condition, will be forwarded on application.)

House of Lords Reports.

The HOUSE of LORDS CASES on APPEALS and WRITS OF ERROR and CLAIMS of PEERAGE. By CHARLES CLARK, Esq., of the Middle Temple, Barrister at Law. Complete in 11 Vols., containing all the Cases from 1847 to 1866.

Clark's Digested Index to the House of Lords Reports.

A DIGESTED INDEX to all the REPORTS in the HOUSE of LORDS from the Commencement of the Series by Dow, in 1814, to the end of the Eleven Volumes of House of Lords Cases; with references to more recent decisions: intended as a Supplementary Volume to CLARK'S HOUSE of LORDS CASES. By CHARLES CLARK, Esq., of the Middle Temple, Barrister, Reporter by apppointment to the House of Lords. (To be completed in 2 Parts.) Part I., price 12s. sewed.

Probate, Divorce Court and Matrimonial Causes Reports.

REPORTS of CASES decided in HER MAJESTY'S NEW COURT of PROBATE, and in the COURT for DIVORCE and MATRIMONIAL CAUSES, commencing Hilary Term, 1858. By Dr. SWABEY, D.C.L., Advocate, and Dr. TRISTRAM, D.C.L., Advocate. Vols. I., II. and III., and Vol. IV. Part I., containing all the Cases decided from 1858 to 1865, price £8 : 4s. 6d. sewed.

Dr. Robinson's New Admiralty Reports.

REPORTS of CASES argued and determined in the HIGH COURT of ADMIRALTY. By WILLIAM ROBINSON, D.C.L. Advocate.
In 3 Vols., containing Cases decided from 1838 to 1850. £4 : 7s. sewed.

Dr. Swabey's Admiralty Reports.

REPORTS of CASES determined in the HIGH COURT of ADMIRALTY, from 1855 to 1859. By M. C. MERTTINS SWABEY, D.C.L., Advocate. One Vol., price 34s. sewed.

Vernon Lushington's Admiralty Reports.

REPORTS of CASES decided in the HIGH COURT of ADMIRALTY OF ENGLAND, and on APPEAL to the PRIVY COUNCIL. By VERNON LUSHINGTON, Esq., Barrister at Law. One vol., 50s. sewed, containing cases from 1859 to 1862.

Browning and Lushington's Admiralty Reports.

REPORTS of CASES decided in the HIGH COURT of ADMIRALTY of England, and on Appeal to the Privy Council, 1863—1865. By ERNST BROWNING and VERNON LUSHINGTON, Esquires, of the Inner Temple, Barristers at Law. One vol., price 40s. sewed. These Reports are in continuation of those by Mr. LUSHINGTON, and comprise the Cases to the end of Trinity Term, 1865.

𝕷𝖆𝖜 𝖂𝖔𝖗𝖐𝖘 𝖕𝖗𝖊𝖕𝖆𝖗𝖎𝖓𝖌 𝖋𝖔𝖗 𝕻𝖚𝖇𝖑𝖎𝖈𝖆𝖙𝖎𝖔𝖓.

Stephen's Questions on the Sixth Edition of Mr. Serjeant Stephen's New Commentaries. In 1 vol. 8vo.

A Manual of Solicitors' Bookkeeping: comprising Practical Exemplifications of a concise and simple Plan of Double Entry, with Forms of Account, and other books relating to Bills, Cash, &c., showing their operation, giving instructions for Keeping, Posting and Balancing them, and directions for Drawing Costs: adapted to a large or small, sole or partnership business. By W. BAYLEY COOMBS, Law Accountant and Costs Draftsman.

A Collection of Mortgage Precedents and Forms of Decrees, intended as a Companion Volume to the General Law of Mortgage.—By W. R. FISHER, Esq., of Lincoln's Inn, Barrister at Law. In 1 vol. royal 8vo.

A Digested Index to all the Reports in the House of Lords from the commencement of the Series by Dow in 1814 to the present time, intended as a Supplementary Volume to Clark's House of Lord's Cases. By CHARLES CLARK, Esq, of the Middle Temple, Barrister at Law. (Part II. completing the Work.)

Shelford's Law of Joint Stock Companies.—The SECOND EDITION. By DAVID PITCAIRN, of Lincoln's Inn, and FRANCIS LAW LATHAM, of the Inner Temple, Esquires, Barristers at Law. In 12mo.

Shelford's Law of Railways.—FOURTH EDITION, containing the whole of the Consolidation and other General Acts for Regulating Railways in England, Scotland and Ireland to the present time and including the Companies Act, 1862; Lord Campbell's Act; the Law of Rating Railways to Local Taxes, with Notes of decided Cases on their Construction and Forms, &c.; the whole brought down to the latest period by W. CUNNINGHAM GLEN and C. W. LOVESY, Esqrs., of the Middle Temple, Barristers at Law. In 2 vols. royal 8vo.

The Commentaries of Gaius on the Roman Law: with an English Translation and Annotations. By FREDERICK TOMKINS, Esq., M.A., D.C.L., and WILLIAM GEORGE LEMON, Esq., LL.B., Barristers at Law, of Lincoln's Inn. In 8vo.

Tomkins' Institutes of the Roman Law.—Parts II. and III. completing the Work. In royal 8vo.

Brandon's Notes of Practice in the Mayor's Court of the City of London. SECOND EDITION. In 8vo.

Glen's Law of Public Health and Local Government.—FIFTH EDITION. In post 8vo.

Swabey and Tristram's Probate and Divorce Reports.—Vol. IV. Part II., completing the Series.

Law Magazine and Law Review for November.—No. 51, N.S.

Law Examination Reporter.—No. 12, for Michaelmas, 1868.